T0305176

Aid, Power, and Privatization

Aid, Power, and Privatization

The Politics of Telecommunication Reform in Central America

Benedicte Bull
Senior Research Fellow

*Centre for Development and the Environment,
University of Oslo, Norway*

Edward Elgar
Cheltenham, UK • Northampton, MA, USA

Published by
Edward Elgar Publishing Limited
Glensanda House
Montpellier Parade
Cheltenham
Glos GL50 1UA
UK

Edward Elgar Publishing, Inc.
136 West Street
Suite 202
Northampton
Massachusetts 01060
USA

A catalogue record for this book
is available from the British Library

ISBN 1 84542 174 4

Printed and bound in Great Britain by MPG Books Ltd, Bodmin, Cornwall

Contents

Figures

Tables

Abbreviations

AGA	General Agricultural Association
AI	Autonomous Institution
AIG	Association of Industrialists of Guatemala
AmCham	American Chamber of Commerce
ANFE	National Association for Economic Growth
ANI	National Industrial Association
ANTECC	National Association of Telecommunication Technicians
ARESEP	Regulatory Authority for the Public Services
ARETEL	Regulatory Authority for Telecommunications
ASDICE	Syndicate Association of ICE
ASIES	Association for Investigation and Social Studies
BMC	borrowing member country
CACIF	Coordinating Committee of Agrarian, Commercial, Industrial and Financial Associations
CACM	Central American Common Market
CAEM	Guatemalan Business Chamber
CARIFA	Caribbean Basin Project Financing Authority
CBI	Caribbean Basin Initiative
CCG	Guatemalan Chamber of Commerce
CCIC	Chamber of Commerce and Industry of Cortés
CDC	Council for the Defense of Constitutionality
CDI	Council for the Defense of Institutionality
CEES	Center for Social-Economy Studies
CIEN	Center for National Economic Research
CINDE	Costa Rican Coalition for Development Initiatives
CNFL	National Energy and Light Company
CODESA	Costa Rican Development Corporation
COHEP	Honduran Council for Private Enterprise
CONADI	National Investment Corporation
CONAES	The National Coordinator for Networking and Follow-Up

CONATEL	National Telecommunication Commission
CRICSA	International Radiographic Company of Costa Rica
DAG	Desarrollo de Autopistas de Guatemala
EBASCO	Electric Bond and Share Company
ECLA	Economic Commission for Latin America
ECOTEL	Costa Rican Telecommunication Company
EENE	National Electricity Institute
ESAF	enhanced structural adjustment facility
FCC	Federal Communication Commission
FD	Democratic Force
FEE	Foundation for Economic Education
FIT	Internal Workers Front
FOL	Organized Labor Front
FRG	Guatemalan Republican Front
FTAA	Free Trade Area of the Americas
GDP	gross domestic product
Guatel	Guatemalan Telecommunication Company
HIPC	Heavily Indebted Poor Countries Initiative
Hondutel	Honduran Telecommunication Enterprise
IBRD	International Bank of Reconstruction and Development
ICE	Costa Rican Electricity Institute
IDA	International Development Association
IDB	Inter-American Development Bank
IFC	International Finance Corporation
IFI	international financial institution
IHSS	National Social Security Institute
IMF	International Monetary Fund
INA	National Agrarian Institute
INDE	National Institute of Electrification
INJUPEM	Institute for Retirement and Pensions of the Public Employees
IPM	Military Previsions Institute
IRA	independent regulatory agency
IRETEL	Regulatory Institute for Telecommunications
ITU	International Telecommunication Union
LIBOR	London inter-bank offered rate

LMFICE	Law of Modernization and Strengthening of the Costa Rican Electricity Institute
MDB	multilateral development bank
MIF	Multilateral Investment Fund
NGO	non-governmental organization
NPE	New Political Economy
OAS	Organization of American States
OPS	Office of Public Safety
PAC	Citizens Action Party
PAN	National Advancement Party
PCS	Personal Communication Services
PCU	Unity Coalition Party
PDCG	Guatemalan Christian Democratic Party
PID	Institutional Democratic Party
PLN	National Liberation Party
PREN	Program for National Reorganization
PRGF	Poverty Reduction and Growth Facility
PSMAP	Public Sector Modernization Adjustment Program
PUSC	Social Christian Unity Party
RACSA	Costa Rican Radiography Incorporated
SAANA	Institute for Water and Sewerage
SAL	Structural adjustment loan
SALES	Workers Stock Holding Companies
SAP	structural adjustment program
SIECA	Secretariat for Economic Integration in Central America
SIGET	General Superintendent for Electricity and Telecommunications
SIICE	Union of ICE Engineers
SIMCATEL	Central American Military Telecommunications System
SIT	Superintendent for Telecommunications
SNE	National Electricity Service
SOE	State-owned Enterprise
SOPTRAVI	Ministry of Public Works, Transport and Housing
SOT	state-owned telecommunication enterprise
SUM	Center for Development and the Environment
Telgua	Guatemalan Telecommunications
TRT	Tropical Radio and Telegraph Company

UCCAEP	Costa Rican Union of Private Sector Chambers and Associations
UDAPE	Unit for Analysis of Economic Policy
UFCO	United Fruit Company
UFM	Francisco Marroquín University
UNAGRO	National Agricultural Union
UNAT	Unit for Technical Analysis
UNDP	United Nations Development Program
URNG	Guatemalan National Revolutionary Unity
USAID	United States Agency for International Development
VAT	value added tax

Preface

This book is a revised version of a PhD dissertation defended at the Department of Political Science of the University of Oslo. The work on it has therefore been conducted in two periods; one leading up to the dissertation and one leading up to this book. During both periods, many debts have been incurred.

The research for the dissertation was conducted in a 'geographic triangle' between Norway, Washington, DC and Central America. Traveling back and forth across the Atlantic and between the Central American countries was an immensely interesting but also a demanding experience. It would never have been possible without generous support from a series of individuals and institutions. Firstly, I would like to thank the Norwegian Research Council for supporting the project financially under its program for research on multilateral aid. Without the scholarship and the travel grants provided, this research would never have been possible. Secondly, the Center for Development and the Environment (SUM) at the University of Oslo has been an inspiring workplace all along. I would like to thank all staff and colleagues, but particularly former director and current research leader Desmond McNeill who has given numerous useful inputs along the way. Thirdly, I would like to thank Helge Hveem, my supervisor at the department of political science at the University of Oslo. Fourthly, I would like to thank Helge Semb, former alternate executive director for Norway in the Inter-American Development Bank (IDB), and IDB representative in Honduras. He provided me with the opportunity to get to know the IDB from the inside, an experience which improved my understanding of both the institution and the Latin American region significantly.

In addition, I have received invaluable support from a series of people and institutions in the different countries where I have conducted fieldwork. There is not space to include all of them here, but in Costa Rica I would particularly like to thank Juliana Martínez and Kemly Camacho at Fundación Acceso, and Cæcar Parall, Alberto Cortés, Mario Devandas and Jorge Arguedas of the Representación Social, and Jim Shapiro for research assistance. In Honduras, I would like to thank Victor Meza at the Honduran Documentary Center. In Guatemala my greatest debt is to Fernando Morales de la Cruz who gave me a glimpse of Guatemalan business life from the inside.

Revising the dissertation in order to prepare the book has been a new, challenging experience. I would like to thank David Levy-Faur for excellent suggestions for improvement of the original product, and the SUM for continued support in this final phase. Finally, I would like to thank Osvaldo Dorich for your endless love, care, engagement and commitment – to me, to Adrian and to a more just future for your fellow Latinos.

1. Privatization Puzzles

Between the late 1980s and the early 2000s, the trend towards privatization of state-owned enterprises swept the entire world. This gave rise to several puzzles for researchers to grapple with. The main question of the early political science literature on privatization was: Why would governments across the world at the same point in time choose to privatize their state-owned enterprises? This question was dealt with from various different angles and by authors with different implicit or explicit political leanings. A whole literature emerged from the effort to analyze and find a way around the obstacles that political interests and institutions posed to privatization policies. The implicit normative goal of this literature was to facilitate the adoption and implementation of privatization policies.

The question of 'Why?' was also dealt with from a more critical angle. The question posed was: What forces are really behind this massive push for privatization? In the developing country context, the answer often given to this question was that it was the international financial institutions (IFIs) – the World Bank, the International Monetary Fund (IMF), and to a lesser extent, the regional development banks – that were behind the push. However particularly within the Latin American context it was early recognized that these institutions could not bear the responsibility alone. There were strong domestic groups that were equally fierce supporters of privatization.

Understanding the driving forces behind privatization was the main motivation for this book. The main argument that it makes is that privatization can not be understood either as a natural result of rational government's response to technological developments and improved knowledge about how to produce goods and services most efficiently, or as a result of the pressure from IFIs. Rather, the impetus for privatization must be sought in the relationship between the state and the local private sector elites. I argue that in Central America, the strength of the local private sector elite and the form of relationship it has developed to the state has been the most important determinant of the inclination to privatize and the kind of privatization policies that have been pursued. This docs not mean that IFIs have not played a role, but that the relationship between the local private sector elite and the state is a key to understanding why different governments react differently to the IFIs' attempts to influence.

However, over the course of the 1990s, new privatization puzzles arose. Firstly, it became evident that privatization is only one element in reforms of telecommunications (and other sectors) that include different forms and extent of private sector participation, different kinds of regulation and different degrees of competition. Thus the question is not so much about what forces are behind privatization, but what composition of forces have been behind the specific kind of reforms in the specific cases. This is an important secondary topic in this book. I argue that governments have many and possibly contradictory goals connected with privatization, including fiscal goals, efficiency goals, political goals and personal economic goals. The degree to which privatization fulfills the different goals depends on the privatization process and the regulatory regime set up for the privatized companies.

Secondly, by 2005 there was an emerging consensus among economists that in Latin America privatization had improved firm performance: profits, operating efficiency and output tended to rise. The telecommunication sector stood out as the one that had been most successful in attracting private investments and in which the efficiency gains had been most noticeable (Calderón and Servén 2004). Moreover, claims about privatization's negative impact on inequality and poverty were largely found to be unjustified (Nellis 2003, McKenzie and Mookherjee 2003). Nevertheless, polls showed that privatization remained extremely unpopular, and protests against privatization arose all over the region. A new puzzle faced researchers and the concerned public: Why did privatization remain so unpopular when to most researchers the gains were so obvious? The argument made in this book is that in order to understand that issue, there is a need to take seriously issues related to state legitimacy. This depends on the degree to which the state is viewed as the instrument of a small elite, and the extent to which the privatization process has reinforced this.

In other words this book does not primarily take issue with the economic benefit of private participation in telecommunications. Rather, it questions the process through which privatization has taken place. In doing so, it focuses primarily on the role of the local private sector elite and the IFIs, and the impact their relationship to government has had on the legitimacy of the states in question.

The remainder of this introductory chapter will provide a review of the development of privatization in Latin America, an introduction to the privatization debates and privatization literature, a presentation of the cases, and an overview of the rest of the book.

PRIVATIZATION IN LATIN AMERICA

The recent wave of privatization has reached every corner of the world. However in Latin America, privatization started earlier and spread farther and more rapidly than in almost any other part of the world (Nellis 2003). After having been the area of origin of structuralist economic theory in the post-war period, Latin America was transformed to a neo-liberal testing ground in the 1980s, starting with the Chilean experiments of the late 1970s and spreading across the rest of the continent particularly after the onset of the debt crisis in 1982. Between 1986 and 1999, 396 Latin American state-owned companies were sold or transferred to the private sector (IDB 2002). As a consequence between 1990 and 1999, Latin America accounted for 55 per cent of the total value of privatizations in developing countries (Chong and López-de-Silanes 2003). From 1990 to 2001, private investment in infrastructure in Latin America totaled US$360.5 billion, most of which was related to privatization (Harris 2003).

By the beginning of the new millennium a consensus had been established among most economists that privatization had brought many benefits. Although varying significantly across countries and companies, profits, operating efficiency and output tended to rise after privatization (Nellis 2003). An IDB study of six Latin American countries found an average increase in profits (return on sales) of 29.8 per cent, and efficiency gains as measured by output per worker or ratio of costs to sales averaged 67 per cent (IDB 2002, Chong and López-de-Silanes 2003). Some of the efficiency gains could be accounted for by the lay-offs that generally have followed privatization. However most of the reduction in employment was short term, and many workers were re-hired after an initial restructuring phase (Chong and López-de-Silanes 2003).

The telecommunication sector experienced a particularly deep transformation. Whereas all 17 major Latin American countries[1] had publicly owned telecommunication companies in 1975 (Levi-Faur 2001), by 2004, only one country (Costa Rica) had only public telecommunication services, 12 countries had privatized their state-owned telecommunication company and opened for competition, and four had opened for private participation, but retained a partially or wholly state-owned telecommunication company.

In the telecommunication sector, privatization was associated with network expansion and price reductions. During the 1985–99 period, mainline penetration in all developing countries tripled (from 2.4 telephone mainlines per 100 people to 7.27 mainlines per 100). A study of eight Latin American countries showed that on average penetration growth increased from 5 per cent to 14 per cent annually after privatization, and the waiting lists were shortened by about 50 per cent (IDB 2002). Some of this could be accounted for by technological developments. However Fink et al. (2002) compared regions that have privatized extensively and those that have not, and found that Latin America and the Caribbean outperformed all other regions, and was also the region that had privatized most extensively. Although they argue that what they call 'autonomous increases' (including technological developments) on average outweigh effects of policy change, they conclude that privatization and introduction of competition had a significant impact on teledensity (number of telephone lines per 100 inhabitants).

Furthermore, privatization and competition have been associated with falling prices. Whereas in most cases there is an increase in fixed-line subscription and local rates immediately following privatization (due to cuts in previous cross-subsidies from long-distance to local telephony), over time, prices have fallen on most services (Estache et al. 2002).[2]

In sum, the conclusion was that privatization brought significant benefits to Latin America. Nevertheless in the telecommunication sector and other infrastructure sectors, evidence accumulated over the course of the 1990s that privatization was not a panacea, but rather one element in a package of reforms that also included regulatory changes aimed at fostering competition. The establishment of a regulatory framework and an independent regulatory institution was viewed as crucial for the benefit from privatization to occur. Also with regards to the establishment of independent regulatory agencies, Latin America outperformed other regions. Whereas less than 10 per cent of the countries had an independent regulatory agency in 1990, more than 70 per cent had one in 1999 (Fink et al. 2002). However, whereas the divestiture of a company was a relatively manageable, technical matter, to set up a regulatory institution with formal and real autonomy from politicians as well as private companies was a much more demanding matter.

In spite of all this, public discontent with privatization rose significantly by the end of the millennium. The well-known opinion polls conducted by Latinobarómetro showed a steady increase in the public's dissatisfaction with privatization. The number of people that disapproved of privatization climbed from 57 per cent in 2000 to 64 per cent in 2001. In the 2003 and 2004 surveys the question had changed slightly. The public was asked whether they were satisfied with the privatization of services in the country, taking into account their quality and price. In 2003, 71 per cent said they were less satisfied than before privatization. In 2004, the number had risen to 75 per cent (Latinobarómetro 2004).

Thus new puzzles arose that the economic literature referred to above was ill-prepared to deal with. However parallel to the economic research, a large body of literature discussing privatization from a political science and political economy perspective emerged. The focus of this literature has evolved due to the developments in the privatization processes referred to above. The initial literature was primarily concerned with answering the question of why Latin American countries privatized so uniformly and rapidly. Later the question turned to why the different countries adopted different regulatory frameworks and models. The final question that should be answered by political economists and political scientists is how privatization has affected the legitimacy of the political regimes. While relating primarily to the two first bodies of literature, this book also aims to contribute to developing the latter.

WHY DID LATIN AMERICAN COUNTRIES PRIVATIZE?

The debate in the literature on privatization in Latin America has been driven by both scholarly advances and political changes. In the following, some of the main issues that have been up for debate and the premises upon which they are based will be reviewed.

Domestic Determinants of Willingness to Reform

In the 1990s a rich literature emerged focusing on political and institutional determinants of the willingness and ability to adopt and implement neo-liberal economic reforms, among which privatization figured prominently. One problem discussed in this literature was that although the introduction of market-oriented policies was assumed to have favorable long-term consequences, the benefits of reforms may belong to the future and they may be less concentrated than the costs. Thus economic reform could be analyzed as a collective action problem. This made it difficult to mobilize potential winners of the reforms, whereas opposition is immediately spurred (Geddes 1994, Haggard et al. 1995). Some authors took as a starting point the idea that the previous state-led model created vested interests and opportunities for rent seeking (Krueger 1993). Therefore an important focus of the analysis was the composition of interest groups and how that prevents or facilitates the introduction of reform (Keohane and Milner 1996).

The interest group approach was challenged by studies focusing on how specific regimes formed the composition of interest groups rather than the other way around (Haggard and Kaufman 1992). The successful economic reform of Chile under authoritarian rule provided the first impetus to this literature. The first hypothesis explored was that authoritarian rule was necessary to overcome the natural opposition against market-oriented reforms that removed privileges from broad groups of the population (Skidmore 1977).

However evidence showing that market-oriented policies were implemented by democracies as well as authoritarian regimes soon accumulated (Maravall 1995). Moreover, privatization was conducted by governments belonging to parties from the political left and right (Wilson 1994, Weyland 2000). Thus the focus shifted to the impact of more specific institutional arrangements. In particular the degree of concentration of governmental authority in the executive has been argued to be a main determinant of successful reform (Haggard and Kaufman 1995). Evans (1992) noted that a capable bureaucracy enhances the possibility for introduction of successful reform. Another argument was that the likelihood of reform depended on how many 'veto-points' the political institutions creates, and how many 'veto players' exist that have to endorse a policy for it to be adopted (Tsebelis 1995, Castiglioni 2000).

The different contributions came up with different answers as to how obstacles to reform could and should be overcome, but much of the literature discussed above had a common implicit assumption that reform was good. Although rarely discussing the normative aspects of their analyses, by formulating reform as a collective action problem they implicitly argued that reform (including privatization) was an expression of collective rationality.

However assuming it is only the privatization opponents that are concerned with personal economic and political gains is a grave error. In Chapter 2, I discuss different formal goals of privatization and different motivations for supporting privatization. The formal goals may be grouped into three: improving efficiency in service production; fostering freedom of choice and facilitating private enterprise development; and reducing fiscal problems. It is argued that these goals may be incompatible, and that different models of telecommunication reform fulfill the goals to different extents. However what model is chosen is equally determined by politicians' motives for introducing reforms. I disagree with the public choice literature referred to above that applies a market analogy to understand the motivation of politicians. Rather than being motivated solely by their attempts to stay in power, I argue that they have a variety of different motivations. In Chapter 2, I group them into political and economic, and general and particular. The desire to stay in power may be considered a particular political motive. However politicians also have more collective political motives, such as security concerns, changing the political system, or strengthening or weakening political groups. They may also have collective economic motives, such as economic development and citizens' welfare. But equally prevalent are particular economic motives including self-enrichment and the enrichment of particular groups.

The more recent privatization literature has moved beyond the assumption of reform as a natural pursuit of development. Murillo (2003) shows for example how politicians have taken advantage of the privatization process to distribute resources in a way that allowed them to constitute or reinforce political coalitions. This book intends to continue this line of research. However whereas Murillo and others take as a starting point a relatively uncontested state with set rules guiding the political game, in some of the cases studied here these are not valid assumptions. The very basis of the state is contested and the control over state-owned enterprises plays an important role in that contestation. Furthermore a perspective on the state as a neutral arbiter of interest groups does not reflect realities in which societal groups are able to capture important policy processes. Therefore I will draw on the literature on state development (see Chapter 2) in order to shed light on the political game in which privatization is entrenched.

A second weakness of the literature referred to above is that it is generally concerned with domestic politics and disregards the international context. While it recognizes that the impetus for reform may come from outside, it analyzes the political process leading to making the decision to reform from an entirely national angle, without recognizing the increasing prevalence of international actors also in what is often called 'domestic politics'. In this case, the most important of these international actors are the IFIs and other aid agencies.

The Role of International Financial Institutions

The IFIs play a key role in the more critical literature on privatization and general neo-liberal reforms. In this literature it is commonly assumed that privatization is imposed on governments in developing countries, including those of Latin America, through the use of conditionalities connected to structural adjustment programs (Green 1995, Harris 2000). However the most pressing task for the critical literature has been to show that the policies introduced are based on flawed assumptions and that they have detrimental social consequences (Veltmeyer et al. 1997, Klak 1999, Zack-Williams et al. 2000, Peet 2003, Robinson 2003, SAPRIN 2004). The literature does not focus explicitly on the question of the degree to which the shift to neo-liberal policies in developing countries is a consequence of the IFI activities. Rather, that the shift is imposed by IFIs in conjunction with transnational capitalist coalitions is mostly taken for granted.

The studies that actually have focused on this question have reached a completely different conclusion. They point almost unequivocally to the conclusion that the connection between a country's embarkation on structural adjustment programs, including conditionalities to privatize state enterprises, is not a good indication as to whether it has actually introduced market-oriented reforms (including privatization). Many countries failed to implement the structural adjustment programs agreed to with the IFIs, and thus failed to privatize or introduce other reforms upon which provision of loans were conditioned. More than half the agreed reforms were never implemented (Haggard 1986, World Bank 1992a, Killick 1998, Mosley et al. 1995). Moreover countries that had not signed an agreement with the IFIs had just as high a probability of implementing market-oriented reforms (Killick 1996).

It would be easy to conclude from the above that the influence of the IFIs has been greatly exaggerated in the critical literature. I will argue that it has been both overstated and understated. The influence they exert through the use of conditionalities is overstated, a matter which many IFI officials also readily admit (Leandro et al. 1999). However, as will be discussed in Chapter 2, this is only one of three different sources of influence that the IFIs have on policy making in developing countries. The influence of conditionalities is based on 'relational power'. This is defined as the ability to make someone do something they would otherwise not have done. In this case the source of power is the ability to withhold funds, and the mechanism is conditionalities. A second source of influence is the production and transfer of ideas and knowledge about development. This may give them 'ideational power' or the ability of 'influencing, shaping and determining [other's] very wants' (Lukes 1974, p.23). Finally, the IFIs may have 'associational power'; the ability to enroll other actors in their own political project. In other words, IFIs may 'create' political actors through supporting specific domestic groups and so on that may become important actors in policy processes leading up to decisions to privatize or otherwise reform the telecommunication sectors.[3] In the remainder of the book I shall sometimes use the shorthand 'soft power' for the IFI strategies that do not include attempts at pressuring governments through the use of conditionalities.

Analyzing all three forms of power requires that we take a longer time-perspective than the single structural adjustment program or the single privatization process. Creating domestic political actors and forging support coalitions are lengthy processes. Therefore I will take into account the long term relationship between the states in question, the telecommunication companies, and the IFIs. Looked at in a long-term perspective, the IFIs appear, not as external forces, but rather as more or less permanent political actors at the domestic scene. Moreover looked at in such a perspective, they do not appear the tough and consistent advocates of neo-liberalism they are often portrayed as. Rather, they appear as complex giants, populated by officials motivated by short-term career concerns as well as ideology, and with leaders constantly searching for new ideas and concepts in development. Their power based on their economic clout and international prestige often fails to translate into influence due to their lack of coherence and consequent failure to attach their support to long-term locally based political projects.

Learning and Policy Emulation

The global wave of privatization and regulatory reform has been treated also from the angle of policy emulation and learning (Ikenberry 1990). From a thorough study of 8000 cases of privatization transactions in Latin America and Europe in the period 1980 and 1997, Meseguer (2003) concludes that pressure from international agencies (here the IMF and the EU) were irrelevant in the decision to privatize. What emerges as the main factor influencing the decision is learning from experience from prior cases within the same country and from neighboring countries. The same is argued by Jordana and Levi-Faur (2004b) who find that particularly in Latin America, there is a process of regional diffusion of regulatory reforms. This is stronger across national boundaries than across sectors.

Learning and emulation are definitely important mechanisms. However this book will add to the discussions about the role of learning in two ways. Firstly, it will dispute that the prevalence of learning and emulation means the IFIs play no role. Knowledge about how to organize the economy does not just 'float' in the international sphere, and it is not value neutral. Rather, it is promoted by actors, and the IFIs are among the most important 'teachers' (Finnemore 1996). The findings of Jordana and Levi-Faur (2004b) may strengthen this hypothesis, as the regional (IDB) and global (World Bank/IMF) IFIs would be more likely to draw on sector experience from other countries than experience from other sectors within the same country.

Secondly, this book will apply a different concept of learning. Underlying the literature above is a concept of learning as involving the transfer of a body of knowledge from one individual or social unit to another. This may be called the 'transportation paradigm', and it involves the transfer of knowledge from one actor to another. An alternative view is that learning is not the transfer, but the transformation of knowledge. This is a process in which everyone in the transformation chain shapes the knowledge according to their different projects (Latour 1986).

I will argue that although many ideas about how to organize the telecommunication sector and the economy in general circulate internationally, and are carried by various powerful international institutions, the actual models that will be implemented in a specific setting will be a hybrid, significantly modified by the ideas and interests of local actors.

In the telecommunication sector, the main local actors have been governments, state elites, private sector elites, and to some extent the military and unions. In many Latin American countries (and two of the cases included here), the military controlled the state-owned telecommunication companies up until the early 1990s. After the transformation of telecommunications from a strategic sector with high impact on national security to a sector which promised the potential of significant profits for the private sector, private sector elites became more central actors. However their access and relationship to national governments varies across countries. Therefore, in order to understand how international ideas are transferred and transformed in different contexts, there is a need to analyze the historically developed relations between different key actors, particularly the state and the local private sector. This, I will argue, is also a key to understanding the final outcome of the process of privatization and regulatory reforms.

WHAT KIND OF STATE EMERGES FROM THE PRIVATIZATION PROCESSES?

In the mid-1990s it was often argued that the withdrawal of the state from key functions (such as the provision of services) signified a retreat of the state (Strange 1996). However it soon became clear that the state and the market do not stand in a zero-sum relationship to each other. With regards to privatization, it was found that those countries where the state invested significantly in the infrastructure sectors were most successful in attracting private investments (Calderón and Servén 2004). Moreover a consensus emerged that privatization was most successful where it had been conducted within a solid institutional framework and where a regulatory institution had been established before the actual divestiture of the company.

Thus it was clear that what we are seeing is not a retreat of the state, but rather a reorganization of the state (Amoore et al. 1997). This reorganization has been interpreted in contradictory ways. It has been interpreted as a 'transnationalization' of the state (Cox 1981), which means that states increasingly adjust national political practices to the exigencies of the global economy. The transnationalization of the state entails a reorientation of state services to private capital, and within private capital, a reorientation of services from national to transnational fractions (Robinson 2003, p. 144). The idea of a transnationalization of the state is in other words connected to the idea of the rise of transnational classes, that are involved in global production and manage global circuits of accumulation (Gill and Law 1989, Sklair 2001). The transnational state is defined as 'a particular constellation of class forces and relations bound up with capitalist globalization and the rise of a transnational capitalist class, embodied in a diverse set of political institutions … the rise of a transnational capitalist class entails the reorganization of the state in each nation (national states) and it involves simultaneously the rise of truly supranational economic and political institutions' (Robinson 2003, p. 43).

This description does not leave much room for an autonomous state. The state was and is an instrument for the ruling classes, with the difference that the ruling classes now are of a transnational character. A partially competing vision argues that we rather see the emergence of 'a regulatory state'. This is suggested to capture the essence of the transformation of the capitalist economy in the late 20th century (Jordana and Levi-Faur 2004b). The regulatory state has given up 'rowing' the economy (running enterprises and provide services), but is still concerned with 'steering' (leading, thinking, directing, guiding) (Jordana and Levi-Faur 2004b). Regulation, in other words, not only means the formal passage of laws, but also informal ways in which the economy is governed. Moreover, it involves both regulation of competition and regulation for competition.

The notion of a regulatory state differs from the transnational state to the extent that it gives more autonomy to the state. The state is not only the instrument of a capitalist class, but may also act independently of it. However the degree to which it does so depends on the historically evolved relationship between the state and capitalist classes. Thus I view the degree to which either of the two concepts above captures the reality largely as an empirical question. Moreover, the specific expressions of the transnational or the regulatory state in different contexts are to some extent path dependent. In other words they depend on the historically developed relationship between the government, state elites and private sector elites.

In order to be able to shed light on the significance of state–private sector relations for privatization processes and the evolving state, I have chosen to study countries that are reasonably similar and comparable, but that differ significantly with regard to state–private sector relations.

PRIVATIZATION IN CENTRAL AMERICA

The cases studied in this book are the processes of telecommunication reform in three Central American countries: Guatemala, Costa Rica and Honduras. The countries of Central America – Costa Rica, El Salvador, Guatemala, Honduras and Nicaragua – have long constituted a popular laboratory for comparative research.[4] The geographical proximity of the five countries and their historical, geographical and cultural similarities provide a perfect backdrop for asking questions about why their economic and political trajectories have been so different. A large body of comparative research has emerged on different aspects of their diverging paths with respect to peace, democracy and development.[5] These have taken different approaches to the explanation of for example why Costa Rica has evolved as a stable democracy, while Guatemala, Nicaragua and El Salvador have experienced brutal dictatorships and civil wars, and Honduras has become a relatively stable, but impoverished backwater. Yet all the studies have attempted to explain the difference between them, in terms of both political regimes and economic policies.

The policy convergence around neo-liberalism occurring from the late 1980s turned Central America into a new laboratory. The five countries provided a focus for studying the puzzle striking observers of economic policy making around the world: Why would these otherwise so different countries all embark on similar strategies of privatization and liberalization?

Although a puzzle to some, for many observers of Central American politics, the culprit was easy to spot. Emerging out of a decade of political crisis in which the United States had played a key role, the turn to neo-liberalism was commonly interpreted as the consequence of US pressure, either bilaterally or through the IFIs. The United States had pressured Costa Rica both directly and indirectly to abandon its state-led development policies since 1983, attempting to shape it as the ideal politically and economically liberal democracy. Only a fear of destabilizing the peaceful haven in the troublesome region constrained the US from using all its powers to pressure for economic reform until peace agreements were coming close in the neighboring countries.

The electoral victory of liberal Violeta Chamorro in Nicaragua in 1990 signified the end of the decade-long socialist experiment of the Sandinistas and the exclusion of a socialist alternative in the region. This also changed the agenda for the US and the IFIs, now being less tolerant of lack of willingness to remove the remains of a state-led development model. For Honduras, it soon became clear that US patience with what was viewed as economic mismanagement and an overgrown state was ending around 1990, when the need for a base for the counter-insurgency forces in Nicaragua (Contras) diminished. The establishment of electoral democracy and the peace processes in Guatemala and El Salvador signified a new phase, not only with respect to the political circumstances, but also to economic policy making.

By the mid-1990s all the countries in the region had embarked on market oriented economic programs and presented plans for the privatization of state-owned enterprises (*Reporte Político* No. 127 May 1997; Larraín and López-Calva 2001). Some commentators seemed to hope that the introduction of market-oriented policies could help the countries to overcome the economic and social problems originating in part from their unstable and contested state structures since independence. Human agency could defeat the structural constraints that history had produced. But could it? Or would history put its mark also on the neo-liberal policies that would be introduced?

This question informed my selection of cases within the Central American region. A general proposition emerging from the historical comparative literature on Central America is that the social forces behind the state consolidation in El Salvador, Guatemala and Nicaragua had many similarities, whereas Costa Rica and Honduras differ from them and also from each other. In a crude and simplified manner, the conclusion of the comparative historical literature could be summed up as follows. In El Salvador, Guatemala and Nicaragua, strong national agro-producer groups emerged around the production of coffee and a few other export crops in the late nineteenth century, oppressing labor and favoring brutal, often military, governments to protect their privileges. Here oligarchic states were established, dominated by informal groups depending on their economic clout for control. The Costa Rican state was also initially dominated by a coffee-growing oligarchy, but a more egalitarian distribution of land ensured less social tension and thus less need for an oppressive state. It also allowed for the changes occurring in the 1940s institutionalizing a welfare democracy and abolishing the military. In Honduras, cattle farming, mining and banana production were the dominant economic activities, none of which had the same potential for producing a national oligarchy as did coffee production. Rather, banana production was to be dominated by US companies, trapping Honduras in a dependency relationship with the Big Brother in the north.

The choice of Costa Rica, Guatemala and Honduras was thus based on a desire to account for privatization processes in contexts that were as different as possible with regards to state development and the relationship to private sector elites.

The choice of the telecommunication sector was based on pragmatic as well as theoretical considerations. By 1997, all the countries involved had presented plans for introducing private participation in their telecommunication sectors. Thus it was a comparable sector. Moreover telecommunications stand at the crossroads between the past and the future in a quite particular manner. The state-owned telecommunication enterprises (SOTs) embodied many of the core features of the states. The Guatemalan and Honduran SOTs (Guatel and Hondutel respectively) had close formal and informal ties with the military, and played key roles in surveillance of the opposition and as income generators for the armed forces. The Costa Rican Electricity Institute (ICE) on the other hand, had been a centerpiece of the Costa Rican state developmental project, being in charge of the extension of both telecommunication and electricity services to poor and rural areas (see Table 1.1 for indicators of the differences between the countries).

By the early 1990s the significance of telecommunications was about to change. Rather than as a developmentalist or surveillance device, a source of state revenue or distribution of spoils, telecommunications were promoted as the key to economic prosperity in the information age. Characterized by rapid technological change and reorganization at the global level, the telecommunication sector provided an arena for encounter between globalizing forces and representatives for the national state development projects. However being a booming sector it also provided an arena for encounters between different ideas about the relationship between profit maximization and distribution of services.

Table 1.1 Economic and social indicators

	Costa Rica		Guatemala		Honduras	
	1990	2000	1990	2000	1990	2000
Population, million	3.0	4.0	8.7	11.7	6.9	8.1
GDP;capita US$[a]	5230	8910	2810	3960	2040	2510
External debt:GDP	61	27	31	20	112	91
Tax income:GDP	17.5[b]	17.9[c]	7.4[b]	8.9[c]	---	---
Teledensity (1995)	9.30	25.70	2.09	6.1	1.73	4.98

Notes:
a. Current US$
b. Average 1990–94
c. Average 1995–99

Source: IDB (1998), World Bank (2000), Government Finance Statistics (IMF).

Focusing primarily on telecommunications, the book will embed the study of this sector in an understanding of the broader processes of privatization and market orientation of the economy within each country.

The study stretches from 1986 to 2000; 1986 marks the beginning of a 'normalization' of politics in Guatemala and Honduras at which point economic reorganization returned to the national agenda after having been overshadowed by security issues. In Costa Rica, 1986 marked the transition to the government of Oscar Arias that actively pursued neo-liberal policies, during which the first proposal for privatization of the telecommunication sector was launched. By the end of 2000, new forms of organization of the telecommunication sector were about to crystallize in the three countries, after having been significantly delayed.

In Guatemala, a new and radically liberal telecommunication law had been introduced in 1996. It allowed for the divestiture of the state-owned telecommunication company (Guatel), full competition in the sector and a minimal role for the state regulator. The privatization was completed in 1998. In Costa Rica, a European-style model which allowed for private competition in the telecommunication sector in which the Costa Rican Electricity Institute (ICE) and its subsidiary Costa Rican Radiography (RACSA) had a monopoly, had been debated for years, but no major reforms had been introduced. In Honduras, a new telecommunication law was approved in 1995. It introduced a traditional Latin American-style privatization, with competition only after a period in which the privatized Hondutel would operate in a monopoly. It also established a separate regulatory institution, Conatel, that was given significant power to direct the sector. However, having been postponed many years, the privatization of Hondutel failed in 2000.

At this point it was clear that privatization had severe political costs. In 2000, the Guatemalan ruling party – the National Advancement Party (PAN) – lost the elections primarily due to the scandals surrounding the privatization of Guatel (now Telgua); Costa Rica saw arguably the most severe public unrest since the 1948 civil war due to public opposition to the proposed reform of ICE and the electricity and telecommunication sectors, and support for privatization plummeted. In Guatemala, polls showed that 98 per cent of the population was dissatisfied with the privatized services. The corresponding number in Honduras was 80 per cent (Latinobarómetro 2004). This book aims to contribute to understanding why.

A NOTE ON METHOD

The methodological approach in this book is qualitative. I have sought to follow the privatization processes in depth, and therefore detailed information has been collected through interviews with involved parties, documents (public and private), newspaper articles, and secondary material (books and articles). The interview material was collected during two trips to Washington, DC (February 1998 and September 1999), two stays in Costa Rica (February 1999 and September–November 2000), two stays in Guatemala (October–November 1999 and November 2000) and two stays in Honduras (November 1999 and August 2001). In total, 130 interviews have been conducted.

Some of the interviews are referred to explicitly and from several there are direct quotes. Most of the interviews in Central America were made in Spanish, and the quotes that appear here are all translated by the author. Due to concerns of confidentiality not all the names are revealed. The main rule of thumb that has been followed is that unless the interviewees have specified otherwise, names of people that have had a high public profile are revealed, and names of people that are not as publicly profiled are not. There is no list of interviews included, due to a desire to protect the informants and particularly those who do not generally have a public role.

In the three countries, access to and existence of documentation of the privatization process differ significantly. This has been a problem, but it has also shed light on some of the issues that this book aims to investigate, as the archival traditions of a state may be an important indicator of its autonomy and capacity. In Costa Rica, extensive use was made of the archives of the Legislative Assembly, where detailed minutes from the debates in the various committees and the plenary and also all the documentation that was presented to the deputies, are guarded. In Guatemala no such information exists in the archives, and the general rule is that the respective committee leader takes home the material after resigning. In Honduras, the situation was largely similar, and access to archives was dependent on the personal approval of the President of the Congress. Similarly, the information available at the ICE was rich and voluminous, whereas in the cases of Guatemala and Honduras, very limited information was available from the former SOTs and I obtained it only through personal contacts.

OUTLINE OF THE BOOK

The remainder of the book is outlined as follows. Chapter 2 spells out the theoretical framework in greater detail. It discusses different goals and motives for privatization and regulatory reform. Further, it discusses how the historically evolving relationship between the state and private sector elites impact upon the privatization process as well as the emerging state form. Furthermore it discusses different sources of influence of the IFIs and how the IFIs relate to different states.

Chapter 3 treats the process of reform in Guatemala. It begins by discussing the relationship between the Guatemalan state and private sector elites. In this, the telecommunication company has historically been a major source of revenue for the government and a surveillance device for the military. The chapter further traces how different private sector elites affected the new telecommunication law and the process of privatization. However it argues that different parts of the local elite had different interests in the telecommunication sector, and that explains to a large extent the contradictory outcome: a telecommunication law opting for full competition and transparency, and a process of telecommunication privatization lacking either. The IFIs played a marginal role in the process, explained to a large extent by the local private sector's ambivalent attitude towards them.

Chapter 4 discusses the case of Costa Rica. This contrasts sharply with Guatemala, with regard to both the main actors and the outcome. The case of Costa Rica shares with Guatemala the marginal role played by the IFIs. As in Guatemala, the only external agency with real influence on the privatization process was the United States Agency for International Development (USAID) that through its strategies to strengthen the local private sector also contributed to creating main proponents of privatization. In spite of this, the private sector was a much weaker actor in Costa Rica than in Guatemala. The actor that emerged as the leading force was the ICE itself. It had become an autonomous institution with significant expertise among its employees and leadership. Therefore, the main policy proposals for reforming it also emerged from the ICE.

Chapter 5 discusses the case of Honduras. Honduras is the only one of the cases in which the IFIs have played a significant role in the process of telecommunication reform. However in spite of the fact that privatization of Hondutel was a condition for loans from the World Bank and the IDB since 1995, and in spite of the fact that Honduras experienced increasingly severe debt problems, the Honduran government did not put up Hondutel for sale until 2000, when it rejected the offer it received. The main explanation given here is that the privatization process was designed in such a manner that the local private sector was effectively prohibited from participation. Therefore those favoring privatization out of collective economic interest did not get the same kind of help from those favoring privatization out of private economic interest, as had been the case in Guatemala. Furthermore, devoid of strong national institutions in which the neo-liberal ideas of the IFIs could be embedded, neo-liberalism did not form a real stronghold in Honduras.

Chapter 6 compares the processes in the three different countries and draws conclusions with regards to the forces behind reforms. It also compares the outcome in terms of the framework for the telecommunication sector and discusses whether we see the emergence of a regulatory state in the telecommunication sector in Central America. It further compares the outcome in terms of a few indicators of telecommunication development. Finally, it discusses implications of the telecommunication reform processes for state, regime and elite legitimacy.

NOTES

1. I do not include the Caribbean nor the 'micro-states' Belize, Guyana and Suriname.
2. To my knowledge there are few studies that have accounted for the autonomous effect of technology on prices.
3. These concepts are based on a pluralist power concept (associated with Robert Dahl), a Gramscian power concept (associated with Steven Lukes) and a Latourean concept of learning, respectively. These are discussed in further depth in Chapter 2.
4. At times also Panama and/or Belize are included in the definition of Central America although for historical and cultural reasons they are set apart.
5. Among the most important are: Rueschemeyer et al. (1992), chapter 6; Paige (1997), Lentner (1993), Dunkerley (1994), Booth and Walker (1989), Vilas (1995), Flora and Torres-Rivas (1989), Yashar (1997). In addition to the explicit comparative literature, there

is a large implicitly comparative literature focusing on one of the cases, but where the interest in the country is dependent on the difference between this and the neighbouring countries. First of all there is a large literature on the 'Costa Rican exceptionalism' (e.g., Gudmundson 1986, Seligson 1980, Franklin 1998, Wilson 1998). There is also a certain literature on the relative stability of Honduran politics (Ropp 1974, Ruhl 1984, Schulz and Sundloff Schulz 1994).

2. The Politics of Privatization

What has driven the recent trend towards liberalizing and privatizing the telecommunication sector? The two most common answers to this are probably technological developments and pressure from international financial institutions. However there are many reasons why these explanations are not sufficient. The first part of this chapter will consider various factors affecting the motivation and ability of governments to pursue market-oriented reforms, including privatization. The second part of the chapter discusses the relationship between privatization processes, state power and legitimacy.

GOALS AND MOTIVATIONS OF PRIVATIZATION

Why do states privatize? One may distinguish between the goals of privatization, which are the official justifications for privatization policies, and motives of privatization, which are the reasons why policy makers choose to support privatization policies.

The Stated Goals of Privatization

Technical improvement and economic efficiency
One main goal of privatization is to ensure a more efficient production of services. This argument is founded on both general economic arguments and arguments more specific to the telecommunication industry. Technical breakthroughs in the telecommunication sector had two major effects. Firstly, telecommunications no longer were a natural monopoly.[1] Therefore the main argument for monopoly no longer applied (Petrazzini 1995, Vogelsang and Mitchell 1997). Secondly, the developments contributed to increase the variety of telecommunication services, improve their quality and the capacity to produce them, and lower their costs. In sum they boosted potential profits to be made from telecommunications at the same time as they lowered the initial investments necessary for production of services. Therefore technological developments made it more attractive to the private sector to participate, and weakened the traditional argument for state ownership (Bulmer-Thomas 1994, p. 352).

However the drive towards competitive markets and privatization is not unique for the telecommunication sector, but a part of a general policy shift. A part of this shift was the increasing dominance of neo-classical economics, designed to elaborate how individual self-interested action may generate optimal solutions to problems of human welfare. These assumptions and methods were the foundation for the so-called new political economy (NPE) that became increasingly influential in development circles over the course of the 1980s. NPE analysis was based in the assumptions of neo-classical economics (methodological individualism, rational utility maximization and equilibrium analysis), and politicians were viewed as individualists who were motivated by rational utility achievements, not by a notion of the common good (Bates 1981, Krueger 1993). One conclusion was that public ownership, due to its incentive structure, is always inferior to private ownership. In the influential World Bank report *Bureaucrats in Business*, one of the main conclusions was that the greater the participation of private agents in ownership and management, the greater the enterprise performance (World Bank 1995a).

A main justification for privatizing the SOT was therefore the idea that private ownership was always more efficient than public. This view was gradually moderated over the course of the 1990s, based partly on empirical analyses of experiences with privatization and partly on the increasing influence of institutional economics. Vickers and Yarrow concluded that private ownership was superior to public ownership only in industries where competition existed. In markets without competitive forces, they argued that the introduction of competition (via the elimination of statutory monopolies for example) or regulatory measures that mimicked competitive forces probably provided greater efficiency gains than could be expected from the transfer of ownership to the private sector (Vickers and Yarrow 1988). It was argued that deregulation aimed at fostering competition was as important as privatization (Guash and Spiller 1994). However it became increasingly clear that competition required not only deregulation but also re-regulation.[2] More recent evidence shows that the establishment of separate regulatory authorities prior to privatization has been a key to success (Wallsten 2002). One main effect of this has been an increasing focus on the need to establish an independent regulatory agency (IRA) with autonomy from the government and other political institutions. Such an institution should ensure transparency in decision making and predictability in operational conditions for the private actors operating in the market.

The increasing focus on the establishment of an IRA led to a focus on the specific interventions of the state, and opened the argument that in some instances these should be strengthened rather than minimized. However this conflicted with another argument for rolling back the state; namely that it was necessary to ensure personal freedom.

Enhancing the freedom of private enterprise
The theoretical justification for neo-liberalism is not only to ensure optimal efficiency in resource use, but also to avoid coercion and ensure freedom, a goal to which the free market is seen as one crucial means. Freedom is generally equated with personal freedom defined as: 'The state in which a man is not subject to coercion by the arbitrary will of another or others' (Hayek 1960, p. 11). According to the liberal philosophers, if given a choice man would choose less over more state intervention. The task of a policy of freedom is to minimize coercion or its harmful effects, even if it cannot eliminate it completely.

In this perspective, state ownership is viewed not only as inefficient, but also as an example of power abuse impeding personal initiative and freedom. As argued by Hayek: 'The reason why many of the new welfare activities of government are a threat to freedom, then, is that, though they are presented as mere service activities, they really constitute an exercise of the coercive powers of government and rest on its claiming exclusive rights in certain fields' (Hayek 1960, p.258). This is echoed by the claim made by Peter Bauer, one of the pioneers of neo-liberalism in development economics, that 'a society resistant to totalitarian appeal implies that the government refrains from substantial government participation in industry and trade' (quoted in Toye 1993, p. 79).

One expression of this totalitarianism was, according to the neo-liberals, privileges given to particular groups. In relation to the telecommunication industry, these groups were often labor unions and private sector groups, such as suppliers of equipment, closely related to the state-owned enterprises. Unlocking opportunities for private sector development through, among other means, privatization and removal of privileges would both increase their productive potential and create a better society (World Bank 1997, p. 61–75). However, the third main motivation for privatization, namely to improve the fiscal situation, could potentially be in conflict with this goal.

Improving the fiscal situation
The debt crisis that hit large parts of the developing world in the early to mid 1980s, struck Latin America particularly hard. Between 1975 and 1982, Latin America's long-term foreign debt quadrupled, growing from US$45.2 billion to US$176.4 billion. In terms of ratio of foreign debt to GDP, it increased from 21 per cent to 44 per cent. In the same period, Central America's average external debt obligations increased from 31 per cent to 77 per cent of GDP (Tavares 2001). With the hike in world interest rates and the

deteriorating prices of non-oil exports of the early 1980s, the current account deficits deteriorated sharply throughout the region. The real interest rates jumped from an average of LIBOR (London inter-bank offered rate) minus 3.4 per cent between 1970 and 1980 to +19.9 percent in 1981, and +27.5 percent in 1982. As a result of the crisis, availability of foreign funds dropped by 40 per cent between 1981 and 1983, and the sources of commercial funds virtually dried up. As a means of covering the deficits and improving credibility towards foreign investors and creditors, most Latin American countries engaged in a process of cutting and restructuring public expenses. In most countries, investment in infrastructure was severely curtailed (Edwards 1995, p. 22). One of the first actions undertaken in order to halt the debt crisis was to put a cap on further borrowing by the SOEs that were an important source of the public debt in the first place (Ramamurti 1992a). The postponement of investment also gradually eroded the quality of services and reduced their public support (Birch and Haar 2000).

In this situation, privatization of telecommunications was both a means of generating income and a means of relieving the state from the burdens of further investment in the sector. The state-owned telecommunication companies often had a particular position with respect to the fiscal balance. Whereas many other state-owned enterprises were loss making, the telecommunication companies were generally producing significant income for the government. In Latin American states, the SOTs were often called the government's 'little cash box' (*la caja chica*), on which it depended in difficult situations.

Theoretically there are not necessarily greater benefits from selling the company than keeping it and capturing part of the increased income stream through taxation and transfer or dividend, but there are many situations in which the one time lump sum is attractive (Raventós 1997). One such situation is when the state is faced with an acute fiscal crisis that does not permit long-term considerations. The privatization proceeds may also be very attractive in cases where the ability to tax is low. Moreover as privatization proceeds are often collected in dollars, privatization may be attractive where the state faces balance-of-payment problems.

The hypothesis that governments privatize primarily in order to raise revenue in the face of high debt burdens and fiscal problems has received considerable attention (Ramamurti 1992a, Ramamurti 1996, Molano 1997, Castelar Pinheiro and Schneider 1995, Yarrow 1999). Attempts to establish a connection are obscured by the fact that virtually all developing countries have experienced fiscal crises and not all of them have privatized, at least not directly following the fiscal crisis. Nevertheless, it is clear that although the revenue from telecommunication privatization has helped some governments out of acute crises, the actual effect of privatization on debt reduction has been minimal (Ramamurti 1992b, Castelar Pinheiro and Schneider 1995).

Moreover an indirect effect of the fiscal crisis on privatization was that it made governments more vulnerable to pressure from the IFIs, which in the mid-1980s started to favor private service providers over public ones. Moreover, the IFIs closed off possibilities for lending to state-owned telecommunication companies, viewed as a sector which due to technological changes could easily find funding on the private market.

Contradictions between the goals
As should be clear from the above, privatization of the telecommunication sector is not a single policy but may involve a variety of different measures that may be defined along three dimensions: divestiture, competition and regulation (including the establishment of an IRA). As sketched in Table 2.1 these may be both be compatible and contradictory.

Table 2.1 Goals and means of privatization of telecommunications

Goals **Priority of means**	Improving fiscal situation	Improved services	Freedom of private enterprise
Divestiture of SOT	High	Low, depending on framework	High
Conditions for sale			
- Competition	Low	High	High
- Monopoly Period -	Yes	No	No
- Forced connection	No	Yes	No
Establishment of IRA	Low	High	Low

The first possible contradiction to notice is between the goals of improving the fiscal situation and ensuring efficient service provision. If the main goal is increased revenue to improve the fiscal situation, the priority would be to divest the state-owned company and one would aim at giving the incumbent carrier a period of monopoly. However, enhancing price through giving the incumbent a monopoly period may conflict with the goal of efficient service production as most would agree that introducing competition may be an important means to that end. Furthermore, in order to realize the benefits of competition, a regulatory framework and an institution that can secure compliance with it, are required (Basañes et al. 1999). However establishment of an agency with the authority to regulate the market may be undesirable to the ideological liberals who would place emphasis on the third goal, namely freedom of private enterprise and favor as little state involvement as possible[3]

Motivations for Privatization

So far we have only considered the goals of privatization that policy makers themselves would point to in justifying their policies. An underlying assumption has been that the goal of the politicians is to enhance citizens' welfare, whereas the exact nature of the policy they pursue depends on their ideas about how to best organize the economy to achieve this. It is clear that this only covers one aspect of the motivation of politicians. The NPE literature referred to above has left largely unresolved the question of what motivates governments to pursue policy reform. This gave root to the 'orthodox paradox' formulated by Kahler (1992). The orthodox paradox originates in the assumption that politicians operate rationally in the pursuit of wealth and power. Part of the justification for introducing policies to diminish politicians' control over the economy was indeed that they were not thought to be motivated by the pursuit of the general well being of society. The dilemma was that if such an assumption should hold, it would be very unlikely that any of the proposed reforms would be introduced. Politicians would most likely meet resistance from groups with vested interests in the prior model, and if dependent on their support, they would have few reasons for going forward with the reforms.

The argument made here is that politicians pursue various motives that may all lead to support for privatization (or not). One may distinguish between economic and political motives, and between motives related to society as a whole and motives related to one specific actor or group. These different forms of motives are not mutually exclusive. Policy makers may pursue different motives at the same time.

One possibility is that politicians are motivated primarily by staying in power, as assumed in the rational choice literature. The main concern of scholars has been that politicians motivated primarily by a desire to stay in power may fail to introduce reforms. However we may also conceive of situations where privatization and other neo-liberal reforms may be used as instruments to weaken political adversaries.

A second alternative is that politicians are motivated by the prospect for personal economic gains. Staying in power may be a means to achieve personal gains, but politicians may also be willing to risk losing power if it provides significant benefit to the person in question or to a group to which he or she belongs. How can these different models be related to the forces behind reforms? Murillo (2003) argues, for example, that the selling conditions of privatized assets is affected by whether the government has potential buyers within its constituency. This issue has been extensively discussed related to the opportunities for corruption in the privatization process (Manzetti and Blake 1996, Celarier 1997). However one may also acquire economic resources through perfectly licit practices. Privatization and neo-liberal reforms may be a means to redirect the organization of the economy in manners that benefit particular groups economically more than others.

A final form of motivation is general political motives. This includes foreign policy motives and security concerns, but also attempts to forge or avoid internal political power shifts. Political motives are no less compatible with developmental policies than economic motives. Indeed they may be a condition for them, as has been thoroughly discussed in the literature explaining the East Asian Miracle (Kohli 1999, Johnson 1999).

A political project as a motivation may be more easily joined with a state-led development project than neo-liberal reforms. Indeed, the origins of a state-led development policy may be found in mercantilist ideas in which the king's political goals and power and the economic development of the nation are viewed as two sides of the same issue. Economic policies were therefore naturally a part of a political project (Hveem and Reinert 1999). However neo-liberal reforms may also be introduced primarily in order to achieve political goals. One example of this is where privatization has been used as a means to weaken organized labor (Gates 2000), or bureaucratic elites (Ramirez 2000). A further theoretical possibility, which has received less attention in the literature, is that privatization may be designed to weaken local economic elites. This may be achieved if, through liberalization and privatization, one succeeds in attracting significant foreign investments. This means not only an additional source of capital, but also possibly a new political actor that could threaten the position of the local private sector.

The discussion above relates to the motives of a government or political elites within one country. However it is clear that the process of introducing market-oriented reforms is not confined to a specific country. Rather, it has been an international process, and in the developing countries, the IFIs have often been considered the main agents of change. In the following I will discuss how their activities may change the equation.

THE INTERACTION BETWEEN THE IFIS AND POLICY MAKERS

Conditionalities and Bargaining Power

The form of influence that dominates the literature on the IFIs and domestic policies is the influence that they exercise through demanding that the borrowing member countries (BMCs) fulfill conditionalities for loans. Policy conditionalities may be defined as 'mutual arrangements by which a government takes, or promises to take, certain policy actions, in support of which an IFI or other agency will provide a specified amount of financial assistance' (Killick 1998, p. 6).

Policy conditionality originated with the IMF, and initially had a relatively specific macroeconomic focus. Conditionalities were intended to substitute for collateral, normally pledged by commercial banks in terms of an asset to be handed over if the borrower failed to pay back loans. IMF conditionalities were to increase the likelihood of loan repayment and give the lender an early warning of potential repayment difficulties (Killick 1998). In the multilateral development banks (MDBs), conditionalities were originally related to project lending and they were set to ensure that the funds were used for what they were intended. With the introduction of policy-based lending in the 1980s, the World Bank and later the regional development banks made general financial support conditioned on policy change.

One way of analyzing the power of the IFIs is to start with the initial positions of the borrowing country and the IFIs and study the bargaining game between the IFI and the borrowing country (Killick 1996, Kahler 1995). The borrowing country in theory applies for a loan due to insufficiency of domestic financing, lack of availability of commercial financing, or better conditions related to IFI financing. The IFIs are motivated by a desire to avoid the borrower running into arrears, or by a broader view of what is beneficial for economic development, demanding that the government fulfill a set of conditions for signing the agreement and for disbursing the loan. Given that the country would not otherwise be inclined to pursue these policies, we could use the outcome of the bargaining to draw conclusions about the power of the IFIs. The underlying concept of power would then be a relational one, defined as A has power over B if A can make B do something it otherwise would not have done (Lukes 1974).

However this is a too simplistic view of the bargaining game. Firstly, neither the IFIs nor the BMCs may adequately be analyzed as unitary actors. In the bargaining process they have to keep an eye on their constituencies, which have to approve any possible agreement. In most cases the government of the BMC depends on approval by a congress or legislative assembly, and the IFI negotiating team needs approval by the board of executive directors (and often several other less formal instances). Moreover recently it has become important to gain ex ante approval by non-governmental organizations (NGOs) and other stakeholders, at least when there are large projects with high environmental or social impacts at stake. Thus the bargaining process may be most fruitfully examined as a 'two-level game' (Putnam 1988, Kahler 1995).

Secondly, the threat of withdrawing funds may lack credibility in both the short and the long run. The loans are normally disbursed in different tranches, and the disbursement of each of them is made dependent on the fulfillment of a set of conditionalities, often called 'trigger actions'. In some cases disbursement is in addition dependent on cross-conditionality (the fulfillment of conditionalities set by other donors or IFIs). However although a tranche is postponed or even cancelled due to failure to comply with conditionalities, bank officials have many incentives to continue to lend to the country at a later point. As Mosley et al. note (1991, p. 172) based on an internal World Bank review (World Bank 1988), even though almost all tranches experience release delays as a result of insufficient progress in fulfilling conditions, almost all tranches have eventually been released. As the Bank's main mission is to lend money, they have little to gain from being too strict with respect to demanding fulfillment of conditionalities for the disbursement of funds after the agreement is signed. The situation is described by Mosley et al. (1991, p.173) as a 'ritual dance':

> All parties now know that they are caught up in a ritual dance: Bank senior staff know that, bearing in mind what other countries have got away with, it will be neither just nor financially productive to make an example of one particular recipient who defaults on conditions by refusing the second tranche; Bank junior staff know that it will not be helpful to their careers to protest the decision to release; and the recipient knows that if it makes amicable noises, plus comparisons with other countries if necessary, it can expect the release of the second tranche within a year as surely as day follows night.

This not only weakens the leverage of the IFIs, it also makes it difficult to analyze the bargaining as a one-time situation.

Bank officials have incentives both for ensuring board approval and subsequently for disbursement of loans. While the former increases the likelihood that the bank official attaches conditionalities reflecting the interests of the board to the loans, the latter decreases the likelihood that they include conditionalities for the loans that delay the disbursement process. However there are several strategies that may be applied by the IFI official to avoid this problematic Firstly, he or she may include conditionalities pro forma, in other words, include conditionalities that have already been fulfilled when the agreement is signed. Secondly, he or she may vary the tranching arrangement. Where it is desired to exert maximum leverage over a government, credit may be back-loaded with a large proportion payable in later tranches. Where there is high confidence in the intentions of a government and it needs finance urgently, one may choose to front-load, with a large proportion of the credit being paid up-front (Killick 1998). If a program is front-loaded and has a series of pro forma conditionalities attached to it, it is easy to conclude that its influence on policy has been greater than it actually has.

Failure to comply by the BMC may be interpreted as some sort of 'moral hazard': policy makers agree to conditionalities they do not intend to fulfill, because they know that the consequences are moderate. However it is equally likely that it is a case of involuntary defection (Putnam 1988) resulting for example from failure to pass agreements in respective congresses. As the IFIs, due to their nature as multilateral institutions, are supposed to be apolitical, they also have to refrain from direct interaction with internal matters and therefore they (at least formally) are excluded from the possibility of making alliances across the two levels of the game.

In the analyses of the case studies, I will take into account various techniques that have been applied in order to attempt to forge reforms through conditionalities. Initial positions will be sketched, discussions referred to (when data has been available) and outcomes analyzed. However, equally important will be the analysis of how the MDBs have attempted to reduce the need for using conditionalities to pressure the governments through different forms of technical cooperation and policy dialogue.

Technical Cooperation, Learning and Power

Both the MDBs and bilateral donors make extensive use of technical cooperation, aimed to convey knowledge and policy ideas relevant for a specific project. Although it is easy to point to policy ideas that have been circulating in the IFIs, and that have been adopted as policies by BMCs, there are several problems with establishing a connection between the two. As Goldstein and Keohane warn: 'Ideas are always present in policy discussions since they are a condition for reasoned discourse. But if many ideas are available for use, analysts should not assume that the sole intrinsic property of an idea explains its choice by policy makers' (Goldstein and Keohane 1993, p. 11). The problem is aggravated by the fact that technical cooperation often follows loan programs that also include conditionalities. Thus it may be difficult to distinguish the policy changes that follow conditionalities and changes that can be traced to transfer of knowledge. A further issue to take into account is that domestic policy makers may be influential in picking the consultants and/or directing their work. The consultant may in turn be dependent on the same policy makers for further contracts and therefore primarily give them what they want (Gasper 1999).

Irrespective of this, we cannot exclude that the IFIs may act as 'teachers' and contribute to policy change through changing policy makers' beliefs about appropriate policy (Finnemore 1996). But if we are able to conclude that the IFIs through dissemination of knowledge have influenced domestic policy making, to what extent can we describe this as a form of exercise of power? The general justification for technical cooperation is that the knowledge transferred is based on the best available research. MDBs are viewed as particularly fit for the task of knowledge dissemination due to their moral standing as institutions endowed with the tasks of promoting the common good, and their legitimacy as 'disinterested institutions' with well-recognized research departments (Gilbert and Vines 2000, p. 29).

This view presupposes that knowledge can be judged according to some objective criteria. There are at least two arguments for rejecting this view. One is that scientific practice is not based on neutral criteria, but on knowledge structures underpinned by belief systems that decide what is to be considered knowledge, what kind of knowledge is to be produced and how it is going to be stored (Strange 1988). The other is the neo-Gramscian argument, which connects this knowledge structure directly to the capitalist structures.[4] The argument is that not only do the capitalist structures affect what kind of knowledge is produced, they shape at a deeper level the categories through which we experience the world, and therefore the questions that we are interested in gaining knowledge about (Gill 2000). International organizations exert power through classification and organization of information and knowledge, they fix meaning through naming or labeling, and establish boundaries for acceptable action (Barnett and Finnemore 1999). Underlying these accounts is a concept of power defined as the ability to shape people's desires and interests through 'influencing, shaping and determining [their] very wants' (Lukes 1974, p. 23).

However underlying this notion is a model of learning depicting the process of knowledge dissemination and utilization as involving the transfer of a body of knowledge from one individual or social unit to another. An alternative view is that learning cannot be understood as transfer of knowledge, but rather as translation, a process in which everyone in the transfer chain shapes the knowledge according to their different projects (Latour 1986). Learning is the joint creation of knowledge by both disseminators and users.

This view of learning has a double implication for understanding the IFI influence on domestic policy. Firstly, if learning does not mean the transfer of a certain policy but the creation of new forms, then we must focus on what occurs in the process of interaction between the MDB representatives and the

BMC representatives. In this process, new policy ideas may be created as hybrids between those of the MDB representatives and the BMC representatives. This also leads to a different understanding of responses to external pressure. The possible forms of reaction are not limited to the adoption of a policy or resistance to it. It includes also adaptation of the policy proposals to suit one's own political project or ideas. Secondly, if power is not only the ability to make someone do something they otherwise would not have done, or to shape their ideas and interests, but also 'the ability to make others carry out or carry on one's will', then we cannot end our analysis at the signing of an agreement and the adoption of new policies. We have to include an analysis of the ability to embed the policy in a political project with the potential to carry forth the purposes and ideas inherent in the policies. Thus, we have to include a third manner in which MDBs may affect the domestic political agenda: through support for actors that promote a certain political project.

The Power of Association and Support for Domestic Actors

Whereas you would find both policy-based loans and technical cooperation in the banks' annual reports, you would not find a column on the amount of funds that has been set off for support for actors and political projects. However through for example the selection of cooperation partners for implementation of loans and technical cooperation projects, the MDBs may contribute to creating actors that may carry on or carry out the will of the IFIs.

Introduction of a role for the IFIs in terms of policy conditionalities means that these actors may change their calculations about costs and benefits of particular policies. Arguing that IFIs may be teachers of policy means that they may also change their ideas and interests. However focusing in addition on their associational power means that they can affect who the actors are. The three different arguments are illustrated in Table 2.2.

Table 2.2 Sources of IFI influence on domestic policy

Means	Power resource	Outcome
Policy conditionality	Relational/money	Changing actors' calculations/strategies
Technical cooperation	Ideational/knowledge	Changing actors' ideas
Institutional support	Associational/money	Creation of new actors

One rationale for such support is nicely captured in Kathryn Sikkink's study of the rise of developmentalism in Brazil and Argentina. She argues that international ideas only achieve lasting impact on policy through becoming embedded in domestic institutions (Sikkink 1991). This means that some domestic actors must adopt them, and that they must become parts of the institutional discourse of a particular state or private institution. However this should also lead to the desirability for the MDBs to support the creation of such institutions that can carry forth a particular idea or viewpoint.

Such support may happen in a conscious and planned manner, or it may be a side-effect of for example the use of a particular institution for technical cooperation services or the implementation of projects. Although the institution in question may be employed for a different project, often great sums of money are channeled through the institution, and in consequence, it may evolve into an independent actor. In this manner, think-tanks, private sector organizations and specific individual 'technocratic' branches of governments have become important political players and important proponents of market-oriented policies in many developing countries.

The ability of the IFIs to enroll domestic groups in their own political projects, make the IFIs political actors. However they enter into political games that differ widely across different countries. In the following I will sketch the most important dimensions along which they differ.

PRIVATIZATION, POWER AND LEGITIMACY

In contrast to the literature referred to in Chapter 1 that focuses on interest groups, coalitions and institutions, this study takes as a starting point elites defined as 'those positions in society which are at the summits of key social structures, i.e. the higher positions in the economy, government, military, politics, religion, mass organizations, education and the professions' (Lipset and Solari 1967, p. vii). The reason why this is found to be most fruitful is that some of the cases involved the state is so weakly institutionalized that interest group politics and institutionally defined political processes can not be taken for granted. A key to understanding the processes of privatization is the competition between elites and how they are linked to the general public. The competition between elites is to a large extent defined by the degree of state autonomy, and the linkages between the elites and the citizens may be characterized by different forms of dominance and legitimacy.

State Autonomy

The first dimension is state autonomy from societal elites. A prerequisite of state autonomy is the centralization of power. A state that has succeeded in centralizing power has overcome resistance from non-state elites and does not need to engage in the politics of survival on a daily basis (Migdal 1988), but may concentrate on pursuing other political projects. One indicator of the centralization of power is the state's ability to extract resources, primarily through taxing the citizenry (Hobson 1997, Moore 1998). A state which has managed to centralize power is not necessarily a centralized state in the sense that the executive or the president is strong in relation to other state entities. Rather it is a matter of the ability of the state to penetrate the territory over which it is supposed to rule, and to make and implement decisions (Mann 1993). In such a process of penetration, state-owned companies played a certain role through making the state visible for the population.

In the states that have managed to centralize power, state institutions develop over time according to their own dynamics, and not only as expressions of the social forces underlying them. This is one of the main arguments of the Weberian historical sociologists (Evans et al. 1985, Evans 1995, Weiss and Hobson 1995). One main aim of the historical sociological literature has been to distinguish the particular institutional features of states that are argued to foster economic growth and development. A main feature of such states emphasized in the literature is their autonomy from societal forces, ensuring a degree of depoliticization of economic decision making. This is argued to have been achieved through a covert separation between reigning and ruling: the politicians set broad goals that the bureaucrats implemented under protection from external pressure by the politicians (Johnson 1987). In this manner the state has been able to create processes of economic transformation even where private interests were inimical to it (Weiss 1998). An important factor enhancing autonomy from state actors was the development of a Weberian bureaucracy characterized by selective meritocratic recruitment and long-term career rewards. This created a corporate coherence and *esprit de corps* that enhanced the autonomy of the bureaucracy from societal forces (Evans 1995). When the state has gained autonomy in such a manner, we may distinguish between the government, which will be responsive to shifting political winds, and the state apparatus that ensures a higher degree of stability and continuity.

However this also means that different state institutions may become social actors distinct from the governments. Although their formal influence on policy would be channeled through the government, they could have great policy impact through for example agenda setting and alliance creation. In states that are based on a centralization of power, it is more likely that autonomous state apparatuses emerge as social actors, and proposals for privatization and liberalization may reflect their interests and ideas.

In states that have gained little such autonomy it is more likely that the impetus of reform comes from non-state elites. In most current states the non-state elites into which most power is concentrated are groups related to business. These may act as a powerful constituency to different political groups. However in some states there is such a lack of balance of power between these private sector elites and the state that we may speak of 'state capture'. Hellman and Kaufman (2001) define state capture as: 'the efforts of firms to shape the laws, policies, and regulations of the state to their own advantage by providing illicit private gains to public officials' (2001, p. 1). I would argue that state capture can occur also when we do not speak of direct corruption. Moreover private sector groups may utilize a broader set of practices than only bribery. Nevertheless state capture is a good concept to describe the degree and intensity of the permeation of corporate policies and functions by private interests and concerns (Bach 2003). As such it is the opposite of state autonomy.

State, Elite and Regime Legitimacy

The second main dimension is whether state domination is based on coercion or some form of legitimacy. A state that has managed to centralize power is not necessarily a coercive state. To the contrary, centralization of power may reduce the need for coercion as it has managed to overcome internal resistance. In these cases, the state is rather based on some form of legitimacy. Dominance based on legitimacy may, according to the Weberian ideal types, take three different forms: 'legal–rational dominance' based on impersonal rule, 'traditional dominance' based on the belief in the sacred character of immemorial traditions, or 'charismatic dominance' based on the prestige of a person because of his extraordinary qualities (Weber 1971).

Whereas most literature on privatization and state reform is based on the assumption that the state enjoys a legal–rational legitimacy, a hybrid between this and a certain form of traditional legitimacy, namely patrimonialism, has been found more appropriate to describe African states after de-colonization and certain Latin American states.[5] This 'neo-patrimonialism' is characterized by the centralization of power in the hands of the ruler who seeks to reduce the autonomy of his followers by generating ties of loyalty and dependence, commonly through complex patron–client linkages. In the process, the public and private interests and purposes within the administration are blurred. In Latin America, the roots of patrimonial rule may be found in traditions of *caudillismo* or 'strong-man rule'. However *caudillismo* also has elements of charismatic dominance, as a lot of power is vested in the figure of the president and his authority is based on his charisma and image as a strong and capable leader. Charismatic rule is further discussed in the Latin American context in the form of populism. It is based on the ruler's superior insight and ability to make decisions based on a divine knowledge. The source of legitimacy is the eternal, that which transcends day-to-day politics, the remarkable and the magic (Taussig 1997). Although populism is also based on clientilist practices characteristic of neo-patrimonialism, one important element in it is that 'a charismatic individual wins and exercises power by maintaining direct, unmediated contact to a largely unorganized mass of followers' (Weyland 2001, p. 5).

However, the Weberian concepts only provide the first take on the issue of legitimacy. Weber talks about the legitimacy of an 'order' or rule. He does not specify how permanent or encompassing this order is. In other words, he does not distinguish between the legitimacy of a state, the regime governing it, or groups dominating it. One could easily imagine a situation where the state remains legitimate, whereas a specific regime (democratic, authoritarian, and so on) does not. Moreover one could imagine a regime (for example democratic) that enjoys legitimacy, whereas specific elite groups that dominate it do not.

In order to distinguish between these levels of legitimacy, one has to introduce two further concepts of legitimacy. The first is democratic legitimacy. This is clearly compatible with a legal–rational dominance, but whereas behavior according to rule of law is the main criterion of legal–rational dominance and legitimacy, participation is the main criterion of democratic legitimacy. A state may in other words be viewed as legitimate if it is considered to be an expression of the will of the population.

Democracy is in other words a way to legitimate dominance. However one may also talk about the legitimacy of democracy. Formal democracy does not necessarily enjoy democratic legitimacy. Moreover participation does not translate into real influence if it does not contribute to solving what are commonly viewed as problems, and if it does nothing to break the dominance of elites, the legitimacy of democracy may be threatened. Here we are in other words talking about consequential forms of legitimacy that we may call development legitimacy (legitimacy based on solving what are commonly viewed as problems), and distributional legitimacy (legitimacy based on counteracting tendencies to inequality and elitism).

The legitimacy of democracy in the face of unpopular economic reforms, failure to deliver on economic promises, and entrenchment of elites has been the focus of a broad literature. The compatibility between capitalist or market–oriented development and a 'real' democracy has been questioned, and much effort has been put into trying to characterize the emerging imperfect democracies (O'Donnel 1994, Boron 1995, Oxhorn and Ducatenzeiler 1998, Oxhorn and Starr 1999). However, the conclusion that is emerging is that although democracy is questioned, and although it has many imperfections, in general it is the most legitimate regime form across Latin America. What is rather threatened is the legitimacy of the political elites. Researching the influence of privatization processes on legitimacy, one has to take into account both the 'point of departure', that is how the state-owned enterprises contributed to elite and state legitimacy, and how the processes of privatization have done so. I will turn to this in the following.

State-owned Enterprises, Power and Legitimacy

Although the opponents of state-owned companies have argued that inefficient state-owned enterprises did a lot to reduce the legitimacy of states across Latin America, in fact state-owned telecommunication companies were intended to, and did indeed, contribute to state power and legitimacy in various different ways.

Firstly, state-owned companies have been important in the processes of centralizing power. For many state leaders in weakly centralized states, gaining control over infrastructure was an important way to extend the reach of the state to the hinterlands. Creation of state-owned enterprises has been one element in the process of making the state present in the citizens' lives.

Secondly, telecommunication companies formed part of the coercive apparatuses of many states; in some cases they have been closely related to the military communication infrastructure and a main function was surveillance (Holden 1999).

Thirdly, SOTs have affected various forms of state legitimacy. In states with neo-patrimonial features, SOTs have been a source of employment in return for political support. Furthermore, contracts were granted to subcontractors and equipment providers in return for political favors. Another practice in which the SOTs were instrumental was to establish infrastructure in communities with the explicit or implicit expectation of political support. In sum, state-owned enterprises have been among the most important conduits for political patronage (Ikenberry 1990). However SOTs have also been important in the formation of the charismatic legitimacy of a state, being expressions of the national pride. In Latin America, establishment of state-owned telecommunication companies was closely related to nationalism and anti-imperialism (Bulmer-Thomas 1994, pp. 350–58), and the SOTs did in some cases emerge as important national symbols. SOTs have also contributed to the distribution of resources. State ownership was generally based on the argument that public enterprise pricing was a more powerful method of redistributing income than more conventional methods of taxation and government expenditure in developing countries (Toye 1993, pp. 78–82). Universal access to services at a reasonable price was thus a central goal for various governments, and where it succeeded it contributed to the developmental legitimacy of the state.

In sum, SOTs did in some cases contribute to state legitimacy. In other cases they were mostly viewed as benefiting a small elite, and therefore did not contribute to enhanced legitimacy.

Privatization, State Autonomy and Legitimacy

The perspectives on the state sketched above have two main implications for the study of privatization processes. Firstly, state autonomy and legitimacy affect how we conceptualize the relationship between state and non-state actors, and therefore how we approach the study of why states privatize. In states with a degree of autonomy and legal rational legitimacy, it may be relevant to study for example interest group formation or institutional features (veto points) in order to understand the inclination to introduce neo-liberal reforms (as is done in the political economy of reform literature introduced in Chapter 1). However in other states economic, military or other elites may have captured the state to the degree that it makes little sense to view the state as a neutral arbiter of competing interest groups. Moreover in states with, for example, neo-patrimonial features, we may gain more from studying the personal networks, including family relations and business acquaintances than institutional features in order to understand the relevant constraints and resources available to policy makers. In systems based on charismatic domination, we should first of all focus on the ideas of the leader. In short, we cannot use the same lenses to study all states. In the following analysis, the main focus is on the relationship between different elites, particularly state elites versus economic (private sector) elites. However their relationship and form of interaction vary widely across the cases.

Secondly, policy makers' ability to strengthen the state and create new bases of legitimacy through the privatization process is of key importance in understanding the public's reaction to the processes. Policy makers do not have equal starting points for doing that. In weakly centralized, patrimonial states for example, policy makers are faced with quite different constraints than in other states. There is, in other words, a certain path dependency. However as in every aspect of life, human agency is both constrained by structures and has the ability to overcome structural constraints. Processes of privatization and regulatory reform may strengthen the legitimacy of elites if they are conducted in such a manner that they improve people's welfare and increase the distribution of assets, but they may also weaken it if they have the opposite effect. The following case studies aim to shed light on how the processes unfolded in the three countries under scrutiny, who influenced them, and how they strengthened or weakened the state's ability to act independently of narrow private sector elites.

NOTES

1. This includes digitalization, optical fiber networks, the development of cellular technology, integrated-circuit technology and satellite technology (Arnbak 1997).
2. See Jordana and Levi Faur (2004b) for a good discussion of different concepts of regulation.
3. Currently, a more decentralized form of regulation in which inter-connection prices are determined through negotiation between the parties and not by the regulatory agency, is gaining popularity. This form of regulation may reduce the conflict between freedom and competition because it limits the regulator's ability to make decisions reducing private sector profitability (often called 'creeping appropriation of the assets') (Rufin and Romero 2001).
4. The focus on ideas is rooted in Gramsci's view of the superstructure which in his account gains a certain degree of autonomy. This is related to his vision of the state, which includes not only the government and the bureaucracy but also their underpinnings in civil society. The state is 'the entire complex of practical and theoretical activities with which the ruling class not only justifies and maintains its dominance, but manages to win the active consent of those over whom it rules' (Gramsci 1971, p. 244). In periods of relative stability, dominating forces come to form a historic bloc with hegemony over the mode of production supported by a set of ideas, depicting: 'the structure of values and understandings about the nature of order that permeates a whole system of states and non-state entities' (Cox 1992, p. 151).
5. See Medard (1996) and Bratton and van de Walle (1997) on Africa, but also Remmer (1989) on Chile and Hartlyn (1998) on the Dominican Republic.

3. Guatemala: Privatization in a Captured State

Guatemala is the case included here that has implemented the most encompassing process of privatization. With regards to the telecommunication sector, Guatemala privatized its SOT in 1998, within the framework of a liberal telecommunication law, but also in the midst of multiple accusations of fraud and corruption. In this chapter, I will trace the roots of the form that the privatization process has taken in Guatemala and shed light on the causes of the public reaction to it. I will argue that in order to understand the sources of reform, we have to disentangle three elements of the reform process: the establishment of the liberal legal framework, the privatization process and later changes made to the legal framework. These parts of the process had different sources and were driven by different groups.

However key to understanding all elements of the process is the relationship and shifting alliances between private sector elites, the state, the military and foreign actors. In particular, the partly antagonistic and partly instrumental relationship between private sector elites and the Guatemalan state is a key to understanding the outcome of the privatization process. I will argue that the relationship between private sector elites and the Guatemalan state can be characterized as an incident of state capture and that this has impacted significantly on the process of reform.

The first part of the chapter traces the role of telecommunications in the development of the Guatemalan state. It shows how attempts at establishing developmental projects have been hampered by a combination of external pressure, and the strategies of the private sector elites that emerged in relation to export agriculture in the mid-nineteenth century.[1] The main impetus for market-oriented policies came from groups opposing the state, which at an early point unified around a political project based on an extreme form of liberalism.[2]

The second part of the chapter discusses attempted and implemented privatization proposals. It traces privatization proposals from the governments of Vinicio Cerezo (1986–91), Jorge Serrano Elías (1991–93) and Ramiro de León Carpio (1993–95), and to the reform process implemented under the government of Alvaro Arzú (1996–2000).

In contrast to its neighboring countries, Guatemala had a relatively low debt with international lenders and was therefore not so vulnerable to pressure from the IFIs when privatization emerged as a conditionality for structural adjustment programs from the mid-1980s. However, it had a private sector with diminishing patience with state-owned companies. This had already made attempts to make the government open up the telecommunication sector to private actors.

TELECOMMUNICATIONS AND THE BASIS OF STATE POWER

Infrastructure and State Development from Independence to the Oligarchic State (1871–1944)

In Central America, the period after independence (1821) was characterized by wars between conservative and liberal groups. By the 1870s, the liberals had gained power across the region. They called for an end to monopoly rights given to privileged sectors of the elite and promoted private acquisition of public or communal land (Del Valle 1963 [1821]). However, the Central American liberals, unlike classical nineteenth-century liberals in the US and Britain, believed in a powerful central state that could intervene to promote economic and technological development. They viewed a technocratic and authoritarian state, supposedly neutral and above politics, as necessary to produce openness, freedom and prosperity (Weaver 1999; Paige 1997, p. 44–47).

Liberal rule in Guatemala started with the rebellions in 1871, led by Miguel García Granados and Justo Rufino Barrios, which ended 30 years of Conservative rule. One main effect of Liberal rule was promotion of agro-export industry and the strengthening of private sector elites based on coffee production. The Liberals contributed to this through securing labor, providing credits and establishing infrastructure and communications. Rural Guatemala was ruled by the coffee planters through the departmental governors and it was only to a limited extent penetrated by the central government (Berger 1992). In 1879, the Liberals codified their development strategy in Article 20 of the constitution, which guaranteed freedom of industry at the same time as it authorized ten-year exclusive concessions to the new industries. This duplicity in the constitution is characterized by David McCreery as a commitment to 'free enterprise but not to laissez faire' (quoted in Dosal 1995, p. 27). The double strategy had the effect of producing monopolies in many industrial sectors and facilitating the diversification of the coffee oligarchy into industry.

The Liberal regime took initiatives to increase the role of foreign capital, and succeeded in attracting US investment in banana production, railways and shipping, as well as German investment in coffee production. However the foreign investors remained a separate group from the local coffee-based elite (Dosal 1993).

The development of the state apparatus occurred primarily in order to satisfy the needs of the coffee-based elite. The regime was not successful in attracting foreign wage labor to work on the coffee farms, and was therefore dependent on control of the rural indigenous population as labor. This made the coffee growers increasingly dependent on the state to provide cheap labor and infrastructure (Yashar 1997). Thus, until the turn of the century, the oligarchs largely controlled the state, and they financed directly the infrastructure developed by the state.

The two long dictatorships of Manuel Estrada Cabrera (1898–1920) and Jorge Ubico (1931–44) represented in certain aspects a continuation of the Liberal dictatorships. They continued the process of state centralization, and the establishment of a system of repression of labor organization, and as such they continued to serve the interests of the elite (Yashar 1997, Grieb 1979). However, the dictators also curbed the elite's direct control with the national government and they gave the state a certain autonomy. But the dictators also oppressed the political freedom of the economic elites, through centralizing power in the dictator's own hands (Dosal 1995, Berger 1992). Consequently, Estrada Cabrera's dictatorship caused a deep disgust for government and bureaucracy among the elite (Dosal 1995, p. 55).

Along with the oppression of the economic elites, Estrada Cabrera invited foreigners to invest in infrastructure. Telephone services were operated by Compañia de Teléfonos de Guatemala, a Guatemalan company with German capital. During the First World War it was converted to a state-owned enterprise, but it was later reprivatized (Ugarte 1999). Subsidiaries of the United Fruit Company (UFCO) acquired monopolies on the operation of ports and railroads through its subsidiary International Railways of Central America (Martí 1994, p. 25). In 1920, the Empresa Eléctrica, Guatemala City's electric plant that had been established by German nationals in 1989, was sold to the Electric Bond and Share Company (EBASCO), a subsidiary of General Electric (Dosal 1993).

The overthrow of Cabrera and the insertion of the liberal oligarch Carlos Herrera (1920–1921) as president meant a strengthening of the drive towards national controls of infrastructure. A new constitution of 1921 established that 'the State reserve the attributes of the postal services, the telegraph, radio telegraph, air navigation, issuing of currency' (Morfín and Montenegro 2000). Nevertheless, in 1925 the US company All American Cables Incorporated started its operations of international telecommunication services. In 1927 the first automatic telephones were inaugurated resulting from a contract with the German company AEG with 2 000 lines and with the possibility of extending it to 6000 (Ugarte 1999).

The oligarchy was unable to stay united under Herrera. This resulted in a political chaos that ended with the takeover by a junta dominated by military personnel. One consequence of this was that the oligarchy lost interest in direct rule (Dosal 1995). After some turbulent years of various military governments, Jorge Ubico, a member of the oligarchy but also with a military background won the 1931 elections, and he held power for 13 years. Under Ubico militarization increased. Particularly the vital dependencies, such as those controlling communication facilities (postal services, telegraph and radio) were led by military appointees. Even schools and the symphony orchestra were militarized (Yashar 1997, Grieb 1979).

Ubico placed strong emphasis on the construction of public buildings, highways, electricity and communications. The construction of electricity and telephone facilities (which were closely related) expanded at a rapid pace, and by 1940 the network encompassed every department of the republic with only two departments containing less than five telegraph offices (Grieb 1979). Ubico's main intention with the establishment of a communication program was to extend his own power and control. He is reported to have been fully cognizant of the political implications of instant communications, enabling direct control of the entire nation from the capital, and more specifically from the Casa Presidencial.[3] Officially communications were the responsibility of the Department of Public Works, but all the projects required Ubico's personal approval. This 'constituted a significant beginning in providing the nation with a modern source of power' (Grieb 1979, p. 170).

However Ubico soon discovered the financial limitations that the meager state income placed on his work. The Guatemalan state has been characterized by severe fiscal constraints, but also by refraining from increasing taxes and taking on foreign loans. The reluctance to incur debts started in the late nineteenth century when local oligarchs preferred to invest directly in infrastructure, rather than accepting foreign loans for it. Thus, as noted by Bulmer-Thomas, before the 1920s the Guatemalan public debt was low by any current standards; in 1920/21 it was merely £1.9 million, or approximately £1.3 per capita.[4] The debt was contracted in gold standard countries, which resulted in increasing debt burdens in local currency (Bulmer-Thomas 1987).

Ubico continued the tradition of cutting costs rather than increasing taxes in the face of fiscal problems. Even during the depression which resulted in counter-cyclical policies in many Latin American countries, Jorge Ubico chose rather to default on the external debt and reduced state expenditure by 30 percent in order to avert a progressive fiscal crisis (Dunkerley 1991, p.

124). However, he did seek foreign investment, the bulk of which came from the US. The UFCO became a dominant owner of infrastructure through its subsidiary Tropical Radio and Telegraph Company (TRT). It established the first telephone lines between the old capital Antigua and Guatemala City, and in 1933 the government signed a contract with TRT for the takeover of the international services as well (Ugarte 1999). North American firms in the end controlled transport and communications, dominated public utilities, and constituted an important segment of the agricultural sector (Dosal 1993).

Although the UFCO control was a major cause of resentment among the Guatemalans, there were few other sources of funds for public utilities. By 1929, US direct foreign investment in public utilities in Central America had reached US$22.5 million compared with US$0.5 million in 1919, with telecommunications dominated by subsidiaries of UFCO (Bulmer-Thomas 1987, p. 40).

At the same time, the private sector was in the process of mobilizing against what they viewed as a highly repressive state. Most accounts of the interests of the private sector in Central America focus on how they have differed between the agro-exporters and the agro-industrialists (Rueschemeyer et al. 1992, Martí 1994). The agro-exporters and the industrialists have fundamentally different interests regarding public investment. The agro-exporters primarily need a transportation and communication system to connect their farms with the sea ports and the capital city. Once this system has been built, they need little more public investment. Therefore they should favor a minimal state. Industrialists, on the other hand, need a more sophisticated transportation and communication system as a prerequisite for the development of the domestic market. They often need substantial amounts of electric energy and a more complex education system, and should thus be more open to increased taxes and higher levels of public investment.

This approach depends on the possibility of treating the two sectors as separate, which is only partly justified as Guatemala indeed has strong sector organizations, but also the strongest private sector umbrella organization in Central America. The first surge of private sector organizations occurred between the dictatorships of Estrada Cabrera and Jorge Ubico. Immediately after the fall of Estrada Cabrera the large-scale agriculture producers established the General Agricultural Association (AGA), and the Guatemalan Chamber of Commerce (CCG) began its work the same year. In 1929, a group of industrialists formed an autonomous private interest group, the Association of Industrialists of Guatemala (AIG). This was part of the movement that contributed to the political uproar in the 1930s.

Infrastructure and the Democratic Interlude (1944-54)

In the late 1930s uprisings were sweeping Central America. By then the Guatemalan state had established an infrastructure in the hinterland. However the state was still heavily dependent on the military, and the communication network that was set up largely benefited them. By 1939, signs of opposition were evident. A series of events coincided and contributed to the establishment of a coalition between students, workers, the oligarchy and parts of the military that together overthrew Ubico in 1944 (Yashar 1997; Handy 1984, pp. 106–7). Ubico turned power over to a military junta that gave powers to General Federico Ponce. Ponce's attempts to continue the policies of Jorge Ubico led the forces that had installed him soon to remove him and replace him by an interim junta composed of Colonel Francisco Arana, Captain Jacobo Arbenz and businessman Jorge Toriello. This called elections in December, in which university professor Juan José Arévalo won overwhelmingly. Arévalo was not himself born a member of the elite, but he had close ties to it, particularly to the Arzú Irigoyen family (Handy 1984, p. 107).

A new constitution was drafted that endorsed the decentralization of executive power, separation of the various branches of government, and reorganization of the army as an apolitical, autonomous institution. In January 1945, the Congress decreed the control of the telegraph, cables and radio communications, but left the foreign enterprises that were the owners of these obliged to provide services (Ugarte 1999).

Alrévalo's social reforms contributed to the alienation of the elites, and within a few months of his inauguration the fronts had hardened among the former allies (Berger 1992, p. 42; Handy 1984, pp. 106–8). In spite of the fact that Arévalo introduced policies that could benefit the private sector, he failed to get much support from it. Indeed, there was an upswing in private sector organization both because Arévalo lifted the ban on private sector organization introduced by Ubico and because the private sector disliked some of his reforms (Yashar 1997). The final blow to the coalition came with the promulgation of a comprehensive labor code on 1 May 1947. After internal disputes, Arévalo was replaced by Arbenz.

Arbenz's policy was more focused on economic than social reforms, and he was clearly nationalistic, launching a campaign against the monopoly of foreign companies in key economic sectors. He initiated the construction of the Atlantic Highway that would run parallel to the UFCO-owned railway (through its subsidiary International Railways of Central America), and planned to build a 28,000-kilowatt hydroelectric plant which would compete with the foreign-owned Empresa Eléctrica. In 1950 he established the national airlines, Aviateca (Decree 733) and in 1952 he passed Decree 900 which called for a modest land reform through redistribution of idle land.

Contrary to the perception at the time, the nationalization of infrastructure was less based on communism than on the recommendations of the World Bank's mission to Guatemala in 1950 (Gleijeses 1991; Handy 1984, pp. 113–17, Dunkerley 1991, pp. 134–35). Nevertheless Decree 900 was interpreted as communist and it sealed the fate of the Arbenz government. Except for the oligarch Guillermo Toriello Garrido who defended Arbenz's actions, a united oligarchy entered into an alliance with the United States and the military (Dosal 1995). Together they staged the overthrow of Arbenz on 18 June 1954 led by General Castillo Armas, who subsequently became the president of Guatemala for the coming four years.

Telecommunications and Military Oppression (1954–70)

Castillo Armas maintained close relations with the US, which in turn granted him generous financial assistance to carry out an ambitious infrastructure program. The US Congress gave the bilateral program the mandate to make Guatemala a 'showplace for democracy' (McCamant 1968), and US financial aid totaled US$61.8 million between 1954 and 1957. This enabled Castillo Armas to build and improve highways, upgrade rail and postal services, modernize the police and military forces, and finance studies on the reorganization of the Guatemalan economy: taxation, budget and accounting, and customs and tariffs systems. Armas was more reluctant to accept multilateral loans. Nevertheless, encouraged by President Eisenhower, Armas accepted a World Bank loan of US$18.2 million (Berger 1992, p. 87). Moreover the five-year economic plan that he implemented, designed to reduce the country's dependence by promoting economic diversification was virtually written by David Gordon, head of the World Bank mission to Guatemala (Dosal 1995, p. 112).

In 1957 Castillo Armas was assassinated, and in the following elections the candidate of the industrial elites and the sugar and cotton producers Miguel Ydigoras Fuentes was declared the winner. The strong support among the economic elite initially enabled Ydigoras Fuentes (1958–63) to introduce a state interventionist development strategy. A main part of this strategy was to develop infrastructure, and he brought energy generation under state control under the National Institute of Electrification (INDE) (Handy 1984). However he did so in the tradition of Jorge Ubico, under whom Ydigoras had been the Minister of Public Works, strengthening his personal role (Dunkerley 1991, p. 138). Through regularly dismissing both high- and low-level bureaucrats, he avoided increasing state autonomy (Berger 1992, pp. 104–20). Lacking any consistent ideological appeal and heavily dependent upon distribution of the spoils of office to sustain its supporters, the regime was confronted by a diverse but growing opposition within its second year in power (Dunkerley 1991, p. 138). Opposition came from the economic elite, dissatisfied military factions associated with the state, and labor suppressed by both the state and the private sector. The latter groups joined together to form the first guerrillas, whereas the economic elite continued to organize. In 1958 AGA, CCG and AIG joined together in the Coordinating Committee of Agrarian, Commercial, Industrial, and Financial Associations (CACIF) (Berger 1992). CACIF would become the most powerful private sector organization in Central America.

The instability caused by economic crisis, conflicts over the Alliance for Progress and other political events, led to a military coup in 1963, and the takeover by Enrique Peralta Azurdia. This coincided with the expiration of TRT's concession to operate international telephony. TRT had been in conflict with the labor union Sttigua (later Steguatel) over the right to negotiate salaries and work conditions, and when the Minister of Labor and Social Security called union representatives to ask their opinion about nationalization of telecommunications, they expressed their full support given that the nationalized company was given autonomy and that labor would have the right to negotiate. Thus Guatel International was established by Decree 4-65 on 26 January 1966 with the mandate to provide international telephone services. Later the same year (March 1966) the Law of Radio Communication was approved, and it established the general management of radio diffusion as a dependency of the Ministry of Communications and Public Works. This centralized the management of the radio spectrum in the Ministry (Toledo 2000).

The nationalization of telecommunications and establishment of Guatel was also related to increasing US involvement in surveillance activities in Central America. The USAID Office of Public Safety (OPS) had responsibility for standardizing procedures in telecommunications, and it provided equipment to the Central America and Panama International Security Telecommunication Network in 1964–65. By October 1966, the Central American Military Telecommunications System (SIMCATEL) had been established with participation of representatives of the US Southern Command. The Americans were particularly active in Guatemala, where the OPS established a police intelligence service (Holden 1999). In August 1964, Peralta also created a Presidential Intelligence Agency, based in the Casa Presidencial, under which was a Regional Telecommunication Center (La Regional) linking the National Police, Treasury Guard, Detective Corps, Government Ministry, the Presidential House, and the Military Communication Center. La Regional also served as a depository for information on activists for purposes of political abduction and assassination (Schirmer 1998, pp. 157–58).

Peralta Azurdia made various attempts to co-opt the private sector elite through appointing particularly industrialists to various commissions and including them in governmental planning. Partly as a result, the military government increased spending on roads, electrification, telecommunications and other infrastructure projects that benefited the private sector (Berger 1992, pp. 121–38). Peralta Azurdia agreed to call elections in 1966 and give power to the popularly elected civilian Julio Méndez Montenegro. The Méndez government was the most reformist one since Arbenz, but it nevertheless expanded the representation of the private sector in important state institutions, and thus managed to create a favorable relationship. However due to an attempt to introduce property tax in 1966, and a sales tax and luxury tax in 1967, support from the Guatemalan elite and the US business community turned to intense opposition. After this 'no new taxes' became the requirement for ascending to power in Guatemala (Jonas 1991, p. 59).

In sum, in this period the state institutions were strengthened through the extension of the spoils system and later through its increasing security functions faced with the emerging threat of guerrilla forces. Infrastructure and telecommunications played important roles in both. However although the state succeeded in some degree of centralization, it was limited by continuous opposition from the private sector. Government-led industrialization was only possible when supported by the private sector, and the ability of the state to extract resources from it was highly limited. Furthermore a large part of the private sector remained strongly opposed to any state involvement, and their opposition to it would be strengthened during the following three military governments.

Coercive Developmentalism and the Establishment of Guatel (1970–86)

The military governments of Colonel Carlos Arana Osorio (1970–74), General Kjell Laugerud García (1974–78) and General Romero Lucas García (1978–82) challenged the limits of the private sector's tolerance through state expansion and increased public expenditure. At the end of the decade they faced opposition from the private sector, the US government and the guerrillas that were gaining a foothold in the western highlands.

The military governments of the 1970s were guided by a philosophy inspired by Peruvian military developmentalism (Martí 1994).[5] Arana Osorio believed that the military was better qualified than civilians to rule due to better discipline, education and experience. Thus he turned to the officer corps to fill top government positions and to make policy decisions (Berger 1992). Under his presidency, the military and individuals within it became large landowners, set up commercial enterprises and industrial projects, and took control over utilities.

Telecommunications were operated by three governmental entities: Empresa Guatemalteca de Telecomunicaciones Internacionales (ex TRT, established by Decree 465) providing international services, the General Direction of Telephones providing local services, and the Telephone Project of the General Direction of Public Works, channeling civil works. On the recommendation of a World Bank mission, the three parts were merged into the new company, Guatel, by Law 14-17 of April 1971. The new company was established in order to improve coordination and planning.

The military governments continued to be disinclined to accept foreign loans. However Guatel had a sufficient degree of autonomy to acquire loans independently of the central government. Guatel's expansion was to a large extent financed by the World Bank. The first loan (Ln792-GU) of US$16 million (January 1972) enabled it to construct approximately 42 000 telephone lines. In April 1975, the Bank approved a second loan (LnL 104-GU) of US$26 million, with the Republic of Guatemala as guarantor (World Bank 1986a, p. 1).

Military intelligence had been supported by the US government from the 1954 CIA coup (Schirmer 1998, Black 1984), but with the establishment of Guatel the call control function was moved from the fourth floor of the American Embassy to the second floor of Guatel. Due to protests from the more technically oriented Guatel staff it was later moved to a military installation.[6]

Guatel was created as an institute dependent on the Ministry of Communication and Public Works, with the minister automatically resuming the position as president of the company. Apart from him, the board consisted of the Minister of Governance, the Minister of Foreign Relations and two further members appointed by the President of the Republic. It was initially proposed that the Minister of Defense should be on the board, but because of objections against direct involvement of the military, this was rejected.[7] The board of directors was the highest authority of Guatel, with responsibility to appoint a manager, and tellingly the first was Arana Osorio's brother. Technical quality was to be ensured through the requirement that all board members should be engineers or lawyers.[8]

General Laugerud continued Arana's modernization programs. He belonged to a military faction that aimed at promoting social change and gradually diminishing inequalities, applying Keynesian-style policies. This caused the state budget to almost triple between 1974 and 1978. This caused not only increased bureaucracy, but provided the military with ample opportunities for self-enrichment. Guatel continued to be a source of state income as well as a means of distribution of spoils. As the World Bank report on the second telecommunication loan concludes:

> Guatel's overall performance was adequate, but organizational efficiency would have been higher if frequent, often politically motivated, changes in senior and mid-level management had not occurred. There were two changes of top management in 1976 and one change in 1978, 1982 and 1983. These changes affected mid-level management and financial and engineering staff to varying degrees (World Bank 1986a, p. 10).

Nevertheless, the number of telephone lines in the country increased substantially, from 46 289 in 1974 to 128 783 in 1978 (World Bank 1986a).

When the Carter administration took office in the US the Laugerud administration's atrocities started to get repercussions also with respect to access to international finance. In 1977, the Carter administration passed the International Financial Institutions Act which included Guatemala on a list of gross and consistent violators of human rights. The Act prevented US representatives from supporting multilateral loans to Guatemala through either the World Bank or the IDB unless they demonstrably financed 'basic human needs'. The act prevented the passage of a US$75 million IDB loan for hydroelectric energy in November 1981, and a US$18 million IDB loan for a rural telephone network, in spite of the change of administration that had occurred in the US in the meantime. The Reagan administration had privately lobbied for the hydroelectric loan, and attempted to steamroller the telecommunication loan through the House of Representatives Banking Sub-Committee, but it was hindered due to arguments that financing infrastructure in military controlled zones would be 'indirect military aid'.

The entering of General Romeo Lucas García and his vice-president Francisco Villagrán Kramer of the Institutional Democratic Party (PID) to power in 1978 was the start of one the most oppressive and brutal periods in Guatemala's history. Lucas soon proved that he did not fear either bloodbaths or foreign condemnation in his strategy to crush the insurgency (Luján Muñoz 1998). Moreover he did not manage to win the confidence of CACIF; he increased the number of officers in the cabinet, and gave the private sector only one sympathetic cabinet officer (Edgar Ponciano), who was also closely tied to the military (Dosal 1995, p. 183). Under Lucás the first experience with privatization in Guatemala occurred. That was his attempt to privatize roads in 1981. However, it did little more than giving privatization an image of being a prime opportunity for corruption.[9]

In the 1982 elections there was only one military candidate, but after accusations of fraud, a group of young military officers staged a coup and named General Efraín Ríos Montt as the president. He was viewed as an opponent of the military developmentalist program of Laugerud, receiving strong backing from the most conservative forces of CACIF joined in the

National Agricultural Union (UNAGRO) (formed in 1984 by AGA and the Agricultural Chamber) (Schirmer 1998, pp. 148–49). By this point, the military and the state apparatus had become so fused that members of military intelligence 'sometimes receive their paychecks from the government agencies responsible for electric power or tourism' (interview with intelligence officer, Schirmer 1998, p. 19).

At the same time, the four main guerrilla organizations had unified in the Guatemalan National Revolutionary Unity – URNG (January 1982). Ríos Montt's main focus was on fighting them, through a plan including extension of local patrol groups and two plans for arming the rural population as well as feeding them to obtain their goodwill – 'Fusiles y frijoles' (arms and beans), and 'Trabajo, techo y tortillas' (shelter, work and food)) (Schirmer 1998).

The political instability caused extensive capital flight in the late 1970s (Bulmer-Thomas 1987, pp. 237–44). Therefore, in spite of the low inclination of the Guatemalan state to take up foreign loans, Guatemala entered into a deep balance-of-payments crisis in the early 1980s. As a consequence, the first stand-by agreement with the IMF was signed in 1981 with a value of US$110 million. The Fund's conditions included interest rate increase in order to reverse capital flight, and reduction in the public sector borrowing requirements. The initial measures undertaken to fulfill these requirements were reversed soon after, and the program was suspended.

In spite of the Ríos Montt regime's continued human rights abuses, on 29 September 1982 the Reagan administration erased Guatemala from the list of human rights offenders. As a consequence of the policy change the six World Bank and IDB loans that had been stopped were now disbursed. These were worth a total of US$170 million, and US$71 million of the IDB funds would be directed to financing of rural telecommunications (Black 1984, pp. 169–71). The lifting of the ban also opened the way for the World Bank to issue a third telecommunication loan (Ln2385-GU) of US$30 million which was approved in March 1984 (World Bank 1986a, p. 1).

In the early 1980s, the main concern for the IMF was fiscal stability achieved through the reduction of budget deficits, primarily through raising taxes. This was fiercely opposed by the private sector, which argued that instead of raising taxes, one should privatize state enterprises (Dosal 1995). Nevertheless Ríos Montt signed an agreement with the IMF in July 1983, which was conditional on the introduction of a value added tax (VAT) at 10 per cent.

The new tax contributed to the fall of Ríos Montt in August the same year, and the replacement by Defence Minister Oscar Humerto Mejía Víctores. The new military government of Mejía Víctores agreed a stand-by credit with the IMF, but promptly lowered the VAT to 7 per cent in October (Bulmer-Thomas 1987, p. 249). In June 1984 the government approved the extension of 146 million quetzals in credit to private enterprise, most of it targeted to the industrial sector, thus worsening the fiscal situation. This added to the fiscal problems caused by the VAT reduction, and provoked the suspension of the IMF agreement in July 1984.

This was the beginning of the relationship between the government and the IMF, which from the start was clearly affected by the dynamics between the government and the private sector. The lesson learned from the early encounter was that negotiating only with the government was insufficient; one also had to deal directly with the private sector. In effect the negotiations with the IMF raised privatization to the national agenda for the first time, although it was not directly proposed by the IMF, but by the private sector.

Although the military continued the brutal anti-insurgency campaign under Mejía Victores, he also started the process towards democratization. As a part of this process, he replaced military officers with civilians in the national communications center, Guatel and INDE, although military officers still held some of the lower-level positions (Schirmer 1998, p. 168). The Mejía Víctores regime also initiated a Grand National Dialogue (Valdez 1998, p. 120). Through this, developmentalist elements of the military were strengthened under the leadership of Hector Alejandro Gramajo (*Reporte Político* No. 32 October 1988).

Mejía Víctores called elections in 1985 in which the Christian Democratic Party (PDCG) candidate Marco Vinicio Cerezo Arévalo won. The victory of Vinicio Cerezo marked a watershed in the sense that it was the first democratic election in 16 years. However, in many ways it was business as usual. In a personal interview, Cerezo pointed out that he had only 33 per cent of the power: the remaining 66 per cent was shared between the United States, the private sector and the military.[10] Moreover the PDCG was traditionally allied with the military (Schirmer 1998, p. 187–92). In the discussions of privatization and other reforms that were conducted during Cerezo's regime, he had to take into account the historically developed antagonism between the military state and the private sector. And although the private sector at times pronounced itself in favor of liberal policies, it just as often supported non-liberal policies if these could serve its interests. It was into this context that the first proposals for privatization of telecommunications were introduced in the early 1990s.

THE PROCESS OF REFORM

The State-led Telecommunication Reform Proposal

One of Vinicio Cerezo's first actions as president was to introduce a four-year

Program for National Reorganization (PREN) which included several measures to restructure the economy towards export orientation and internal deregulation, and a state reform program aiming at increased participation and decentralization (Sosa 1991). This also had a telecommunication component.

The reform plans of Cerezo were influenced partly by an attempt to sign an agreement with the IMF. Although low compared to the neighboring countries, the debt:GDP ratio was at a historical high (27 per cent) when Cerezo took power, and he started to negotiate a stand-by agreement with IMF. IMF looked favorably upon various measures undertaken under the PREN and approved a stand-by agreement worth US$126 million in November 1988. Of this, a US$70 million tranche to support PREN was disbursed without further conditionality (*Reporte Político* No. 30 August 1988, No. 33 November 1988).

In 1989 the Cerezo government initiated a shift toward a neo-liberal, export-driven model of economic growth, which President Cerezo referred to as the 'modernization' of the economy, summarized in two economic plans, the Plan for 500 Days and Guatemala 2000. The programs centered on development of nontraditional exports, combined with a trickle-down approach to social justice (*Reporte Político* No. 47 March 1990, Trudeau 1993, Sosa 1991). Public services were now under discussion and the state enterprises were targeted for increased private participation and restructuring. However in the case of telecommunications, only a goal of increased efficiency was included.

In spite of the new policy measures, due to total arrears of US$200 million with the IFIs, the disbursement of agreed foreign loans was stopped in large parts of 1989. In the beginning of July 1990, the Bank of Guatemala was again put on the 'black list' by the World Bank (*Inforpress* 19 July 1990). Consequently, the World Bank suspended six loans in March 1990 (World Bank 1995b, p. 7), and the IMF agreement was suspended with US$40 million left of undisbursed funds.

The Cerezo government had two remaining sources of foreign exchange. It succeeded in attracting some capital from abroad through issuing so called Cenivacus bonds with an interest rate of 25 per cent (Bjørsvik 1993, p. 35). Further, it received some funding from the Japanese government which increased its lending to Guatemala. Among this was a US$170 million loan for development of telecommunications and electricity *(Inforpress* 22 March 1990).

Thus the relationship with the IFIs was anything but smooth. Moreover Cerezo was no convinced neo-liberal and the PDCG incorporated those favoring military developmentalism and more liberal ideas. In 1977 Cerezo published a pamphlet entitled 'The Army as Alternative' in which he endorsed General Laugerud's concept of the army as an institution for social change (Dosal 1995, p.162, Schirmer 1998, pp. 187–92). Moreover Cerezo appointed Hector Gramajo as his Minister of Defense, and the government's economic program was clearly influenced by his ideas. The idea of a 'social debt', developed by Gramajo under Mejía's Grand National Dialogue was central, justifying the call for increasing salaries for teachers and social workers, subsidies for medicine, fuel, wheat, agricultural goods such as fertilizer, and the creation of temporary jobs in rural service (Dosal 1995, p. 167; Cerezo 1987).

In the mid-1980s, a division occurred within the military between the soft-liners or 'institutionalists' supporting constitutional democracy and developmentalist policies following Gramajo, and the hard-line, right-wing officers. Among the issues dividing the military was the necessity to modernize the state (for example through tax reform) (Schirmer 1998, p. 207). While the institutionalists worked closely with the government, and shared many of Cerezo's viewpoints, the ideas of the hard-liners had, according to Schirmer, a lot in common with the position of the most right-wing of the UNAGRO members, primarily the sugar growers. Schirmer (1998, p. 211) reports that:

> Like UNAGRO, the group of officers believed that by 'limiting [economic burdens],' such as taxes, 'eliminating privileges,' being 'anti-monopolist,' especially against US corporations, and 'totally eliminating state intervention into the economy, they would have a better solution than the Christian Democrats ...' The idea is to destroy, sell, and put into private hands – national and foreign (depending on who offers better services to the Guatemalan people) – the telephones, the railroads, the electric company, and so forth.

As a reaction to Cerezo's handling of popular demands for economic and human rights, a group of hard-liners calling themselves the Officers of the Mountains staged two coup attempts, one in May 1988 and one in May 1989. Among the group identified to be behind the first coup were three former officers, among them Major Gustavo Adolfo Díaz López, and a group of civilians (Schirmer 1998, p. 219). As Díaz López was a member of the Guatel board, the coup attempt was launched with Guatel as the staging ground.

Cerezo was able to fend off the first attack, agreeing that he would halt negotiations with URNG and terminate plans to carry out agrarian reforms (Dosal 1995, p. 171). A second coup was launched in May 1989 in which Díaz López, by then stripped of his military credentials due to his involvement in the May 1988 coup, also played a central role. The second coup attempt also failed (*Reporte Político* No. 38 May 1989). However Díaz López kept his position on the board of Guatel, and from there influenced the development of the plans to reform the telecommunication sector, as will be discussed below.

There were also more liberal Christian Democrats. In 1982 the Association for Investigation and Social Studies (ASIES) was founded in 1982 as one of several think-tanks in the region established to educate the Christian Democrats in liberal ideas. It was increasingly dependent on funding from the USAID and other international donors, and started to promote economic policies that, although having carried over many elements from the developmentalist era, also had clear neo-liberal features.

The main representative of this form of Christian Democracy in the Cerezo government was Lizardo Sosa, the first Minister of Economy (1986–88) and later the President of the Central Bank. He was also the main proponent of privatization, and had frequent confrontations with his successor as Minister of Economy, Oscar Piñeda Robles, who insisted on keeping some state control.[11]

The telecommunication proposal developed under the Cerezo government was characterized by what could be called a hybrid between neo-liberalism and military developmentalism. Cerezo favored a use of private capital in which the state was still in control and still able to keep some of the profits. The plan aimed at involving foreign companies in the development of infrastructure and the provision of services. The idea was not full privatization, but concessioning of various functions of the sector. It included development of satellite telephony, cellular telephony and the installation of 75 000 community telephones. Agreements were reached with various equipment providers and operators (among others Ericson, AT&T, Telecom Italia) to participate in the project, which had a total value of US$250 million.

The only part of the plan that was implemented was the issuing of a 20-year concession on the cellular band B to Comcel, a joint venture between the international cellular company Millicom and local minority investors in 1989. The condition for the concession was that Comcel would have monopoly on cellular services the first five years, and had to pay 20 per cent of the profits to the government in return (CIEN 1999b).[12]

Cerezo had initially counted on the support and cooperation from CACIF in implementing the economic programs. However the PREN had a social agenda that the private sector resisted fiercely. Moreover although Cerezo appointed several private sector members to his cabinet, he did so without consulting CACIF.[13] The attempt by the government to pass a series of tax reforms led the relationship to deteriorate further. In response to disagreement over taxes and what was viewed by CACIF as Cerezo's repeated violation of agreements with the private sector, a national strike was organized beginning on 7 October 1987. An agreement between the government and CACIF was made and accepted by the president on 3 November, including the establishment of a public–private commission which later worked out modifications to the tax bills. However, when Congress on 3 December approved the tax reforms without amending them to contain the modifications to which the executive and CACIF had agreed, the relationship with the private sector broke down completely (McCleary 1999, Valdez 1998).

With a lack of confidence in the government, the private sector also rejected the privatization policies that it was in essence for. For the government, on the other hand, privatization was partly a means to curb the power of the private sector elites. As argued by the president himself:

> What we wanted was to develop a process of privatization. We wouldn't sell everything and leave the state with no capacity to influence. ... This process would enable us to acquire some money for the sale of frequencies, authorizations and concessions, without necessarily giving the impression to the people that the state was dismantling itself too quickly because that would send the wrong message ... I understood that the process of liberalization would allow us to diminish the power of the internal private sector. Because allowing the foreign enterprises to compete in the same conditions with the internal would allow us to balance, establish rules of the game and we would find a point of balance, right? It would give power to us, right? Not to continue the traditional routine.[14]

Cerezo failed to implement the plan, largely due to accusations against him of misapprehension of funds. During Cerezo's government privatization acquired a negative image in the public opinion. Cerezo's first action was to privatize the state-owned airlines (Aviateca). After transforming it into a stockholding company, Cerezo sold most of the state's shares to a group of Guatemalans in a joint venture with the Salvadoran airline, TACA (CIEN 1999a).[15] However, he was publicly known for having ownership interests in the business himself.

Later Cerezo was also accused of having ownership interests in Comcel. Among Comcel's minority investors were series of persons close to the governing Christian Democratic party, including the Minister of Foreign Affairs and the General Secretary of the Christian Democratic Party, Alfonso Cabrera and Cerezo himself. For these two actions, and the US$2 million purchase of three Sikorsky helicopters from Jordan, Cerezo was charged with graft in 1991. However as he at the time was a member of the Central American Parliament, he enjoyed immunity and was not sentenced (McCleary 1999, p. 213 n. 44).

In conclusion, the economic ideology of Cerezo was based on a mix between neo-liberalism and military developmentalism. Part of the neo-liberal influence came from the Christian Democratic think-tank ASIES who had emerged as an actor partly due to support from the IFIs. However equally important motives for his proposals for reorganization of the telecommunication sector were a desire to curb the influence of the local private sector elites, and to gain political support by giving benefits to elites close to the government. Such motives also dominated in the succeeding government.

Privatization Attempts and Democratic Setback

The government of Jorge Antonio Serrano Elías is more frequently described as neo-liberal than the Cerezo government. However Serrano was also known for his close relations to the military and his religious leanings. Serrano was elected on a conservative economic program, as the head of a diverse coalition government. It suspended the plans to reform the telecommunication sector developed under Cerezo due to charges of corruption. However he kept some of the members of the board of directors of Guatel from the Cerezo government. Among them was Major Diáz López, who attempted to continue the process that had started under Cerezo.

Serrano's position on privatization was dubious, as he expressed to the press: 'With respect to the size of the state, in my opinion it should not be smaller or bigger, but sufficiently large to satisfy the basic needs of the people.'[16] The President of the Central Bank, Federico Linares, who had argued that Guatel should be the first company to be privatized, also expressed that Serrano did not share his position. Linares said in the aftermath that: 'I wonder why he [referring to Serrano] never gave me a reason either for or against privatization [of Guatel], but what I can tell you is that his opinions were unpredictable.'[17]

The fact that Serrano's support for privatization was not ideologically motivated, or motivated by a desire to enhance efficiency, did not mean that his government did not undertake actions to promote it. This was related to solving the international debt problem, but not so much the multilateral aspect of it.

Jorge Serrano took over a troubled economy. Inflation reached 60 per cent during the Cerezo administration, the fiscal deficit increased and the total foreign debt reached US$2490 million (World Bank 1995b). In 1991 the government attempted to renegotiate the debt that had expired in 1990 (US$145 million), of which US$33.8 million was with the IDB and US$79.7 million was with the World Bank.

Guatemala managed to clear all arrears in 1992, and reached a Paris Club agreement in March 1993. This also opened for the rescheduling of 80 per cent of the bilateral debt with the US under the Initiative for the Americas, and the release of US$50 million of USAID funds that had been held up due to the lack of an agreement with the IMF. In October 1992 the President of the Central Bank announced the signing of a Framework Agreement with the IMF and the following stand-by agreement ensured Guatemala new access to World Bank funds.

As a result of this, in November 1992 the World Bank issued the first structural adjustment loan, the Economic Modernization Loan (EML, Ln. 3533-GU) for US$120 (World Bank 1995b, *Inforpress* 10 December 1992), aimed at liberalizing the economy. However, with respect to privatization, only a vague statement that one should conduct a 'revision of the state enterprises' was included.

What was of more importance to the long-term process of privatizing the telecommunication company was the attempt to renegotiate the bilateral debt with Mexico. In March 1991, Minister of Foreign Affairs, Alvaro Arzú, went to Mexico with the purpose of renegotiating US$70 million of the bilateral debt Guatemala had with Mexico. Mexico had at this point started to carve out its role as a new regional leader, and expressed an interest in restructuring debt in exchange for shares in privatized state agencies. The convention that was signed by Arzú said that the debt would be restructured 'in the context of a flexible scheme, that take into account mechanisms for debt reduction through programs of interchange of this for state assets, in the frames of the policy of privatization of public enterprises that the government of Guatemala adopts' (quoted in *Inforpress* 21 February 1991). Among the public enterprises mentioned was Guatel.

Thus deals were struck on the international level to prepare for privatization, but also at the national level preparations were made. In 1991 Serrano appointed a blue-ribbon commission including representatives of the government (Leonel López) and the private sector (Victor Suarez and Fernando García Molina) to outline a policy for the privatization of electricity companies. The commission turned out to have little support from the president,[18] but by July 1992 it had drafted a bill on the restructuring of the INDE. The Congress approved the bill, but Serrano vetoed it and instead proposed his own privatization bill that he signed into law by executive decree. In early 1993 the government began seeking political support in Congress (primarily through purchasing votes) for electricity rate increases and the removal of subsidies, but was met with widespread opposition. The President of Congress, José Lobo Dubón, called on the population not to pay its electricity bills until Congress had an opportunity to vote on the administration's proposal for privatizing INDE. At the same time Serrano was pressured by a group of deputies and supported by the head of the Supreme Court who threatened to block the government's bill and consider corruption charges against him after he was stripped of immunity, if they were not granted concessions for operating electricity plants under the new law (McCleary 1999).

The corruption charges and privatization conflicts related to the INDE were among the factors that led Serrano to set aside the constitution and attempt a 'self-coup' in May 1993. Serrano's anti-democratic actions were met with resistance from the popular sectors, CACIF and parts of the military, and with international support – particularly from the Organization of American States (OAS) – they managed jointly to recover constitutional rule.

The private sector took the initiative to establish an ad-hoc commission (Instancia Nacional de Consensos) as a forum for reaching agreement between the different sectors about how to reestablish constitutional rule. The Instancia agreed on installing Human Rights Ombudsman Ramiro de León Carpio as an interim president, and congressional elections were planned for 1994, after corrupt members of Congress had been purged successfully. De León got a mandate to rule until the new presidential elections, scheduled for the autumn of 1995.

Serrano's attempted self-coup brought about some important changes in the Guatemalan political landscape: it confirmed constitutional democracy as the basis for conducting politics in Guatemala (Holiday 1997); it led to an agreement about the division of labor between the private sector and the military in the running of the country (McCleary 1999); and it showed that insurgency was no longer a significant element in political decision making (Cameron 1998). This all opened the way for increased influence by private sector groups that for years had organized in order to change the direction of Guatemalan economic policies.

'Soft Power' Strategies of the US and Private Sector Groups

Groups within the private sector elite had for years attempted to pressure the government directly to privatize, but there were also groups that had applied indirect and long-term strategies. In order to analyze the role of the private sector in the privatization process, there is a need to distinguish between different private sector groups, and their different strategies and ideas. Moreover one has to take into account that private sector attitudes and strategies are not directly derived from their economic interests, but are also influenced by ideas. In the following, I will analyze the strategies of the private sector in Guatemala, and how they have been influenced by changing ideas and by the strategies of foreign actors – first and foremost the USAID.

In 1984, the private sector had already started to blast the state-owned enterprises in the press, charging that the poor performance of Inde, Guatel, Corfina, Aviateca and other state companies was a proof of the failure of the military's development model (Dosal 1995, p. 159). Starting with the Serrano government, there were two main parts to the private sector strategy. Firstly, CACIF and several of its individual chambers started to analyze the possibilities for privatizing state-owned enterprises, and made elaborate policy recommendations. In 1991, the Guatemalan Business Chamber (CAEM) presented a study with a prioritized list of over 32 public enterprises that were recommended for privatization or de-monopolization, on which Guatel figured at the top (Cabrera 1997). Privatization was also a main recommendation in the CACIF 'Yellow-Book' outlining desired economic and social policy for the Serrano government (1991–95),[19] where electricity and telecommunications figured among the core areas for reform in Guatemala. CACIF further established a Private Sector Commission for the Sale of State Assets[20], which prepared a General Privatization Law, and established sector commissions analyzing possibilities for demonopolization for each sector.

In the elaboration of proposals, CACIF was indirectly supported by external agencies. For example it was assisted by previous director of the Department of Economics of the University of Chicago, Arnoldo Harberger, in the development of the 'Yellow-Book' prepared for the incoming Serrano government in 1991. He had been hired by the Center for National Economic Research (CIEN), a think-tank established in 1982 on the initiative of USAID (Palencia Prado 1998). CIEN also elaborated a Law of de-monopolization as a means to prepare a privatization process.

The second part of the strategy was to place private sector representatives in core governmental positions. In the Cerezo government, Minister of Finance Rodolfo Paíz Andrade, a Harvard economist and the co-owner of a supermarket chain (Martí 1994) was viewed as the main representative of the private sector. Also, President of the Central Bank Lizardo Sosa, who came from the position as Dean of the Faculty of Economics at Rafael Landívar University, had close ties to the private sector primarily through Pedro Lamport Rodil (Dosal 1995, pp. 162–63). The Serrano government was often viewed as a government of the private sector (*Inforpress* 17 January 1991, *Central America Report* 11 January 1991). Among the private sector representatives was Richard Aitkenhead Castillo, former president of the sugar industry association, and a descendant of one of the most powerful families in Guatemala (Dosal 1995, p. 11; Martí 1994, p. 217)

However in the mid-1980s there was also a split between the private sector organizations, due to foreign influence. Traditionally the strength of the Guatemalan private sector organizations staved off foreign influence. This reflected the relatively weak position that foreign investment has had in Guatemalan industry. The majority of foreign investments occurred in sectors in which Guatemalan capital was either unwilling or unable to develop, or it happened in partnership with Guatemalan capital. Moreover US owners and managers of multinational firms did not integrate into the domestic elite. Since 1967, US companies have been organized in the American Chamber of Commerce (AmCham).

Beginning in the early 1980s, there was a perception in USAID that CACIF represented a too narrow set of interests. An alternative group was proposed as a means of 'opening up' the private sector, broadening participation in productive activities, and promoting policy reform. After having failed to get congressional approval for using funds from the

Caribbean Basin Initiative (CBI) to create a new business organization, a more modest project established the CAEM in 1981 (Crosby 1985). However it never managed to become a real challenge to CACIF, and it was co-opted by it in 1985. Beginning in 1987, CAEM's focus shifted to providing technical assistance, training workshops and seminars on privatization, management-labor relations, regional integration, and legal reforms to enhance foreign trade (McCleary 1999).

This co-optation was a part of a larger process of restructuring of CACIF, that began in 1983 on the initiative of the CCG. The aim was to prepare it for the anticipated transition to procedural democracy which would demand a unified and flexible organization. The stated objectives were to eliminate the practice of clientilism, introduce fundamental market principles that would guide CACIF's activities, to promote industry as the priority of national economic policy, and to unify the private sector's voice for effectively lobbying government. McCleary (1999) points out that a main reason for this initiative was the rise of a new generation of leaders in CACIF that was influenced by classical liberalism. Also Dosal (1995) argues that liberal ideas have unified the private sector:

> The fragmentation of the private sector that occurred during the Lucas and Ríos Montt regimes certainly weakened the oligarchy, but with neoliberalism sweeping through influential academic circles and CACIF, the elites would play a leading role in the construction of a new political and economic model. Antagonized by excessive state spending and corruption, the various factions of CACIF gradually united behind a new political agenda calling for privatization, free trade, lower taxes, and administrative efficiency (Dosal 1995, p. 152).

In my view Dosal's account is only partially correct. Neo-liberalism has not entirely unified the private sector, but it has contributed to its unification, and this was a conscious strategy by those who promoted these ideas in Guatemala.

The spread of neo-liberal ideas in Guatemala can be traced to the work of a small group of businessmen connected to different parts of the private sector, led by businessman and member of the board of the Chamber of Industry, Manuel Ayau Cordón. His work started with the founding of the Center for Social-Economy Studies (CEES) in 1958. CEES was established by a group of seven friends, most of them descendants of influential families in Guatemala, but evenly spread between agro-exporters and industrialists.[21] They had three main concerns: the international dominance of ideas promoting a strong state and limiting the liberty of the individual, the lack of interest in discussing long-term development issues in Guatemala, and the lack of intellectual alternatives to what they saw as the socialist San Carlos University. The group shared a basic concern for individual freedom, and despised the state which was viewed as synonymous with illegitimate privileges. Moreover they shared a conviction that in the long run ideas govern: 'if our country should enjoy peace and prosperity, without oppression of ideological groups, it was necessary that enough influential people understood clearly the organization of a free society, and acquired the conviction and courage to defend it' (Ayau Cordón 1992a, p. 3). Thus Ayau's strategy to change Guatemala was through the changing of people's minds.

CEES soon established international contacts and started to discuss ideas developed in the United States and Europe; the Foundation for Economic Education (FEE) in New York, the Mont Pellerin Society in Austria, and through them personalities such as Milton Friedman and Friedrich von Hayek that became sources of inspiration for Ayau and his group.

CEES started its work to divulge ideas of the 'free society' through a daily radio program and a weekly column in the newspaper *El Imparcial*. At the top of the agenda for the early years were the fight against income tax, the minimum wage, tariff protection and exchange rate controls.

Initially Ayau contemplated establishing a political party. However, learning how Keynesian ideas had become dominant all over the world, he decided that a more efficient strategy was to establish a university. As he recalls himself:

> At this point, the whole world had gone to the left. I never believed in conspiracy theories because I thought whenever there are more than two people in a conspiracy, one of them will talk about it and it will not be a conspiracy anymore. And so I started to study how the success of the ideas came about and I found the explanation in how the Fabian society had spread their ideas. They had a lot of power. They had induced Lenin to take power. Keynes was not the first one, he was the student of people like G.B. Shaw, of H.G. Wells and Webb. They founded the London School of Economics, it was much to the left back then. The people from Harvard went to the LSE to learn. The students from Louisiana did not go to the LSE, but they went to Harvard. The people from Latin America did not go to Harvard, but they went to Louisiana. In that manner, ideas were propagated down in the system.[22]

Finally, in 1972, Ayau founded the Francisco Marroquín University (UFM) with the explicit purpose of divulging political and economic liberal theory.

Ayau also worked directly through political channels. He gained a seat in the parliament (1970–74), a position from which he launched fierce attacks on the establishment of Guatel in 1971 and the nationalization of electricity in 1973. In 1979, Ayau and his friends developed a fully fledged governmental program. In this he not only proposed economic policies, but gave them a solid theoretical explanation and provided both ideal and 'politically feasible' solutions. Thus proposals for privatization or de-monopolization of all the state-owned enterprises, including INDE and Guatel, were complemented by thorough explanations of how and why it should be conducted. Moreover he designed a political strategy for the achievement of the goals. One of the points on the program was to conduct 'psychological warfare' against myths and distorting explanatory categories such as 'oligarchs, multinationals, rich people' (CONSECA 1979).

Although running for president at one point, Ayau had little success as a politician. But the UFM grew in both size and prestige. It acquired the reputation as the best private university not only in the country, but in the region, and its graduates started to fill various positions in government and business.

Through these channels, the CEES group divulged their story about the Guatemalan state, picturing it as oppressive and as depriving the individual of freedom. Harking back to the days of dictatorships, CEES argues for respect for individual rights, and the establishment of clear rules. However the state is also pictured as overextended, employing a large state machinery that has crowded out private investment and thus hampered efficiency of production: 'For the last 50 years, Guatemala has stuck to a governmental model of the Welfare State which slowly has obtained multiple functions and attributes which previously were fulfilled voluntarily by members of the society' (CEES 2000). This state, so the story goes, has been financed through taxation of the elite hampering employment and development.

Based on the story of the state emphasizing overextension, oppression, privileges and domination, CEES developed economic ideas that were radical even to most Chicago-style economists. Ayau argues for full privatization of all state activities and state property, which should be followed by a minimum of new legislation. According to Ayau's liberalism, there is no need for public concessions or laws encouraging private actions where the state withdraws (Ayau Cordón 1992b).

In sum, there were strong private sector groups that for many years had pressured for the privatization of state enterprises. Their viewpoints were shaped by both the experiences with the former dictatorships and the role of state-owned enterprises in them, and by ideas adopted from abroad. In the end they established a story about the Guatemalan past that was taught to the new generations of business leaders and politicians. These would finally be influential in the coming administration, that of Ramiro de León Carpio.

The Interim President and the Ideological Right Wing

The interim government of Ramiro de León took significant steps towards privatization of Guatel by appointing the committed liberal, Dr Ayau, as a 'governmental privatizor'. This occurred in spite of the fact that De León himself was far from a convinced neo-liberal. He came from the position as a human rights ombudsman and was a self-declared socialist. Moreover with

Jacobo Arbenz as a role model, he saw infrastructure not as a sector for private gain, but as a key in a national development strategy.

De León's ideological orientations were reflected in his choice of economic advisors, several of which came from ECLA. It was commented in the press that De León's economic program could be the first experiment in ECLA's new response to the neo-liberal trends, namely the 'adjustment with a human face' (*Central America Report* 10 September 1993). Furthermore, neither his appointee as Minister of Communication Ernesto Ramírez nor his appointee as General Manager of Guatel Gustavo Adolfo Diáz López supported privatization.

Thus although there also were proponents of privatization within the government, few shared the radical beliefs of Manuel Ayau, and nor did the president. Asked about his motive for appointing Ayau, he answers:

> What I asked of him was that he helped me to privatize under transparency. I had the experience of the B Band in the back of my mind and therefore I wanted a competent person. ... But there was opposition even within the government. I had an advisor that daily told me that if I privatized Guatel, that would be my main legacy. I would go into history as the privatizor.[23]

Thus Ramiro de León was faced with the dilemma of Cerezo: that privatization could be a means to curb the power of the private sector if done right, but it could also enhance it if it was done wrong. In order to limit the power of the national private sector, it was important that ownership was disbursed, that the sector was opened up to international investors, and that the process was transparent. If not, privatization could easily lead to continuation of the local private sector's traditional control through other means.

Thus it was far from solely ideological convictions that led to the first governmental initiatives to reorganize the telecommunication sector. Rather it was a mix of ideology and a desire to diminish the power of the private sector. But private sector groups also had political motives and did not give the government unconditional support, even for policies that they in principle supported.

De León could initially count on backing from CACIF, as a compromise candidate in the process of restoring constitutional rule after the Serrano self-coup. However, before De León took office, private sector representatives had already expressed their doubts that he had the leadership skills and congressional trust to take on such a task as it would be to privatize the state-owned companies (Lionel Toriello, President of the Bankers association to *Central America Report* 29 October 1993). The actions he took with respect to tax reform and electricity privatization, made them more convinced that he was not the man for the task.

Tax issues were again the cause of conflict between the private sector and the government, and Minister of Finance Ana de Molina was the personification of the private sector's animosity. She had a personal interest in tax issues (De Molina 1999) and designed a tax reform that would increase the social profile of the Guatemalan tax system.[24] CACIF reacted immediately and argued that rather than increasing taxes one should privatize state-owned enterprises, among them Guatel, in order to reduce the fiscal deficit (Jorge Briz Abularach to *Reporte Político* No. 93 May 1994). A month after the plan had been presented to Congress, CACIF presented a study where the argument that it was more important to privatize and demonopolize the state-owned enterprises than to reform the tax system was repeated (Palencia Prado 1998).

The IFIs attempted to pressure for the adoption of Ana De Molina's tax reform by making it a condition for an IMF Shadow Agreement and the disbursement of tranches worth US$80 million of loans from the IDB and the World Bank. They also threatened that a failure to pass the reform would lead to the cancellation of an upcoming Consultative Group Meeting (planned for 21 June 1995) at which further aid to Guatemala should be discussed with various donors. Even the US ambassador Marilyn McAfee attempted to press for tax increases. She pointed out that Guatemala had one of the lowest tax rates in the hemisphere, and warned that 'the international community wants to help out, but won't if Guatemalans don't contribute their fair share' (*Central America Report* 29 October 1993). According to De Molina, the international support was crucial in her struggle to reform the tax system, as it strengthened her position faced with the massive CACIF opposition.[25]

Although the IFIs gave priority to tax reform, they were not uninterested in privatization. According to the 1995 World Bank country assistance strategy, privatization is necessary, but not urgent (World Bank 1995b, p. 3).

What rather limited the IFIs' influence on the privatization process was parts of the private sector's attitude towards them. Ayau was of the generation that still remembered the World Bank's involvement in Arbenz's nationalistic policies. He strongly opposed foreign intrusion in policy making, and claimed that the IFIs were too 'statist'.

The government managed to pass the tax reform in April 1994, but after this the relationship between the government and the private sector was beyond mending and the government could not count on support for any initiatives. De León's veto of a new law of INDE aimed to de-monopolize the electricity sector, on 9 January 1995, added insult to injury. De León's argument was that it should await the passage of a General Law of Electricity. However it was soon discovered that a proposal for a new electricity law had been contracted by USAID and elaborated by Sebastian Bernstein of the Chilean consulting company SYNEX, and that it was supported by the World

Bank.[26] This enabled CACIF to use a nationalist discourse to oppose it, winning support even among the unions. In a paid advertisement in the press CACIF charged that: 'the attempted General Law of Electricity is nothing but an imposition of the World Bank which is used as a pretext for postponing the process of demonopolization' (*Inforpress* 26 January 1995). Also Ayau reacted strongly and argued that: 'You don't have to read much to notice its institutional vices. It is founded in a vision which is very far from a demonopolized market economy. This is rather an example of a dirigiste economy.'[27]

Yet the agreement between Ayau and CACIF did not last long. Although in essence in favor of the privatization policies proposed by Ayau, CACIF failed to give him strong support. When directly asked about whether CACIF supported him, Ayau answered:

> No. They wanted to buy the companies. And I told them to go through the bidding process. But they were not that bad. They were not really supporting me, because of my position on other matters. Not because they were against it, they were in favor. So if they were acting in favor of the privatization, they were doing it, not coming through me. Because by this time our relationship had been one of antagonism.[28]

In sum, although the private sector in principle favored privatization, governmental privatization attempts were opposed due to the private sector's refusal to cede power to the state, even when it was in order to implement policies that would increase private sector participation in the economy. Former Minister of Finance Ana de Molina, described the relationship between the private sector and the government as an octopus and its prey.[29] Thus although the possibility for privatizing state companies was used by the private sector as an argument for avoiding increased taxes, it did not mean that it would support government attempts at privatization.

The Strategies of the Guatel Management and its Unions

Another factor hindering the implementation of reforms in the telecommunication sector was the continued presence of military hardliners on the Guatel board. When De León came to power, he appointed Diáz López as the General Manager of Guatel. While his appointment of Ayau was seen as a move to appease the private sector, the appointment of Diáz López as General Manager of Guatel can hardly be interpreted as anything else than an attempt to appease the hardliners of the military.

However although the general ideas of his military faction were anti-state, the ideas that Diáz López presented as a manger of Guatel brought in various statist elements, aiming not to lose control over the institution.[30] The plans resembled closely ones that had been presented under Cerezo. The aims were to increase private sector participation while retaining a role for the state. One of the first actions of the new Guatel management was to contract the International Telecommunication Union (ITU) to prepare the bidding documents for the concessioning of a second cellular band. According to the documents, the contract would be awarded depending on not only the price offered for the concession, but also a series of other attributes such as plans for development of the network and the prices offered to the consumer. In other words, what was planned was a so-called 'beauty contest' (Guatel 1994).

The bidding process based on this study ended in a power struggle between the Guatel management, the government and competing investors, characterized by incompetence as well as corruption. This was the background for the failure to concession a cellular band and it contributed to the steadily deteriorating relations between Diáz López and Dr Ayau, who to start with disagreed about the model to be implemented.

The final blow to Dr Ayau's plans came from the unions. Guatel had two major unions, and a few smaller ones. The main unions were Steguatel and Sindicato 22 de Febrero. Steguatel was established in the Arbenz period, and had been instrumental in the creation of Guatel International in 1965. By former Guatel managers it was described as left wing, but moderate. Sindicato 22 de Febrero was aligned with right-wing forces, and described as 'rebellious'. It was created as a means of counteracting anti-governmental forces after public demonstrations against Ríos Montt in 1982.

When talk about privatization reached Guatel during the De León regime, various groups started to form. With support from the Friedrich Egbert Stiftung, the unions started to elaborate alternatives and divulge them to the public. This resulted in a public campaign where the message was that Guatel had provided generous benefits to the population, and should be restructured and given full autonomy in order to make it a real instrument for development. The unions also attempted to use a carrot strategy, promising to install 725 300 new telephone lines if the government refrained from privatization (*Prensa Libre* 12 January 1995). In early 1995, the unions presented their proposal which was called 'Reaffirm the decentralization and autonomy'. This involved various changes to the Organic Law of Guatel (71-14), which would give Guatel significantly increasing financial and administrative autonomy from the central government (*Prensa Libre* 25 January 1995).

Furthermore the unions pressured the government to make Ayau resign. In an open letter to the President of 24 November, Steguatel demanded that De León suspend the process immediately and leave the appointment of Dr Ayau without effect.[31] Under the leadership of Sindicato 22 de Febrero, the unions also went on strike and threatened to paralyze the entire communication network. They finally managed to make the government suspend the process for a month, and to ensure the unions participation in it.

Thus the first major attempt to privatize telecommunications in Guatemala failed. Nevertheless the work of the ideological right wing and Dr Ayau would turn out not to have been in vain, as their ideas would become influential in the elaboration of the new telecommunication law of 1996.

The 'Private Sector Government' and the Radical Telecommunication Reform

In December 1995 the National Advancement Party (PAN) and President Alvaro Arzú won the elections and in January 1996 he took power on a wave of support from the international community. This was based on his determination to continue the peace process, and in December 1996, the final peace accords that ended the 36-year-old civil war were signed with the guerrillas. In the socio-economic agreement that formed a part of these accords, a clear obligation was placed on the government to develop improved infrastructure in poor and rural areas, especially those areas hardest hit by the war.

PAN had its main support basis in the private sector, but due to its anti-corruption and anti-clientilist image, it also had relatively broad support in the population.[32] PAN was nevertheless viewed as clearly market oriented, and the main thrust of its governmental plan was to modernize the state through extensive use of the market, 'desincorporation' and 'decentralization' (but not privatization) of state enterprises (Segeplan 1996).

One of the government's first actions was to elaborate a new telecommunication law. This was approved by the Congress of Guatemala on 17 October 1996 (General Law of Telecommunications, Decreto Legislativo 94-96).[33] It was widely acclaimed for being the most liberal and modern telecommunication law in Latin America (Belt 1999, Raventos 1997, *Wall Street Journal* 25 September 1997); it established a regulatory framework which privatized not only the operation of telephone services, but also the management of the radio spectrum and many regulatory functions. The rights to use the radio spectrum would be given as so-called Use Entitlements (Titulos de Usufructo) that were almost equivalent to private property.[34]

The regulatory framework had two main innovative features: it allowed a high degree of competition and it established a regulatory body, the Superintendent For Telecommunications (SIT), with very limited powers to enforce it. In order to ensure competition it first avoided granting any monopoly rights. Furthermore the law guarantees the access of operators of the radio frequencies and other services to 'essential facilities'.[35] Thus according to the law, any operator is obliged to provide interconnection to competing companies' networks and allow its customers to freely shift service provider. Prices and conditions for interconnection were not to be regulated, but to be established by agreements between the different operators. If negotiations between different operators regarding price and conditions should fail, the SIT would be called upon to authorize an expert as an arbiter in the dispute.[36]

The law established an innovative procedure that the expert arbiter was to follow settling a dispute about the price for interconnection or access to any other 'essential resource', called 'final offer arbitration.' The formula was based on game-theoretical reasoning and it is aimed at removing any incentive for the parties to demand unreasonable prices.[37] Another aspect of the law was that final prices were completely deregulated. This was facilitated by the system of interconnection settlement, and it ensured that the role of the SIT was reduced to facilitating arbitration. It could not intervene directly, but had to await a complaint by one of the parties.

Initially the idea was also to establish a SIT as an autonomous institution. However as creation of autonomous entities required a 2/3 majority in Congress and the governing party PAN only controlled a simple majority, this was not approved. Thus, the SIT was established as a dependency of the Ministry of Communication.

The law further established a fund (Fondetel) for realization of telecommunication projects in rural areas and/or low-income urban areas, replacing all other governmental subsidies. For the first eight years of operation, 70 per cent of the income from the auctioning of the radio frequencies was to be channeled to Fondetel.

Parallel to the elaboration of the telecommunication law, Guatel was prepared for sale. In order to overcome the constitutional requirement for a 2/3 majority in Congress for divestiture of autonomous institutions, changes were made to the Public Procurement Law based on the ideas elaborated by Eduardo Mayora in his period as Ayau's advisor (Proyecto de Modificación 20-97). In its modified version, the law allowed the possibility to transfer state property to a new or old stockholding company. On 28 June 1997, the board of Guatel issued Decree 11-97 where the privatization process was laid out. Subsequently Guatel was transformed into a hitherto unknown organizational form, a Unitary State Property, resembling a state stockholding company. Thereafter 85 per cent of the stocks of Guatel were transferred into a new subsidiary, Telgua, leaving Guatel only with the rural infrastructure. Finally, the government announced its intention to sell up to 95 per cent of the 28.8 million stocks (worth approximately US$440 million) of Telgua to a strategic investor, and these were transferred to Citibank, New York.

The main condition for presenting a bid was that the company should have more than 1.5 million telephone lines in operation, or annual sales worth

US$10 million in the telecommunication sector. This effectively excluded local investors, unless they had entered into partnerships with international telephone companies. Five companies pre-qualified for the auction: MCI, Southwestern Bell, GTE, Teléfonos de Mexico (Telmex) and France Telecom. Initially scheduled for September, the auction was postponed twice, and it finally took place on 17 December 1997. At auction day, only Telmex made a bid, of US$529 million for 27 360 570 stocks (95 per cent) at a price of US$19.34 each. The offer was rejected by the committee because it was considered not even to cover the value of the assets, estimated at US$563 million, and the process was declared closed.

A few days before the failed auction, on 19 November 1997, congress approved an amendment to the law (Decree 115-97) which changed some of the basic ideas of the 1996 law. Firstly, the formula for settling disputes about charges for interconnection was changed in favor of the incumbent carrier. While the expert that was to be involved in case of a dispute originally was to set the price at 'long-term incremental average cost', according to the 1997 law, it should be based on average historical costs. This meant that the cost would be higher as it would not take possible technological innovation into account. The incumbent carrier would be favored further by a new paragraph stating that the provider of the local connection should be given 70 per cent of the international settlement income.

Secondly, the 1997 amendment delayed the introduction of obligatory interconnection. The original law stated that any commercial network provider with more than 10 000 access lines should permit the users to freely connect to other providers' networks and that the subscriptions should be flexible in order to make this feasible (Article 49). The new law removed the note about flexibility and added a condition that this should happen on 31 December 1998, with possible prorogation until 1 July 1999. In consequence it would give the incumbent carrier a monopoly of at least one year.

In short, the amendment weakened some of the liberal criteria established in the 1996 law. It placed the incumbent carrier in a position to charge higher prices from entrants, and with the ability to delay competition.

On 7 January 1998, Giovanni Musella, Vice-Manager of Telgua, announced that a second attempt to sell the company would be made by the end of the month. Before this, an important change had been made to the conditions for participating in the auction, namely that the requirement that participants had to be international operators of telecommunications was removed. It was open to investment groups and banks to participate. They could be international or national, but the former would need at least 10 per cent national participation.

This time around, the government publicly announced a lower-end price which was set to US$700 million, but argued that it hoped to get up to

US$800 million. The auction was postponed several times, but finally on 30 September it was announced that Telgua would be auctioned the morning after. A Board of Notables that included Minister of Communications Fritz García-Gallont, Minister of Finance Pedro Miguel Lamport, General Manager of Telgua Alfredo Guzmán, and representatives of JP Morgan, was to pick the winner. At this point only two of the six companies that had pre-qualified remained as interested parties. These were Datacom, a subsidiary of Deutsche Telecom, and Luca, S.A., a local investment group. Telmex, GTE, Telefónica de España and the local group TeleRed had withdrawn. The Board of Notables had an easy job as only Luca, S.A. finally made a bid, of US$700.1 million, representing US$25.59 per stock or US$6.25 more than the offer made by Telmex the year before.

Soon after, it was revealed that Luca, S.A. had made an agreement with the government for paying off Telgua in tranches: US$200 million at the closure of the contract (5 November), US$150 million 18 months later and US$350 million 36 months after that. Of the first payment US$120 million would go to paying the debt with Hamilton Bank that Telgua had contracted to pay severance to the workers on 28 August 1997. Moreover JP Morgan received US$4.45 million for consulting services.

It turned out that it was not France Telecom, as initially announced, but Telmex that had formed a strategic alliance with Luca. According to a Telmex statement it had negotiated a call option to purchase 49 per cent of stock in Luca. However Telmex gradually gained greater control over Telgua. Firstly, the PCS part of the company was separated out into a different company, Telred, of which Telmex acquired 51 per cent of the stocks. At the beginning of 2000, when the deadline for payment of the second installment for Telgua approached and it became clear that Luca did not have the funds, Telmex purchased 79 per cent of the stocks of Luca. By purchasing Luca Telmex gained control over Telgua without violating the clause in the contract between Luca and the Guatemalan state prohibiting Luca from passing Telgua on to third parties.[38] Thus it was not revealed how much Telmex had paid for the stocks, but there was little doubt that the investors in Luca had profited generously from the transaction.

In sum, Guatemala first passed the most liberal telecommunication law in the world. It could, if successfully implemented, ensure a high degree of competition assumed to benefit the consumers. In 1997 some reforms were introduced that decreased the liberal nature of the framework, but Telgua was nevertheless privatized in a competitive framework. In spite of this, the process surrounding the privatization was viewed by the public as characterized by fraud and lack of transparency, and benefiting primarily the elite. In the following I will discuss the role of the government, private sector elites and IFIs in producing such an outcome.

The 'Private Sector Government' and the Private Sector

The entering of the PAN government has been widely analyzed as the return of the traditional elites to power (Casaus Arzú 1992a). President Arzú was connected to the oligarchic family network (the Arzús and the Toriellos) that has produced some of the most reformist elite politicians (among them Jorge Toriello who was a key person in the 1944 October Revolution). While certainly pro-private sector and also a graduate from the UFM, he was not known to be convinced about the virtues of privatization.

Moreover it is clear that his political goals also included attempting to curb the power of competing elites. Although he was a part of the oligarchy himself, he worried about the possibility that a privatization process should further strengthen some parts of the private sector. When Ayau served as a governmental privatizor he had gone to see Arzú who was then a presidential candidate, to discuss his plans for Guatel. In Ayau's own account:

> When I was going to privatize, I went to see him. I said I want your backing. It could be good for the country. And if you give it you would be better off. And he said on one condition. He said, that you don't sell it to the oligarchy. I said, you can be sure of that. I won't sell anything under the table.[39]

Arzú also had several openly left-wing representatives in the government, partly as a result of the peace process, and partially based on contacts that Arzú made in his youth. Furthermore, the Minister of Finance, José Alejandro Arévalo, did not come from the private sector, but from his position as the President of the Central Bank. He supported privatization but within a strong regulatory framework. He argued for a model of selling 51 per cent to a strategic investor, and the rest to the workers and the general public.[40]

Thus although the Arzú government was clearly intending to forge private sector development, had it not been for the long-term work of Manuel Ayau and the linkages that his followers established to international actors, it is not likely that it would have chosen such a liberal law as the one that was adopted. However in order to understand why it was adopted, there is a need to take into account the process occurring across the border in El Salvador.

The Sources of the New Telecommunication Law

When the right-wing Arena party came to power in El Salvador in 1995, President Calderón Sol appointed Alfredo Mena Lagos as the head of the Presidential Commission for the Modernization of the State, and his friend Juan José Daboub as president of the state-owned telecommunication company, Antel. Mena Lagos was of one of the old coffee-growing families in El Salvador, the founder of the Salvadoran Nationalist Movement,[41] and one of the leaders of Arena. He was deeply committed to the ideas of the Austrian liberals and, as reported by the *Wall Street Journal*, he was 'seldom seen without his Ludwig von Mises tie'.[42] The right-wing movement in El Salvador never managed to establish the kind of ideologically based institutions as CEES and UFM.[43] Thus one of Mena Lagos's first actions in office was to hire Manuel Ayau as an advisor. His clear objective upon taking the job was to privatize the company as soon as possible, and to ensure a liberal telecommunication law. With support from the IDB, World Bank and USAID, Mena Lagos collected various proposals for technical advice. He ended up with the one proposed by Berkeley professor Pablo Spiller, a choice in which Manuel Ayau was highly influential. Says Mena Lagos:

> I asked my assistant from the commission to give me all of the offers for technical analysis on the law and I wanted to go through them, and I read through them on the flight and I discovered that the one that came closest to a free market model was the offer that Pablo Spiller had made, so I asked Manuel to go over that with me and you know, then we decided upon Pablo Spiller.[44]

Spiller's ideas were based on the experiences from Chile and New Zealand, some of the pioneers of privatization. While their legal frameworks were aimed at ensuring free competition in the telecommunication sector, several problems had occurred due to the incumbent carrier's resistance against providing interconnection to entrant operators. This had resulted in prolonged lawsuits delaying competition (Belt 1999). In order to avoid such problems, Spiller developed an arbitration system designed to avoid having to go through the legal system.[45]

With such elements in place, there would be no reason to grant the incumbent carrier a monopoly as had been done in most other Latin American countries. The system of arbitration was also intended to remove the need for strict price controls. In short, it rendered it unnecessary to establish a regulator with a high degree of discretionary power, both elements of which suited the liberals Manuel Ayau and Alfredo Mena Lagos well. However Spiller also proposed elements that did not suit the disciples of Ludwig von Mises. Among these was to create a very detailed law that included a tariff regime. This was recommended by Levy and Spiller (1996) in order to avoid frequent governmental interference. However, due to Mena Lagos's and Ayau's aversion to detailed regulation, it was not included in the laws.

The World Bank and the IDB supported the process in El Salvador through the Public Sector Modernization program, a US$51 million program implemented by the Presidential Commission that Mena Lagos headed (World Bank 1996a). The goals of the program were to de-bureaucratize the state and privatize public agencies, among them the telecommunication company Antel.[46] However, it was a local USAID representative that was most active in assisting Mena Lagos and Daboub in putting the ideas of Spiller into a law. In the autumn of 1995, CIEN researchers met the USAID representative in El Salvador. At this point, the prospects for a PAN victory in the Guatemalan elections looked bright. With support from USAID, CIEN had set up an office in Congress in order to support elaboration of law proposals that matched the liberal market-oriented philosophy of the institution. The young Congress deputy Alfredo Guzmán had made contact with CIEN's office in Congress discussing the prospects for a new telecommunication legislation

Upon hearing that the party that was most likely to win the upcoming elections was interested in a radical telecommunication reform, the USAID set apart a modest sum of US$5000 in order to finance a trip for a CIEN researcher and Guzmán to Berkeley, California to meet with Pablo Spiller. The USAID also took the initiative of presenting various other models to the small self-appointed team consisting of Guzmán, a CIEN researcher and a private sector representative, Victor Suárez.[47] But Guzmán in particular became enthusiastic about Spiller's model, and he returned to California to continue discussions with him. Guzmán also continued the discussions with Manuel Ayau who connected Guzmán with Giancarlos Ibargüen, a young engineer who had worked on privatization of the radio waves since the early 1990s.[48] Guzmán liked Ibargüen's ideas, asked him to write them into a law proposal, and brought the draft to Spiller. Through the discussion with Spiller, Ibargüen's idea of privatizing the radio spectrum developed further, and Spiller brought it in turn to El Salvador, where it became a part of the legal framework.[49]

Thus when PAN won the elections in December 1995, the telecommunication reform was already well under way. When the new government took office in 1996, Arzú changed the entire Guatel management. He appointed Guzmán as General Manager of Guatel and gave him the responsibility for privatizing the enterprise together with Minister of Communication Fritz García-Gallont.

USAID's main priorities at this point were poverty reduction and support for the peace process. However through programs for private enterprise development and trade and labor liberalization, directed towards the Ministry of Economy and CAEM, the USAID officials were able to find funds for development of the law and find them fast. Avoiding the start-up process of a new program, the process could start within a time frame of two months with a donation of US$85 000, and the aforementioned team drew up a plan for elaborating the telecommunication law within nine months. On 17 October 1996 the new law was approved by Congress, and PAN deputy Mario Roberto Paz was chosen as the first SIT.[50]

In sum, two processes were going on in the preparation of the telecommunication legislation. Firstly, there was a transfer of the ideas of Berkeley professor Pablo Spiller to Central America, facilitated by the regional USAID representative based in El Salvador. However it was no coincidence that Spiller was chosen. He was chosen because his ideas fitted with those of Manuel Ayau and the Guatemalan liberals. Therefore it is difficult to argue that the Guatemalan law was the result of influence from foreign consultants. As for example Guzmán argues when asked why he chose Spiller's model: 'Listen, first of all I am a graduate of the University of Francisco Marroquín. Thus, from there, we have gotten the theoretical ideas about the economy of the free market.'[51]

Moreover ideas were not only transferred from Berkeley to Guatemala. There were also elements of the legal changes that were transferred from Guatemala, with the international consultants as 'couriers'.

Secondly, there was a process of transformation of the ideas and adaptation of the ideas to Guatemalan ideas and interests. The ideas were primarily those that had been cultivated at the UFM. However, the final framework was also a result of the adaptation of those ideas to strong interests of the private sector elites, and to the fiscal needs of the state.

The IFIs and the Role of Fiscal Constraints

Due to the extremely narrow tax base in Guatemala, fiscal problems were a recurring problem for all Guatemalan governments and even more so for the Arzú government that had committed to significant social investments in the socio-economic agreement of the peace accords. Due to the changing political situation, all the IFIs placed increasing attention on Guatemala and they refocused their strategies towards support for implementation of the peace agreements.

In the autumn of 1995, a team of PAN representatives visited the World Bank in Washington, DC, presenting the plans for a thorough reform of the telecommunication sector and soliciting a loan to support the process. The team was met with limited enthusiasm, as few believed the government would be able to carry out its plans. Experiences from both Guatemala and other Latin American countries showed that the road towards privatization of state-owned enterprises was paved with political difficulties, and to issue a loan depending on its implementation was viewed as too risky. It was argued that it would be wiser to make a 'Christmas-tree loan' where several sectors were included under the heading of state reform. The team left empty-handed and with its initial skepticism against the Washington institution confirmed.[52]

Early in 1996, when the PAN government had taken office, a meeting was held in Guatemala with all the main donors, among them the IDB, the World Bank and the USAID. Here the governmental reform agenda was presented, and among the reforms were plans for the privatization of Guatel and reform of the telecommunication sector. The World Bank representatives were less than enthusiastic about the drafts of the new legislation, arguing for a more traditional legislative framework with a strong regulatory body and a five year monopoly for the incumbent carrier. It offered to support such a privatization process within the framework of the general state modernization loan, and to provide technical assistance in drafting new legislation. However at this point the governmental team had lost patience with the World Bank and rejected the offer.

The IDB was from the start much more positive towards the law proposal. Thus the government continued the negotiations with the IDB for a Sector Reform Program for Infrastructure and Investment. It included a US$100 million loan, a US$7.45 million technical co-operation grant and a US$1.15 MIF donation. IDB chose to establish its own unit for program coordination within the Ministry of Economy, instead of using the World Bank-supported Commission for State Modernization,[53] and appointed a member of the PAN team that had prepared the governmental program, as the program coordinator. The technical cooperation was primarily directed towards the civil aviation sector (privatization of airports), but advancements in telecommunication reform were included in the conditionalities. The disbursement of the first tranche of the loan was dependent on the approval of the telecommunication law. This was a pro forma conditionality as the agreement was not signed until 20 October 1997, and by then the telecommunication legislation had already been in effect for a year. For approval of the disbursement of US$20 million from one of the three proposed floating tranches, completion of the Guatel privatization process was required. This process had also started when the agreement was signed.

Finally, as the process proceeded and the government proved that it was serious about telecommunication reform, the World Bank approved a US$13 million technical assistance loan directed towards the preparation of Guatel for privatization, strengthening of the Superintendent of Telecommunications, assistance in the management of the radio spectrum and purchase of software for the management of the radio spectrum. The sum set apart for the preparation of Guatel was primarily meant for allowing the government to pay the severance for the workers, until receipt from the sale had been collected. The funds could also be used for public campaigns to increase support for privatization. However the funds were never used. Instead, Guatel's own funds were used for the preparation, and the sum set off for this purpose was later renegotiated to be support for the SIT.

Thus privatization was in the end included as a conditionality for an IDB loan, but it is nevertheless difficult to argue that the government privatized due to IFI pressure. It is also difficult to show a direct connection between fiscal issues and privatization, although it was at the time a main issue of concern. Of the US$700 million that the international community had committed to support the peace process, by July 1997, only US$101 million had materialized. This left Guatemala in a precarious fiscal situation. By mid-1997, the connection between privatization of Guatel and finding a resolution to the fiscal situation, and particularly the internal debt became a main focus of the public debate. The government had in the first six months of 1997 spent 41 per cent of the budget on down-payment on the public debt and foresaw a serious fiscal deficit if no solution was found. The total public debt was at this point at US$1749.8 million (*Prensa Libre* 7 November 1997). In November 1997, a mission from the IMF was expected to negotiate a shadow or stand-by agreement, either of which would be dependent on a satisfactory fiscal situation (*Prensa Libre* 3 November 1997).

Guatel had made annual profits of approximately Q 500 million between 1992 and 1996, and although this was expected to fall due to new investments, transfers were approximately Q150 million in 1997 (US$24 million) and Q225 million in 1998 (US$34 million). However these transfers were small compared to the sum that the government expected to receive from selling Telgua.

In August 1997 the Vice-Minister of Finance, Irma Luz Toledo Peñate, announced that the budget for 1998 was calculated with an expected income from the sale of Guatel of Q1500 million (US$220 million). This number was later lowered by Minister of Finance Alejandro Arévalo who in December declared that the budget of the coming year was based on an expected income of Q1519 million for the sale of public enterprises of which Q1200 million (79 per cent) was expected to come from Guatel. Telgua manager Guzmán announced that Q300 million of the funds obtained from the sale of Guatel would go towards severance payment, Q98 would be destined to the company's pension fund, while the rest would be split between payment of the government's internal debt and social expenses (*Siglo Veintiuno* 30 August 1997).

Nevertheless the fiscal demands contributed directly to the reforms that were introduced in the telecommunications law in the autumn of 1997. Initially there were accusations that the changes had been introduced due to pressure from the prequalified foreign firms. This was rejected by the SIT, Mario Roberto Paz (*Prensa Libre* 7 November 1997). Also most of my informants argued that the measures were rather intended to increase the price of the company for fiscal reasons. Team leader Guzmán emphasized that the main reason for the changes in the law was that it had been difficult to find an investment bank that was willing to take on the job of selling Guatel within the existing legal framework.[54]

However the first sale attempt failed and when it became evident that it would not be possible to conduct the sale before the closure of the fiscal year, Arévalo announced that the government might have to seek new loans in order to cover the deficit. The solution found to the lack of privatization proceeds in the budget was finally to issue Q1500 million (US$236 million) worth of governmental bonds (*Prensa Libre* 27 November 1997).

The failure to sell Telgua not only made the government's financial situation difficult, but also Telgua's. The main problem was how to find money to pay the US$75 million that the 6000 workers of Guatel had negotiated as severance pay for being laid off. The deadline for the payment to the workers was set to 6 April, but by 3 April, application for approval for seeking a loan for this had not even been sent to the Congress. Mystery continued to surround the issue of where Telgua should get the money from until it was revealed that Telgua had obtained a US$100 million loan from the Hamilton Bank. This had been issued to Telgua at an unusually high interest rate (Libor + 6.75 per cent). In the final sales agreement between the Guatemalan state and Luca SA, the loan was deducted (including interest), and in the end the Guatemalan state's coffer lost from the deal. In sum, the Guatemalan state gained little from the process and the main winners were indeed the members of the private sector elite. Without understanding the private sector business strategies and their connections to the government, it is impossible to understand the process of privatizing Guatel.

Private Sector Business Strategies

The Guatemalan private sector elites had started to prepare for the possibility of privatizing Guatel since the government of Jorge Serrano Elías. Alvaro Arzú was then the Minister of Foreign Affairs and had, as discussed above, already discussed privatization with the Mexican government related to a renegotiation of the debt that the Guatemalan government had with the Mexicans. The private sector had further made two forms of preparations. Firstly, a series of smaller companies operating a limited number of lines, mostly connecting businesses in Guatemala City, had been established. Various banks established their own telecommunication companies in order to take care of internal communications, as well as ATM services.[55] One of these was Telered, which had been established in 1991.[56] Telered had aquired a significant debt due to investment in equipment, and needed new capital. This was the start of the connection between Luca, SA and Telered.

Luca SA had been registered on 11 December 1996, with a capital of Q5000. At the point of the purchase of Telgua, Consortio Luca SA had 75 per cent Guatemalan capital and 25 per cent Honduran. Among the investors were several investment groups and banks.[57]

However Luca also had connections to private sector groups as well as governments of the other Central American countries. The manager of Luca was Ricardo Bueso Derás. Originally from a Honduran family, Bueso had been the Guatemalan ambassador to Belize during the government of Jorge Serrano, and he had investments in various sectors. On the board of Luca SA was also Carlos Chaín Chaín, a Honduran businessman who had served as the Minister of Economy in the Callejas government in Honduras (1990–94) and was closely associated with the Arzú family in Guatemala. Bueso had initially been interested in buying Comcel (*Prensa Libre* 11 December 1998).

Thus it is clear that the political elites had close connections to groups in the Guatemalan businesses that were interested in investing in the telecommunication company. It was also clear that after privatization, parts of the governmental privatization team ensured themselves a position in the telecommunication sector. Eduardo Mayora Alvarado, who had designed the changes in the public procurement law, became one of Telgua's two company lawyers after privatization. The other company lawyer was Hector Mayora Dawe, Eduardo Mayora Alvarado's uncle and brother of Eduardo Mayora Dawe. Mayora Dawe had during the 1980s run the ultra right-wing Solidarity Action Movement party together with José María Marroquín Samayoa (*Inforpress* 10 July 1998), who was Guatel's main legal advisor in the privatization process as the representative in Guatemala for Shaw Pittman, Potts & Towbridge.

Thus traditional private sector elites managed to get a share in the new economic sector by taking direct control over the government. Other members of the government team such as Minister of Communications Fritz García-Gallont and General Manager of Guatel Alfredo Guzmán, were not part of the oligarchy but managed to ensure themselves a place in the telecommunication business after privatization. Guzmán continued his career in the telecommunication business in Nortel, the company that acquired the license for operating the PCS band by Guatel in 1997. There were allegations about Fritz García Gallont's personal involvement in the purchase of Telgua through the coffee-export company Agro Commercial SA where he had been the vice-president in 1992 and responsible for inscribing the company as an offshore enterprise of the Virgin Islands (*Prensa Libre* 14 December 1998). However he primarily ensured himself a place among the elites as the new Mayor of Guatemala City after the elections in 1999.

In addition to the actors benefiting directly from the sale of Telgua, there were several traditional private sector actors that started to invest in companies competing with Telgua. A series of smaller companies had been established in order to compete in the cellular sectors. Among them were Grupo Londrina and Guatemala Cellular. Victor Suárez, ex CACIF president (July 1990–January 1991) who had been the private sector participant in the team that elaborated the new telecommunication law, was one of the main investors in Grupo Londrina, who in 1991 had filed a complaint to the Constitutional Court against Comcel's monopoly. After a series of attempts, finally the court awarded the injunction. He also had a long list of merits in terms of being a member of blue-ribbon committees. Grupo Londrina later entered into partnership with Telefónica de España and started to offer cellular services as the first company competing with Telgua.

Conclusion

After having been in the hands of US companies in the first part of the twentieth century, infrastructure in Guatemala was developed first as a means to penetrate the countryside by dictators. Later, infrastructure and telecommunications in particular became parts of the Guatemalan military's developmental project, but also of their coercive strategies.

A main effect of the process of democratization in the mid-1980s was a weakening of the military elites related to the private sector elites. These had throughout history been in a contradictory relationship to each other; whereas the private sector elites needed the military to protect against popular opposition and insurgents, they also resented their tendency to expand the state apparatus.

The democratic opening and the gradual move towards the end of the civil war in Guatemala made the private sector less dependent on the military and more willing to rule themselves. This led to an increasing state capture by private sector elites. This occurred at the same time as telecommunications came to be considered the most lucrative business in the war-torn country.

This is the main background required to understand why Guatemala chose to privatize rapidly and within a highly liberal framework, and also why the actual privatization process was conducted in a manner that primarily served parts of the private sector elite.

The influence of the IFIs in this setting was minimal. They initially alienated the private sector by insisting on tax reform, and decided to support the privatization process only when it was well under way. They did supply some ideas and consultants, but in the end the ideas that were adopted were first and foremost in the interest of their domestic counterparts.

NOTES

1. The economic elite in Guatemala is often referred to as an oligarchy, defined as the family networks that control the means of production: land, labor, commercial institutions, banks and industries (Dosal 1995, p. 3). I will primarily use the word 'elite', as I will keep the question open as to whether the elites emerging around the new economic activities in the

telecommunication sector belong to the dominating family networks or not. I will use 'oligarchy', when I refer to groups belonging to these networks.

2. See Martí (1994), pp. 105–6, McCleary (1999), pp.56–57 and Dosal (1995), p. 152. It should be noted that McCleary uses the term 'classical liberalism' and refers to Milton Freedman and the Chicago Boys. As noted below, I think this is a more correct description than neo-liberalism.

3. There was a special Presidential Telegraph Office housed in the Casa Presidential, and Ubico always included a telegraph operator and mobile transmitter among his party whenever he left the capital.

4. As British banks were among the main lenders, foreign debt was still commonly measured in pounds sterling.

5. The Peruvian military attempted to define itself as nationalist and place itself on the ideological left, and undertook reforms of existing structures in order to accelerate social development (Rouquié 1973).

6. Interviews, former Guatel officials.

7. Interviews, former Guatel officials.

8. Ley Orgánica de la Empresa Guatemalteca de Telecomunicaciones, Recopliación de Leyes, República de Guatemala.

9. Lucás had given concessions worth millions of dollars to a company (Desarrollo de Autopistas de Guatemala – DAG), which was   registered with a capital of only Q5000.

10. Interview, Vinico Cerezo, 15 November 2000.

11. Interview, Vinicio Cerezo, 15 November 2000.

12. In fact Comcel kept the monopoly until June 1999, when Telgua started to offer cellular services (CIEN 1999b).

13. Asked whether he did so by a FLACSO researcher, he answered: 'Listen, what angered the private sector was that for the first time since Arévalo, the president has the authority to demand. I was not placed here by the businessmen … thus I make the decisions' (quoted in Valdez 1998, p. 116).

14. Interview, Vinicio Cerezo, 15 November 2000.

15. In fact what was privatized was the concession, as AVIATECA at that point could not count on a single airplane.

16. *Prensa Libre* 12 December 1990.

17. Quoted in Palencia Prado (1998), p. 191.

18. Interview, Richard Aitkenhead, 12 September 1999.

19. Beginning in response to the actions of General Ríos Montt in the early 1980s, CACIF had produced an economic plan upon the entering of each new government. CACIF continued to do so until the Arzú government took power in 1996. At this point CACIF viewed the private sector party PAN as capable of elaborating its own development policies (interview, Peter Lamport, former President of CACIF, 7 November 2000).

20. The following persons were members of this commission: Edgard Heinemann, Peter Lamport, Juan Luis Bosch, Alfredo Chincilla, Gustavo Anzuato Vielman (Comisión Nacional del Agro) and Victor Suárez.

21. The founding members were, apart from Manuel Ayau: Alejandro Arenales, Antonio Aycinena, Imrich Fischman, Enrique García Salas, Enrique Matheu and Ernesto Rodríguez Briones. The Ayau family is not one of the main oligarchic families in Guatemala, but has its roots in El Salvador where it is connected to one of the main families (the Hills) through marriage (Paige 1997, p. 363). However, the connection of the rest of the group to the Guatemalan oligarchic families is clear and the family lines can be traced in Dosal (1995), p. 9–11, 132–33 and Casaus Arzú (1992b), pp. 75–96.

22. Interview, Manuel Ayau, 23 November 2000.

23. Interview, Ramiro de León Carpio, 19 October 2000.

24. It would re-establish the personal income tax at 34 per cent, eliminate various exceptions to the sales tax (IVA), increase the taxes on alcoholic beverages, increase the departure tax, place a 34 per cent tax on international calls, and increase the tobacco tax by 100 per cent (Inforpress 28 April 1994).

25. Interview, Ana de Molina, 10 December 1999.
26. USAID-Guatemala. Office of Program Development and Management, PDM. Project No 520-02353. Contract No 520-0353-C-00-5037-00. Republica de Guatemala. Proyecto de ley General de Electriciedad. Borrador No1. Santiago de Chile. 20 de Enero 1994.
27. Memorandum to the President of the Republic, 5 February 1995.
28 Interview, Manuel Ayau, 11 November 2000.
29. Interview, Ana de Molina, 10 December 1999.
30. Interview, Gustavo Adolfo Díaz López, 31 October 2000.
31. Letter to Mario Sierra, General Secretary of Steguatel from Hector José Luna Troccoli, General Secretary of the Presidency, 7 December 1994, Presidencia de la República, Declaración de Antigua 16 December 1994.
32. This image was strengthened as during its first months in power, the government managed to break Red Moreno, the mafia that had corrupted the Guatemalan state since the 1970s (Presidencia de la República de Guatemala 1997, pp. 306–316).
33. Entering into effect on 19 November when it was published in Diario Official.
34. The owner of a Use Entitlement may not only sell it, but alternatively lease and/or mortgage it. Use Entitlements can also be fragmented vertically (if new technology allows a more intensive use of a given band), geographically and in time. The Use Entitlements were to be given for 15 years at the time, but with automatic prorogation unless the SIT finds evidence that the frequency has not been utilized at all. Anyone can bid for a radio frequency, and they are to be auctioned by the SIT whenever someone has expressed interest in a certain frequency, unless they are already utilized. According to the law, all transactions of Use Entitlements would have to be registered in the Telecommunications Registry, but no further permits are needed (Part IV Decreto 94-96).
35. This includes: the right to terminate a call in another network; signaling; automatic caller identification; billing data; number portability; right to publish user data in the white pages of any telephone directory; and access to databases to permit publication in the white pages of any telephone directory.
36. The procedure established was as follows. When an operator requires access to essential resources or facilities of another network, it will send a request to the company from which it requires the services with copy to the SIT. The parties have the duty to negotiate and have a period of 40 working days to reach an agreement, but the period for negotiations can be extended by mutual agreement of the parties. If no agreement can be reached, the parties should submit to the SIT an analysis of the points of divergence, and a best and final offer on each point. If one of the parties does not present a final offer on any point of dispute, the SIT would be obliged to resolve it in favor of the other party.
37. The formula can best be illustrated by an example: if one party offers to pay 2 cents for interconnection and the other demands 10 cents for providing it, and they fail to reach an agreement through negotiation, an expert will be brought in. He or she will determine which of the two prices is closest to the real costs.
38. Americatel, AT&T, Elite Telecommunications, ITT and MCI World Com complained to the Federal Communication-Commission (FCC) of the US arguing that Telmex would be too dominating on the long-distance traffic between the US and Central America. However, FCC resolved the issue in favor of Telmex (FCN-NEW-20000114-00001, 28 February 2000 reported in *Prensa Libre* 2 March 2000).
39. Interview Manuel Ayau, 23 November 2000.
40. Interview, José Alejandro Arévalo, 2 December 1999.
41. This was a group of young business-men sharing right-wing ideas who had organized to plot against the weakening President Carlos Romero in 1979 (see Stanley 1996, p. 124–27).
42. The *Wall Street Journal* wrote: 'Seldom seen without his Ludwig von Mises tie, Mr. Mena Lagos, who heads the presidential comission to modernize, is a zealot for free markets. A warm Latin smile masks a dead serious determination. This man is a committed disciple of classical liberal economics' (*Wall Street Journal* 8 March 1996, p. A11). *The Economist* noted: 'An open admirer of Margaret Thatcher, Mr Mena Lagos would make her look a pinko' (23 March 1996, p. 40).

43. The possible equivalents would be the think-tank 'Friends of Freedom' and the Mathias Delgado University. But as Mena Lagos argues: 'the Mathias Delgado University was captured by the mercantilists, and the Friends of Freedom is essentially only Orlando de Sola, Enrique Tamirrano and I', interview, 10 November 2000.
44. Interview, Alfredo Mena Lagos, 10 November 2000
45. The interconnection from day one was to be ensured through splitting up the infrastructure into a chess board of blue and red areas, and subsequently by selling the blue to one company and the red to another. This would force a degree of competition from the first day and avoid delaying competition in the 'local loop'. The arbitration mechanism was based on negotiation between the different parties rather than the direct intervention of a regulatory body.
46. The program received US$24 million from the World Bank and US$19.7 million from the IDB. The governmental co-financing was US$7.8 million.
47. For example was the man behind the Chilean model, Gregorio San Martin, was invited to give a seminar.
48. Interview, Giancarlos Ibargüen, 26 October 2000.
49. Interview, Alfredo Guzmán, 16 November 2000.
50. Mario Roberto Paz was PAN member and businessman, but had no experience from the telecommunication sector.
51. Interview, Alfredo Guzmán, 16 November 2000.
52. Interview, senior official, World Bank, Washington, DC, 23 September 1999, and members of the Guatemalan team.
53. Also the IDB supported the Presidential Commission, but through a modest technical cooperation of US$750 000 (signed in March 1997, first disbursement in August) for the contraction of various services directed to implement the modernization of the executive. ATN/SF-5457-GU.
54. Interview, Alfredo Guzmán, 16 November 2000.
55. For example Totalcom, established by Bancared to operate their ATM machines, and Cablenet, established in 1995 to give services to Banco de Construción.
56. Telered was owned 50 per cent by Banco Industrial, 25 per cent by Banco Granai & Towson and 25 per cent by Grupo de Cheppe Mirón.
57. It included 22 Guatemalan and Honduran businessmen. The largest four stock holders were Grupo Finsa-Banco Americano (40.91 per cent), Grupo Optimal Investment (36.36 per cent), Grupo Banhcrecer (18.18 per cent), and Centrans International (4.45 per cent)

4. Costa Rica: In Defense of the Welfare State

The case of Costa Rica contrasts sharply with that of the Guatemalan case. By the beginning of the millennium it could be considered the last refuge of state ownership in Latin America. Its electricity and telecommunication company Costa Rican Electricity Institute (ICE) was still state-owned and the private sector had only been allowed to participate in marginal parts of the business. That does not mean that the government and private sector elites had not attempted to privatize it. Rather it was public resentment and the strategies of the unions that contributed to the rejection of privatization attempts.

This chapter tells the story of the rise of ICE as a centerpiece in the project of state-led growth and welfare in Costa Rica. However it also tells the story of the political struggles between the presidency and the autonomous institutions in which ICE came to play a key part. Thus whereas in Guatemala the IFIs entered into a situation where the government attempted to regain control from a strong private sector (and vice versa), in Costa Rica it was the ICE management that attempted to regain autonomy from the government.

In spite of the fact that Costa Rica faced a severe debt problem and was under strong pressure from the IFIs to cut back on state expenditure, their influence was significantly curbed by the dynamics of the internal political situation. It was eventually the influence of 'new public management ideas' in the ICE management that set the basis for the telecommunication proposals that were merged into the so-called Combo-ICE; a proposal to reform ICE and allow for the participation of private capital. This proposal provoked a serious public uproar in Costa Rica in March 2000, leaving one person dead and many injured and arrested. The government had to withdraw the proposal, and after new discussions a consensus was achieved about the need to strengthen ICE and give it greater autonomy; but no consensus was found on the issue of private sector participation.

TELECOMMUNICATIONS AND THE BASIS FOR STATE POWER

Infrastructure and State Development from Liberal Rule to the Decade of Reforms (1870–1941)

The starting point in Costa Rica – as in Guatemala – was the victory of the Liberals over the Conservatives in the rampant nineteenth-century civil wars. The Costa Rican counterpart to Barrios in Guatemala was Tomás Guardia who launched a successful coup in 1870, and assumed dictatorial powers for 12 years. Under General Guardia the public sector expanded, the ability to collect revenues increased, and the national infrastructure improved. Nevertheless the state never penetrated the countryside or the cities to the same extent as the more militarized Guatemalan state did (Yashar 1997; Ferraro Castro 1998).

From the mid-nineteenth century, coffee developed as the dominant crop in Costa Rica. There is significant debate about the consequences of the introduction of coffee. One version of the story is that pre-coffee Costa Rica was a rural democracy with small farms worked by yeoman farmers. The rise of coffee production transformed the traditional small holding pattern of Costa Rican agriculture, and led to dominance by large estates, unequal land distribution and the growth of a landless proletariat (Facio 1978, Seligson 1980). This paved the way for the development of a class deriving its social power from the control of land, which in turn established the Liberal state. Revisionists argue that the introduction of coffee advanced a more equitable land tenure and wages that traditional historians had attributed to the pre-coffee era (Gudmundson 1986, Samper 1990). Furthermore whereas the development of a coffee market in Costa Rica preceded the Liberal reforms, the Liberals reinforced the predominance of an already established coffee-based political economy through a significant role of the state (Yashar 1997). Thus a class-based interpretation focusing on economic structures cannot account for the relatively unoppressive state in Costa Rica. Rather it was the other way around: the Liberals encouraged coffee production which ensured a more equitable distribution of land.

Irrespective of who is right in this, there is little doubt that by the end of the nineteenth century the distribution of land in Costa Rica was significantly more equitable than in the neighboring countries. Costa Rica had both yeoman farmers and large estates, but most importantly, the elites did not derive their economic, political and social power only from control over land, but also from control over coffee processing, credit and commerce (Armeringer 1982; Yashar 1997). This has become an essential part of the explanation for Costa Rican exceptionalism. The Costa Rican oligarchy was less dependent on cheap labor, and therefore it was not as dependent on a coercive state in the countryside to establish the basis for capital accumulation (Flora and Torres-Rivas 1989, Stone 1990). Rather, it depended on the state primarily to regulate the market (Yashar 1997). This did not preclude conflicts between smallholding farmers and the elite. However it did make the elite less dependent on a military apparatus to check labor than in the neighboring countries, which in turn made it possible to abolish it in 1948.

The other side of the story was the early development of a political system which, although it was far from egalitarian, had a certain ability to incorporate competing interests to the elite. The period after Guardia's dictatorship is often characterized as oligarchic politics, similar to the 1920s in Guatemala. Political parties emerged in 1889, but they were primarily temporary organizations created to mobilize electoral support around a candidate from the dominant agro-export class. The Republican Party, representing coffee growers, commercial importers and private bankers, maintained power for 50 years after its establishment. Apart from the short dictatorship of the Tinoco brothers (1917–19) there were periodical elections, but they were notoriously fraudulent and frequently followed by revolts and coup attempts (Lehoucq 1996).

However the private elites not only conserved their own interests, but also established institutions aimed at general economic growth and welfare. Although the social reforms are most often credited to the social-Christian and social-democratic governments of the 1940s and 1950s, several of them were established in the Liberal period (Ferraro Castro 1998). The Liberals also established state control over electricity in opposition to US interests.

Towards the end of the 1920s, opposition against US companies' domination of electricity production and the banana production on the Atlantic coast rose. The opposition was represented in the Legislative Assembly through the newly formed Reformist Party, but it was primarily influenced by the Civil League (the Liga Civica), an intellectual group linked to the regional movement against US dominance, led by Peruvian Victor Raúl Haya de la Torre. As a result of this, a new Autonomous Institution (AI) was established in 1928, the National Electricity Service (SNE) which was given authority to exploit energy sources, give concessions and supervise their utilization (Araya Soto 1988).

In sum, the Costa Rican state was based on a weaker agro-export elite, with less of a need for a military apparatus to control labor. This allowed for a greater centralization of power in the state, but also the emergence of a liberal oligarchy with a project also to promote welfare and development. Thus Franklin (1998, p. 76) concludes:

The Costa Rican oligarchic parties did not fit easily into the common portrayal of a class-based group seeking only to protect and promote their own wealth and interests. They also established state institutions aimed at development and welfare. And the democratic opening allowed for movements that opposed excessive international influence and absorbed ideas from abroad. However the traditional parties were not prepared to relinquish control of the political system to the new groups.

Therefore, the main change did not come until the landslide election in 1941, bringing Dr Rafael Angel Calderón Guardia of the Republican Party to the presidency (with 85 per cent of the votes).

The Decade of Reform (1941–48)

Calderón Guardia was handpicked by his predecessor Leon Cortés, who saw him as a candidate that could continue the traditions of the oligarchy – and in many aspects of the state administration he did. He retained the spoils system and was infamous for awarding public contracts to friends and supporters. Moreover he promoted coffee exports and production by cutting municipal and national coffee taxes, leading to a grave fiscal crisis.

However he also introduced social reforms. In 1941 the administration passed a social security law designed to cover costs incurred for sickness, maternity, old age, and death for all workers below a certain income. With this legislation Calderón further upset the oligarchy, which had already reacted negatively to his conduct due to his failure to appoint Cortés's son Otto as President of Congress. Calderón further established two more AIs: the Costa Rican Social Security Institution (Caja Costarricense de Seguro Social) and the University of Costa Rica, which had been closed since 1888 and now opened as an independent state institution.

Cut off from the backing of the elite, Calderón turned to the Communist Party to get support for his policies, and signed a formal accord with the communist leader Manuel Mora in 1943. This alliance has often been pointed to as a key to understanding the further development of democracy in Costa Rica. However it was far from unique in wartime Latin America, where anti-fascism temporarily took precedence over the domestic labor agenda (Yashar 1997, Franklin 1998).

In the 1945 elections, characterized by unrest and accusations of fraud, the Republican Party candidate Teódoro Picado won. He continued some of Calderón's social policies, but his election weakened the alliance with the Communists. There was also growing opposition against the Calderón/Picado–church–communist alliance.

By this time, independent businessman and social thinker José Figueres Ferrer had already formed the Democratic Action Party. In conjunction with the Center for the Study of National Problems (the 'Centro'), a study group formed at the newly reopened University of Costa Rica and with participation from the Civil League, he now formed the Social Democratic Party, on an anti-Communist, developmentalist and reformist platform. In its opposition against the alleged corruption and fraud of the government, the conservative publisher and former congressman Otilio Ulate joined it.

In the period 1945–48 the government continued to face both political and economic problems. In preparation for the 1948 elections, Ulate of the Democratic Party and Figueres joined to run against Calderón who sought a second term. Ulate was the presidential candidate while Figueres was appointed his 'chief of action' (Longley 1997). The 1948 elections ended in chaos and lack of clarity about the election results. On 11 March, Figueres launched the 'war of national liberation', with the aid of forces from the Caribbean Legion.[1]

The war cost between 1000 and 1300 lives and ended on 19 April with a victory for the opposition coalition. A revolutionary junta headed by Figueres took power on 8 May 1948, and declared the founding of the 'Second Republic'. During the 16-month junta period both the political and economic power of the old elite was challenged. The junta sent the old oligarchic leaders into exile and banned the Communist Party. Most importantly, they introduced a set of reforms that challenged the elite's economic powers.

Two AIs were established during the junta period: ICE and Oficina del Café (the Office for Coffee). Oficina del Café was to regulate prices for coffee and credit to small coffee farmers, whereas ICE was given the monopoly on electricity generation and supply. Decree No. 449 of 8 April 1949 established ICE, stated that the main responsibility of ICE was to ensure the availability of electric energy as a means to strengthen the national economy and the welfare of the Costa Ricans. In order to enhance autonomy from the politicians, ICE was given full independence from the executive power and was to be 'guided exclusively by its Board of Directors' (Art. 8). The board was to be put together by representatives of the private sector, the engineering school and various other civil society organizations. ICE was further given authority to enter into any form of contract to make necessary purchases, sales, and so on, and it was exempt from any present and future tax.

Thus state intervention in the economy was from the beginning a part of the political project of the Figueristas, aimed at modernizing the Costa Rican economy, but also aimed at keeping the traditional elites at bay. However at the same time state intervention was firmly based in the Costa Rican political culture even before the establishment of the development project of the 1950s and 1960s. Thus most Costa Rican authors view the development of state institutions in the period after the 1948 civil war as a continuation of Costa Rican traditions, rather than as a rupture of them (Ferraro Castro 1998, Masís

Iverson 1999). Volio Guardia et al. argue that the ideas discussed in the late nineteenth and the early twentieth century 'teaches us clearly a very Costa Rican doctrine in this matter: not prescribe State intervention, but allow it when special reasons for the good of the society makes it necessary, in a temporary or definite manner' (Volio Guardia et al. n.d., p. 19). However in the following decades, the political project in which the state institutions were embedded changed, and so did the conditions for their operation.

Telecommunications and the 'Developmental State' (1949–65)

The development of the post-war Costa Rican state may be divided into three periods, defining different forms of state involvement: 'the developmental state' (1949–65), the 'paternalist state' (1965–75) and the 'businessman state' (1975–early 1980s) (Villasuso 1992).

The first phase was characterized by the establishment of a series of new autonomous institutions and the involvement of the state in establishing physical infrastructure as a basis for development. The constitution of the Second Republic was created by a Constituent Assembly in 1948. It assigned a significant role to the AIs, granting them constitutionally a high degree of autonomy from the executive powers.[2]

Otilio Ulate took power in 1949 in accordance with the agreement made with Figueres after the war, but much of the economic strategy was already spelt out in the new constitution. Ulate also continued some of the more popular social programs of the two reformers of the previous decade (Longley 1997, p. 111).

In 1951, the Figueristas founded the National Liberation Party (PLN or 'Liberacíon') and issued a 'Carta Fundamental' outlining beliefs and plans for the future that Figueres put into action when he returned to power in a landslide victory in 1953. The PLN strategy was partly indigenously produced and partly inspired by external ideas, particularly those of the Economic Commission for Latin America (ECLA). Among the 'home grown' parts was a strong emphasis on the development of national sources of energy through the establishment of ICE (Carballo Q 1992).

The privileged position given to ICE and other AIs had its background in the intellectual endeavors of the aforementioned Centro. The ideology that was developed in the Centro was a mix of various pieces of foreign influence.[3] Marxist ideas also became a source of inspiration, although the Centro was staunchly anti-Communist (Solís 1993).

However a main principle was that one should avoid the direct application of 'exotic' solutions as this could 'lead to dictatorship of the right or the left' (Franklin 1998). Thus at the Centro 'foreign' ideas were adapted to Costa Rican realities. A part of these realities was the always present possibility of domination of political life by the old elites. The constitution gave the state responsibility for the economic and social well-being of all people, while at the same time separating the machinery to carry out the task (the AIs) from the authority of those responsible for overall policy making and the conduct of government (Armeringer 1982, p. 41). Thus state responsibility for the welfare of the population should be combined with the protection from politicization of the implementing institutions. Rodrigo Facio, for example, argued that the intention of the AIs was: 'To permit the administrative extension of the State in a period which requires all the time more state intervention in the economic and social life, but avoid that this extension is transformed into an increase in the power of the Executive.' (Quoted in Masís Iverson 1999, p. 50).

Moreover as a means to delegitimize the opposition from traditional elites, it was important for the Centro to present an image of democracy in Costa Rica as something which had existed in a longed-for past, but which was lost due to the corrupt, oligarchic elites running the country in the early twentieth century. This 'myth of the rural democracy' was both for internal use, where it has been an important basis for social cohesion, and for external use as 'Costa Rican officials actively cultivated their friendship with the US and strategically promoted the image of a country full of happy, peaceful Costa Rican peasants' (Franklin 1998, p. 131). This myth served as an important ingredient in the strategies of Figueres to gain leeway for the introduction of developmentalist policies without arousing suspicion of communist sympathies in the US. Gudmundson concludes that this image of Costa Rican democracy is 'one of the most attractive and widely disseminated national mythologies of any Latin American nation' (Gudmundson 1986, p. 1).

The AIs played an important part in the new discourse of the Costa Rican state. They became the symbol of the path from the rural democracy to peace, welfare and prosperity. As argued by Figueres in a speech to the Inter-American Association for Democracy and Freedom (IADF):

> Another type of association appears to be better suited to the development of Latin America: the autonomous authority. This is a state-owned enterprise, which combines some of the operating advantages of 'private' corporations with the protection of general interests. The success of the autonomous agencies depends to a large measure on the method followed for appointing their directors. Appointments should be as non-political as possible, and changes should be made gradually, one man at the time (José Figueres Ferrer, Unity and Culture, address delivered to IADF, Havana, 12 May 1950; Davis 1963, p. 469).

In the discourse on the Costa Rican developmental state, ICE was a cornerstone and it was given highly favorable working conditions to fulfill its developmental role. Not only was ICE given formal autonomy from the executive, also the informal relations between ICE and the government during the first years ensured its independence. Figueres took a personal interest in the well-being of ICE. As the first director of the board of ICE, he appointed Alex Murray McNair, a coffee grower, but nevertheless a *liberacionista*,[4] and one of Figueres's close allies during the revolution (De Witt 1977). Figueres trusted Murray's judgment and gave him the full responsibility for the development of the institution.

After one presidential period of opposition government, PLN returned in 1961, this time with Figueres's close friend Francisco Orlich as president. Although more conservative than his predecessor, he continued the developmentalist policies, and among his main accomplishments was the continued development of a national plan of electrification and telecommunications (Armeringer 1978, p. 204). One of the means to encourage this was to enhance ICE's possibilities to seek independent finance. In 1961 a paragraph was added that gave ICE the authority to issue bonds. Article 17 of this amendment states that the Government is not entitled to derive any part of the profits that ICE generates, as 'the Institute should not be considered a source of generation of funds for the government'. Rather ICE should use the funds it generates to increase the production of electric energy as a basic industry in the country. According to the law, the tariffs were to be regulated by the SNE.[5]

ICE soon became one of the electricity companies with the highest productivity and highest levels of technological development in Latin America. The coverage of electricity increased rapidly (see Table 4.1). However as of the early 1960s there were only approximately 10 000 telephone lines in the country, all of them in the area of the capital San José. The National Energy and Light Company (CNFL), a subsidiary of EBASCO, operated telecommunication services. In 1963, the Legislative Assembly passed the necessary legislation to incorporate the infrastructure operated by CNFL into ICE, which was given a constitutional monopoly on owning and operating telecommunication infrastructure (ICE 1994).[6] With a staff of five engineers dedicated to the purpose, ICE started to develop plans for extending the telephone network to the entire territory.

There were three main reasons for the government to place telecommunications within the same company as electricity. Firstly, ICE had gained a reputation for efficiency and high technical standards, and was thus viewed as competent for also developing telecommunication services. Secondly, telecommunications were seen as a luxury good of which profits could be used to subsidize electricity development in poor and rural areas. Thirdly, the recuperation rate for investments in telecommunications was approximately one quarter of the rate of recuperation of electricity

investments. Thus the income from telecommunication services would ensure
liquidity in phases of large investments in electricity development.[7]

Table 4.1 Social and economic indicators in Costa Rica, 1930–88

Indicator	1930	1940	1950	1960	1970	1980	1988
Life expectancy	42	47	56	62	65	73	76
Infant mortality (per 1000)	172	137	95	80	67	21	14
Homes with electricity (%)			40	51	65	79	86
Population with running water (%)			53	65	75	84	91
Telephones (per 1000)		7	11	12	23	70	135

Source: Carballo Q (1992), Franklin (1998).

The development policies of post-war Costa Rica were to a large extent
funded externally through grants and loans. During the first Figueres
administration the governmental expenses increased by 11.9 per cent,
whereas the income only increased by 3.9 per cent. The rest was covered by
external assistance. The total flow of grants and low-interest loans received
between 1951 and 1966 was US$226.9 million, the highest of all the Central
American countries (if the extraordinary US support for Guatemala in the
early 1950s is kept apart), in spite of the fact that it had the smallest
population and the highest GNP per capita (Denton 1969).[8]

The main source of financing for the telecommunication sector was the
World Bank. A certain division of labor developed between the IDB and the
World Bank, where the IDB focused more on the electricity sector. The first
phase of telecommunication development started with a US$22 million loan
from the World Bank.[9] A second loan of US$6.5 million allowed for the
opening of the first automatic telephone exchange in Costa Rica, and a third
(US$17.5 million) permitted expansion of services to various provinces
among them Puntarenas and Limón.[10]

The performance of ICE not only buttressed the support of PLN by the
beneficiaries of its subsidized services, but also earned the PLN
government's respect within the opposition. The AIs had a double function in
relation to the PLN opponents. Several members of the old elite assumed
positions in these AIs and thus gained control over important economic
sectors (Yashar 1997, p. 218). Furthermore ICE gained a certain acceptance
among the old elite, and also contributed to the gradual establishment of the

legitimacy of the regime in the eyes of the opposing forces (Paige 1997, p. 257).

However the extended autonomy given to ICE also made it an actor in and of itself. It came increasingly to resemble a state within the state, as depicted in its nickname 'the autonomous republic of ICE'. This was a perhaps unintended consequence of the support it had gotten, and one that had great impact on the policies in the years to come.

In sum, the first post-war period in Costa Rica signified the establishment of a state apparatus that was given a high degree of autonomy from political interference and capacity to direct the economy. The background for this was the Figuerista political project which on the one hand was based on a state-interventionist ideology, but which also used the AIs as a part of the establishment of a myth of the Costa Rican exceptionalism with the purpose of gaining political support at home and abroad.

ICE and the 'Paternalist State' (1965–75)

The transformation into the paternalist state was motivated by the discovery that in spite of the efforts of the Costa Rican state to achieve a more equitable society, a large part of the population was still marginalized (Villasuso 1992). As an attempt to reduce the social gaps, new state institutions were established, particularly in the area of social provision. Thus the state started to intervene more directly in order to fulfill the constitutional duty to provide social welfare to the population.

However in this period the state also became paternalist in a different sense. The establishment of the Central American Common Market (CACM) in 1963 marked the beginning of a new industrialist model. With the CACM, industrialization could take place in the shadows of the world's highest levels of protectionism, combined with fiscal incentives for national industries (López 1995). The result of this policy was an unprecedented economic growth (averaging 6 per cent annually between 1950 and 1975) and a strong growth of the share of industry in the GDP (increasing from 13.8 per cent in 1960 to 19.7 per cent in 1973) (Barahona Montero 1999). However another consequence was that the national industry, which up to this point had been weak, now emerged under the state protection umbrella, in what has been called a 'parasitic-capitalism'.[11] Costa Rican businesses emerged as suppliers to AIs with generous protection from competition abroad, and they depended increasingly on political connections. Under the leadership of politicians and the leaders of the AIs, a new symbiosis emerged between the state and Costa Rican industry. Entering Costa Rica into the CACM further changed the balance between different private sector groups. Whereas the Chamber of Industry was deeply involved in the entry of Costa Rica into the CACM in

1961 and in the following period had increased influence, the loser was the Chamber of Commerce with its emphasis on trade (Wilson 1998, p. 71; Ramírez-Arango 1985, p. 391–93). In 1975, an umbrella organization, the Costa Rican Union of Private Enterprise Chambers and Associations (UCCAEP) was established by six influential private sector organizations. Although its membership grew to 30 organizations in the following five years, its influence has been relatively limited due to its weak resource base and institutional rules (Ramírez-Arango 1985; Wilson 1998, p. 70–71).

At the same time, the politicians struggled to regain control over the ever more independent AIs. According to Armeringer, Rodrigo Facio and the other thinkers of the Centro did not foresee that there would ever be a conflict between the AIs and the central government, except from where there might be an administration hostile to the concept itself (Armeringer 1982). However it soon became evident that the autonomy given to the institutions not only enhanced their operating capacity, but also strengthened them as political actors. This was viewed as a problem by the executive, which argued that its hands were tied. The impetus for recentralization of the state therefore came primarily from elites connected to PLN who saw their influenced curbed by the existence of strong AIs (Rottenberg 1993).

Figueres was a main proponent of this view. He re-entered the presidency in 1970, still with ideas of social welfare and development, but this time more inclined to support industrialization, arguing that 'Coffee is a colonial product which produces a feudal society' (*La Nación* 17 August 1971, quoted in Armeringer 1978, p. 250). But another new feature of his ideas was that while he originally had promoted the AIs, now he attempted to extend his own authority over them (particularly the Central Bank) (Armeringer 1978, p. 251).

However the perception that the decentralized state was a problem was also influenced by international concepts of planning laid down in for example the Alliance for Progress (Cerdas Cruz 1979, p. 90). The ideal was to establish centralized administrative and economic planning that could ensure optimal use of scarce resources, and various external consultants pointed to the problems of the decentralized nature of the Costa Rican state. A study from 1969 concludes for example, 'One of the principal problems of the Costa Rican public administration is that the chief of the executive has very limited powers' (Denton 1969, p. 148).

As a response to this, starting in 1968 a series of laws that curbed the independence of the AIs were passed. The first was the constitutional reform of 1968 that eliminated the political autonomy of the AIs stating that they are subject to the decrees submitted by the government (Araya Soto 1988). When Figueres entered power, he passed Law No. 4646 (1970), better known as 'Ley de 4/3' (Law of 4/3). This dictated the composition of the board of directors of the Autonomous Institutions. From now on they would all have four members from the current government, and three members from the opposition party. This increased the board's dependence on partisan politics, and reduced continuity. Instead of a gradual one-by-one switch of board members, the whole board would now be exchanged with a change of government. Nevertheless Figueres continued to talk of ICE as a symbol of the heroism of the Costa Rican development project:

> Only in poetic terms can we talk about this work. This said Figueres commenting on the construction of the tunnel in those seven years. It is a victory, repeated Figueres, of the man over the rocks, the water and the harshness of the weather. These are heroes, he said [referring] to the workers. (*La Nación* 28 March 1974, quoted in Amador 2000, p. 4).

The development of telecommunications and the institution of ICE thus became an important part in the strategies of signification of the Costa Rican elites. Amador (2000) argues that ICE has become a complex symbol for the Costa Rican population. ICE has come to be connected with words such as: 'innovation, cutting-edge technology, modernization, economic solvency, national success, education, knowledge, ability to work, machines, equipment, publications, power, the skill of Costa Rican labor, technological sovereignty, social solidarity, democratization of services, welfare of the popular sectors, human projection, and solidarity of the communities' (Amador 2000, p. 1).

The external myth of ICE was coupled with a strong internal myth. Costa Rican sociologists who worked with ICE argued that it was creating a 'new man', characterized by a 'messianism': a collective sentiment that they possessed a historic mission to serve the Costa Rican people (Amador 2000). ICE even had its own hymn:

> Companion with pencils and tools, companion with mantle and staircase, join me to sing a hymn, a hymn with a strong beat. In the honor of, the honor of the seed, that they planted, people of toil and progress, with an open mind and with horizons, they saw it emerging in the light. A seed that put down strong roots, over the ashes of those who fell, in the battle for making it possible, that served the country of peace. Sing to what flourished in progress, from countryside to city, from Tabarca to the Universe, using the creation that God gave us. Sing to those who lit up the nights, that communicated countries and villages, that protected rivers and forests, all that have not yet died, companion with shovel and suit, companion with helmet and courage, the heart of Costa Rican tradition, Costa Rican Electricity Institute (*The Hymn to ICE*, author's translation from Spanish).

In sum, by the early 1970s the autonomy of the AIs had been significantly curbed, and party politics had started to influence their operations to a larger extent. However it was with the establishment of the Costa Rican

Development Corporation (CODESA), that the distinction between the state and business was seriously challenged.

ICE and the 'Businessman State' (1975–85)

The transformation into what has been labeled a 'businessman state' (Estado Empresario) is most often related to the establishment of CODESA in 1973 (Cerdas Cruz 1979). Through CODESA the state became a direct participant in various enterprises, either as a majority investor, a minority investor or by giving cheap loans or guarantees. By 1977, CODESA was present in a variety of economic sectors: agriculture, industry, mining, oil exploration and transport. In this period Costa Rica more than doubled its manufacturing value-added, from US$251 million in 1970 to US$540 million in 1980 (Gayle 1986). The board of CODESA in which the private sector had the majority, gave it unprecedented power over governmental activities, but it also became the arena for clashes between the private sector arguing that the state had become too dominant, and the government (Ramírez-Arango 1985).

The rise of the businessman state also led to a split in the PLN. By the end of the PLN presidency of Daniel Oduber Quirós (1974–78) who succeeded Figueres, the perceived excessive state involvement in the economy had led an important group of private sector leaders to leave the PLN and move to the new loosely formed alliance of the traditional elites, now called Unity Coalition Party (PCU) (Ramírez-Arango 1985, p. 399).[12]

At the same time, the process of 're-centralization' of the AIs continued. The reforms that had been introduced during Figueres's government had been of little help and President Oduber Quirós described the situation as follows:

> It was not possible to work or to make political changes with a series of separate worlds, small feudal societies, as the autonomous institutions had become. Every one of them planned in their own way, in accordance with their own perspectives, with no order or coordination with the others or with the central government. But since a country is one and its economy is an integrated system that does not permit fragmentation, this situation drew us towards a dispersion of resources and efforts. The President in such conditions is nobody and the responsibility for administrative and political management evaporates. Apart from putting the three-colored ribbon on him and playing him the national hymn, there is not much more of importance for the President to do. (Quoted in Masis Iverson 1999, p. 51)

Consequently in 1974, a further reform was introduced through the passage of the Law of Executive Presidents (Ley de Presidencias Ejecutivas, Ley No. 5507). This applied to 14 of the most important AIs, among them ICE. From this date, the main link between the Central Government and the AIs was the Executive President that was appointed by the government. This added a new layer of management to ICE, which was now run by the

Executive President, a general manager and two sub-directors, one for the electricity part and one for the telecommunication part.

These internal tensions increased in strength as Costa Rica came under pressure from the IFIs due to the rapidly evolving debt crisis.

The Debt Crisis and the Beginning of the End of ICE's Glory Days

In 1978 Rodrigo Carazo Odio of the PCU took power on a platform of reduction of the size of the state and better control over the AIs. As a part of his plan, he added a further layer of control on ICE through the establishment of the Budget Authority to control the efficiency in the execution of the budgets of the institutions in the public sector (Autoridad Presupuestaria, Ley No 6821).[13]

However his focus had soon to be directed towards the worst economic crisis since the great depression. Partly due to the expansion of the public sector, the Costa Rican external debt increased by 27 per cent a year between 1970 and 1980. Towards the end of the 1970s, the pace of growth of the external debt increased, and in terms of per capita debt it increased from US$320 in 1976 to US$1200 in 1981, one of the largest per capita debts in the world. The cost of servicing the debt rose from a manageable US$60 million in 1977 to US$510 million in 1982. Three-quarters of the ten-fold increase in public external debt between 1970 and 1979 is explained by the debt incurred by the AIs, and ICE was the largest of them by far (Contraloría General de la República 2000).[14] At the same time, economic growth slowed down and terms of trade plummeted. Thus Costa Rica experienced a 40 per cent decline in purchasing power between 1978 and 1983.

In order to resolve the crisis Carazo signed two agreements with the IMF. Firstly, a stand-by agreement in February 1980, and secondly, an extended service agreement worth US$300 million of three years validity in May 1981. The main goal of the IMF agreements was to reduce the current account deficit from 14.5 per cent to 11 per cent, as well as to apply a restrictive fiscal policy in order to reduce the fiscal deficit (Salom Echeverría 1992).

Carazo attempted to adjust taxes, the domestic price of oil products, and the colon's international exchange rate in order to meet IMFs demands, but attempts were repeatedly blocked by the Legislative Assembly in which he had very little support (Wilson 1998). However it was not just the Legislative Assembly that contributed to a failure to comply. According to several authors Carazo himself was by no means convinced of the virtues of the IMF/World Bank medicine, and he never really intended to comply with the agreements (Rivera 1982, Salom Echeverría 1992).

The IMF responded to the government's failure to continue the reforms and its unwillingness to address the rapidly growing deficit by ending the loan disbursement and ceasing negotiations with the Costa Rican government. In 1981 President Carazo became so frustrated with the IMF demands that he expelled the IMF's Costa Rica mission and declared a unilateral debt moratorium in July 1981, one year before Mexico sparked off the global debt crisis by doing the same (Edelman and Monge Oviedo 1995).

In this context, ICE was under increasing pressure. The World Bank had already in the early 1970s started to pressure ICE to separate the telecommunication and electricity sectors, and the fifth and final telecommunication loan that was issued in 1979[15] had as a key condition that ICE 'operate each of its Telecommunication and Power Directorates separately, maintain separate records and prepare separate financial statements'.[16]

The purpose of this condition was to clarify the extent of transfers between the two sectors. The exact amount of the transfer was difficult to determine due to the internal accounting procedures, but in 1981, the ICE management believed that the transfers were in the orders of US$5 to 6 million per year.[17] The World Bank and later the IDB wished to change the practice of transfers in order to gain a better overview of expenses and costs. However there was a second reason. The electricity and telecommunication projects started to get different treatment internally in the IDB and the World Bank. As telecommunications had increasing possibilities for getting private finance, willingness to fund that sector decreased.

In sum, by the early 1980s Costa Rica found itself in a difficult situation with regards to foreign debt. ICE which had been given significant autonomy in post-war Costa Rica, now faced pressure both from the government that wanted control over the 'autonomous republic of ICE' and from the IFIs. This was a pressure that would become significantly more vocal in the years to come as the debt crisis unfolded in Costa Rica. In spite of this, the direct influence of the IFIs on telecommunication reform was never very significant.

THE PROCESS OF REFORM

The Neo-Liberal Turn and the Early Privatization Attempts

After the incident with the IMF during the Carazo administration, the incoming PLN government headed by Luis Alberto Monge (1982–86) initially signaled that it would handle the relationship to the IFIs quite differently. Upon taking office, Monge signed a stand-by agreement with the IMF, leading to an agreement with the Paris Club in 1983. Subsequently he introduced a freeze on government expenditure, tax increase and a change in the tax burden from production to consumption taxes. By 1983 the fiscal deficit had dropped from 14.3 per cent to 3.4 per cent. However as popular protest increased, Monge sided publicly with the protesters and argued that the austerity measures were the result of IMF conditionality and were undermining the social fabric of the country (*La Nación* 20 December 1983, quoted in Wilson 1998, p. 117). He subsequently refused to sign a new IMF stand-by agreement, ended some austerity measures, and increased social spending.

Nevertheless after a major Cabinet reshuffle in 1984, the Monge administration changed its direction with respect to development policies. In April 1985, the convention for the first structural adjustment loan (SAL I) was signed between the government of Costa Rica and the World Bank, facilitating credits up to US$80 million.

The main focus of the first Structural Adjustment Program (SAP I) was the achievement of macroeconomic stabilization through reduced fiscal spending. In order to achieve this goal, a series of measures were agreed upon, many of which affected ICE. Firstly, it was agreed to freeze public sector jobs for three years, which meant that ICE could not hire any new staff. Secondly, the government agreed to improve the mechanisms for controlling spending through the Budget Office and the Comptroller General's Office. This included a new auditing procedure aimed at discouraging the AIs from 'buying now, paying later'. Third, it was agreed to limit public investment equal to 6.4 per cent of GDP during the period 1984–86. The consequence was that during the Monge administration the investments in telecommunications fell from an average annual increase of 16 per cent to 4 per cent. ICE had to cancel the planned project of investment in rural telephony and waiting lists for getting a telephone installed increased to 11 000 (Monge 2000). Fourth, the government agreed to a periodical adjustment of the public utility charges. Consequently, ICE had to raise tariffs four times between 1978 and 1985. This was also a requirement for meeting the obligations agreed with the World Bank under the Fifth Telecommunication Loan of 12 per cent rate of return on its revalued telecommunication assets (Sojo 1995, Castro 1995, Mideplan 1992). ICE also undertook a rescheduling of its commercial debt, obtaining a grace period of three years, followed by a repayment period of 3½–4½ years. However in return, interest rates were raised substantially (to LIBOR + 3 ¼ per cent) (World Bank 1986b). In short, ICE's ability to provide high quality telecommunication services was severely constrained. This would later become a main argument for bringing in the private sector during the following PLN administration.

In the 1986 election campaign, implementation of neo-liberal economic reforms was a contentious issue. Part of the reason why Oscar Arias Sánchez won the elections was that he focused on the Central American peace process rather than on economic policy, and attempted to present himself as an 'old-style' interventionist Liberacionista (Wilson 1998, p. 141). However by 1986 neo-liberalism had gained a stronghold within a significant fraction of the PLN. Arias clearly belonged to the neo-liberal fraction, along with some of his cabinet members (among them were Carlos Manuel Castillo, the first President of the Central Bank, and Fernando Naranjo, Minister of Finance. He later appointed Eduardo Lizano, a declared neo-liberal, as President of the Central Bank, in spite of his association with the conservative opposition, that from 1983 had unified in the Social Christian Unity Party (PUSC). His endorsement of neo-liberal strategies was also connected to the tension with the US over the Central American peaceplan. The peace initiative was Arias's main political project, but he met fierce resistance from the Reagan administration, which repeatedly attempted to jeopardize Arias's peace efforts. Following the US's recommendations with respect to economic policies was viewed as a small price to pay for maintaining some political goodwill from the US (Honey 1994).

In 1988, Arias initiated the negotiations with the IFIs over a new SAP (SAP II), and in October 1989 the Legislative Assembly approved a US$100 loan supporting it.[18] In addition, the government signed a convention with the Japanese Overseas Economic Cooperation Fund for the same amount. SAP II included measures to further commercial openness, reform of the financial system, limit governmental controls on agricultural prices, and improve the administration of the public sector (Barahona Montero 1999).

Privatization of ICE was never a part of the agreements related to SAP II. However ICE was indirectly affected by entering into the accounts of the IMF. Previously only the central government's finances had been taken into account in the estimation of the fiscal deficit. After 1986, the main autonomous institutions and public enterprises also entered into the account, putting stronger pressure on the institutions to avoid deficits.

Of more importance for ICE was the Arias administration's decision to stop external borrowing, which meant that the government had to depend on internal sources of funds. One way to acquire funds to cover the fiscal deficits was to force AIs to purchase state bonds. This placed increased financial burdens on ICE. The debt that the government had in relation to ICE increased steadily and by 1999 it amounted to 80 000 million Colones (US$275 million).

Also, the implementation of the programs to reform the state and 'democratize services' (COREC 1991, Castro 1995) under SAP II had a certain impact on ICE. The 'Plan for transferring services from the public to the private sector' aimed at transferring activities of a non-strategic and non-regulatory character to the private sector. These activities could be carried out primarily by former workers of the affected institutions who voluntarily agreed to transfer to the private sector and set up a co-operative, an association or a company, so-called Workers Stock Holding Companies (SALES). This form of 'sugaring the adjustment pill' resulted in the establishment of a series of SALES by ICE workers in the telecommunication sector that further blurred the boundaries between the public and the private sectors.

SAP II did undoubtedly provide an important backdrop to the proposal to privatize ICE that was developed during the Arias government. The proposal would separate out the telecommunication part of ICE to form the Costa Rican Telecommunication Company (ECOTEL) in which ICE would have 40 per cent of the stocks and the remaining 60 per cent would be sold to private investors.[19] ECOTEL would in turn control 40 per cent of ICE's subsidiary RACSA, and the remaining 60 per cent would be sold.[20] ECOTEL would be ensured monopoly on most services as no opening of the market was considered in the proposal (ICE 1988a). Wilson (1998, p. 133; 1994, p. 773) argues that this was a part of Arias's plan for the democratization of services. And indeed it was Arias that asked ICE to evaluate the possibilities of privatizing parts of ICE (July 1987).

However by that time, ICE's Manager of Telecommunications (and later President of ICE) Antonio Cañas had already started to explore various options for privatization.[21] The solutions he proposed were primarily affected by the institutional questions that the ICE management had grappled with for years: the consequences of having placed both telecommunications and electricity in one company, the increasing financial controls placed on the company by the General Comptrollers office, and the politicization of the company resulting from the introduction of the 'Law of ¾' and the Law of Executive Presidents.[22] Moreover it was affected by attempts to handle the technical revolution in the electricity and telecommunication sectors. By 1988 the two sectors faced very different challenges. Technological developments had led to a diversification of services in the telecommunication sector, whereas in the energy sector, it had led to an increase in plant size, which required larger investments. Moreover, the energy sector was faced with a possible crisis, and as long as the two sectors were in one company, this could spill over into the telecommunication sector.[23]

Although the top management also mentioned pressure from the World Bank and the IMF as an impetus for their proposal, they argue that the main motivation for their proposal was to end the increasing politicization of the company. According to Cañas:

We saw the glimpses of a political change in the country, one of politicization of the state companies. In the period when I was [in the management], it was first and foremost a technocracy. We who held the highest positions of ICE in this period were career officials, whether it was from ICE or other companies. We were career administrators or professionals, almost all of us engineers.[24]

With regard to IFI influence, another member of the management argues that:

Of course, they looked upon it with sympathy, but the World Bank did not participate. More like giving us a general culture, about what is the method. Of how to 'go public', how to finance it ... But we only participated in some seminars. There was no direct support. This was entirely an ICE issue.[25]

In addition to improving the situation for ICE, one cannot exclude the importance of other personal motives of the ICE management. A series of companies were established providing services in which ICE did not have monopoly (for example beepers), but whose stated objectives were to provide various types of telecommunication services, currently exclusively under ICE's authority. This included a series of companies in which the top management of ICE was involved, and they may have intended to provide services after ICE had lost its monopoly.

Regardless of the motives, the proposal soon met fierce resistance from the unions and the general public, and the management decided to withdraw it.[26] However a new attempt was soon made to introduce private sector participation in telecommunications, and this time the impetus came from quite different actors.

Bringing the Private Sector in by the 'Back Door': the Millicom Case

Already in the 1970s, ICE had developed plans to establish a network of mobile telephony, and obtained funding for it under the Fifth Telecommunication Project of the World Bank. However due to fast increasing demand for regular telecommunication services, ICE decided to increase the component of regular services of the project and postpone the mobile telephone service component. Thus when demand started to increase for cellular services in Costa Rica in the early 1980s, ICE did not have its own funding for it, and the World Bank had by then adopted a strategy not to fund mobile telephony as it was considered eligible for commercial funding.

Faced with these financial limitations, ICE attempted to establish a joint venture with Millicom to develop cellular services. Millicom was the first international company to develop cellular services in Central America. It had various investors, but in its Central American investments, the private sector arm of the World Bank, the International Financial Corporation (IFC) was an important source of finance.[27]

In order to establish a joint venture with Millicom, the government needed a special permission from the Comptroller General that it did not get. ICE continued to develop plans for its own cellular service, but this was also stopped due a new governmental policy that limited financing for the development of public services, particularly for services that could be exploited by private companies.[28] Thus ICE was in a no-win situation: it was cut off from public funds due to the debt situation, and it did not get permission to use private capital.

By this time, another company, Comcel, had already started to construct a private cellular network. In August 1987, the Office of Control of Radio gave a concession to Comcel to exploit the frequencies between 830 and 840 MhZ and between 868 and 878 MhZ.[29] Some months later, President Oscar Arias and Minister of Governance Rolando Ramírez ratified the concession which was later transferred privately to Millicom.[30] With these permissions in hand Millicom started to develop its own cellular system and in April 1989, Millicom started to operate. Three years later Millicom could count on approximately 10 000 telephone lines although it never had more than 2000 subscribers.

Millicom's position would not last long. In 1990 a special commission to study the telecommunication sector was established in the Legislative Assembly, and Millicom soon became its primary occupation.[31] In October 1993, the Union of ICE Engineers (SIICE) filed a complaint to the Sala IV (the constitutional chamber of the Supreme Court) arguing that the concession given to Comcel was unconstitutional. The claim was endorsed by the special commission, which moreover accused 16 ICE officials of having acted in ways that were damaging to the interests of the country. In 1994, the Supreme Court approved the injunction filed by SIICE, and ruled Millicom's operations unconstitutional. The ICE officials were found not guilty on the charges. With this verdict, the two first attempts to privatize telecommunications in Costa Rica had failed. ICE had maintained its monopoly.

Not only did privatization fail, but the Millicom case also contributed to giving private participation in telecommunications a negative image. A main reason for that was that both the president himself and a series of politicians were publicly known to have ownership interests in Millicom.[32] Due to this and other incidents, the Arias administration was viewed as the start of a new blurring of the boundaries between the public and the private sector. Whereas in the period of the 'entrepreneurial state' the private sector was crowding around state enterprises, now governmental elites were increasingly also investors and businessmen, a tendency that continued during the government of Calderón.

ICE Under Structural Adjustment

Rafael Angel Calderón Fournier of the PUSC (son of Dr Calderón Guardia) entered power in 1990 on an anti-adjustment platform. However the pressure he faced from abroad was massive. Before his inauguration (in April 1990) USAID gave him a clear message that it would no longer give Costa Rica special treatment (*Inforpress* 19 April 1990). Subsequently, support was further cut from US$65 million in 1990 to US$50 million in 1991 (see Table 4.2).

Table 4.2 US aid to Costa Rica 1982–90, million US$

	1982	1983	1984	1985	1989	1990	1991
Total aid	$54.3	$216	$179	$ 219	$117	$65	$50

Source: Clark (1997), Salom Echeverría (1992).

Moreover Arias had achieved partial conventions for the renegotiating of the US$992 million bilateral debt with Japan, France and Great Britain in the Paris Club, and he started to renegotiate the US$1800 million of the commercial debt under the Brady Plan (*Reporte Politico* No. 45 1990). However finalizing these agreements as well as rescheduling the multilateral debt was left to the incoming government. In May 1990 Calderón achieved an agreement to repurchase the commercial debt under the Brady Plan,[33] and by the end of 1990, Costa Rica had cleared most of the outstanding arrears with the multilateral banks (World Bank 1992b). Subsequently, in spite of his electoral promises, Calderón's government embarked on a program of strict economic policy measures, backed by the IMF.

The main focus of the emergency measures was to reduce the fiscal deficit, which was thought to be 6 per cent at the end of the Arias administration, but turned out to be 7.1 per cent on closer examination. As a means to reduce the deficit, tariffs on public services (telephone, electricity, water) were increased. The government also announced that it intended to privatize the remaining companies under CODESA.

Due to the failure to reduce the fiscal deficit to 1 per cent of GDP, the government repeatedly failed to sign a new agreement with the IMF. Finally, in April 1991, Calderón reached an agreement with the IMF which ensured disbursement of US$120 million in support for SAP II from the World Bank.

Simultaneously the government initiated a dialogue with the World Bank and the IDB about a possible SAP III (World Bank 1996b). The final result of the negotiations was a total credit of US$350 million under four different credit lines, all of which came with a series of conditionalities, many of which were crossing conditionalities (see Table 4.3).

Table 4.3 SAP III: structure and resources

Component	Area	Source	Amount US$
Third structural adjustment loan	Public sector reform	World Bank	100 million
Public sector adjustment program	Public sector reform	IDB	80 million
Sector investment loan	Financial sector reform	IDB	100 million
Multi-sector investment loan	Productive transformation	IDB	70 million

Note: In the strict sense, SAP III refers to the first two loans. However because they are related to the structural adjustment process, it is common to talk about all four as a bloc and as integral parts of the SAP III.

Source: MIDEPLAN (1993).

A wide range of public institutions was targeted for privatization, de-monopolization or new regulations under SAP III. Calderón committed to passing a Public Works Concession Law allowing for private investment in the physical infrastructure of ports, roads, airports and railroads, and an Economic Democratization Law, allowing for privatization of ancillary state activities (including four CODESA enterprises) and a reduction in the public payroll, cutting 2500 jobs (World Bank 1992c, *Inforpress* 19 March and 23 April 1992).

There were only two conditionalities that related directly to ICE. First, ICE was required to develop and implement plans for financial and administrative separation of the telecommunication and electricity sectors. Secondly, the National Electricity System (SNE) should be transformed into an autonomous regulatory authority for the public services.

No attempt to privatize ICE was put into the SAP III program. [34] Moreover privatization of ICE was not seriously discussed in the talks with the IFIs. Part of the reason was that it was not a priority even for the most clearly neo-liberal of the governmental representatives, for example Minister of Finance Thelmo Vargas:

I philosophically thought we could leave telecommunications to the end because I thought ICE would be very difficult with respect to the public opinion. And at the moment, I don't think it was put in the SAP as condition for disbursement, not in the 'bold conditions', those that have to be fulfilled before the first disbursement and in the second. The most difficult we would always leave to the end. And I thought at the time that we should leave telecommunications to the end. [35]

The process of putting SAP III into practice proved long and painful. The first obstacle was an attempt by US Senator Jesse Helms to stop the approval of the Sector Investment Loan by the board of the IDB. The reason was a dispute over the appropriation of land from a US citizen in Costa Rica that owned property in a protected area considered to be the last reserve of tropical dry forest in Central America. When the board approved the loan in January, Helms went on to pressure the US government to boycott a disbursement of the first tranche of the Multi-sector Investment Loan (*Central American Report* 29 January 1993).

This was only the beginning of Calderón's troubles. The total SAP III program reportedly depended on the passing of 17 different laws in the Legislative Assembly,[36] and entering into an election year, this revealed itself to be more and more difficult. The opposition to the reform program focused on the target for public sector downsizing that was set as a reduction of 25 000 employees, and the de-monopolization of the insurance and petrol markets (*Reporte Político* No. 98 October 1994).

However it was not only due to legal troubles that Costa Rica did not fulfill the requirements. Calderón himself was considered to be far from a convinced neo-liberal. In the policy dialogue with the IFIs related to SAP III, his ideas about economic reform were far from consistent. Calderón's lack of consistency and his pursuit of political rather than economic goals alienated the more ideologically motivated government members. In November 1991, he announced that he wanted to add US$12 million to the budget for the four state universities, suspend the program to cut down the number of public employees, and drop plans to privatize a series of public enterprises. These changes led the main neo-liberal ideologue in the government, Thelmo Vargas, to resign (*Reporte Político* No. 67 November 1991).

Calderón's relations to ICE were also characterized by lack of a clear strategy. Early on, Calderón did take some initiatives to get a process of privatization going. It was revealed that the government in August 1991 had established contact with the US company, Paine and Webber, which had offered advisory services for the privatization of ICE. However as this soon spurred resistance from the ICE management as well as the unions, the government backed off (*Central American Report* 14 June and 5 July 5 1991; *La Nación* 19 July 1995).

In sum, although Calderón's government had clearly neo-liberal members, Calderón himself was not one of them. He was rather motivated by a desire to keep his popularity and privatizing ICE would not be the best recipe for success in that respect. Moreover the IFIs did not want to heighten the risk of holding back the disbursement of funds, which would have been a consequence of putting it into the SAP as a conditionality. It was not until new public management ideas became influential in ICE that new propositions were formulated.

New Public Management 'á la Tica'

The PUSC government of Calderón was succeeded by a PLN government headed by José Maria Figueres in 1994. Figueres was the son of the mythical founding father of the second Republic. His government (1994–98) is often described as a turning point at which the private sector perspective became dominant in Costa Rican politics. He had dedicated most of his life to his private businesses, and although he also entered power on an essentially anti-structural adjustment platform, he was not perceived to have any strong ideological commitment. During his campaign he had made few statements about what to do with ICE.

However during the summer of 1995, the voices arguing for the necessity of opening the telecommunication sector to private participation had become stronger, and Figueres announced his inclination to develop a plan to modernize ICE. In the ministries, in the ICE management, and even among the unions it was reported that there was support for limited opening of the sector (*La Nación* 23 July 1995). In November 1995, the discussions about privatization and about the future of ICE became the main source of tensions in internal meetings in the two majority parties, but particularly within PLN's which never had been able to stake out a unified policy on privatization. Three factions emerged in PLN: one opposing privatization, one that was for it, and one taking on an intermediate position, arguing that ICE should be allowed to enter into strategic alliances. President of the PLN, Rolando Araya, led the latter group, arguing that: 'My fear with respect to ICE is that we end up enrolled in copper cables not worth a peseta if we don't make the right decision in time' (*La Nación* 21 November 1995).

Figueres was also under financial pressure, as he had inherited a deeply troubled economy. In 1994, the overall public sector deficit increased to 8 per cent of GDP from 0.9 per cent in 1993, growth declined from 6.4 per cent to under 4.5 per cent, and inflation more than doubled to 20 per cent. He was also under pressure from the US which threatened to block funds from the MDBs due to the Millicom ruling. The Costa Rican constitutional court's decision that Millicom's operations were illegal and that it had to cease operations by 10 May 1995, caused fears that Costa Rica would be victim of the US Hickenlooper amendment. This created the possibility for the US to withhold funds from the multilateral organizations from countries threatening US investments.[37] This was seen as likely, particularly since the IFC – in which the US government is the largest stakeholder – held a majority of stocks in Millicom. Millicom representatives also asked the US Congress (March 1995) to exclude Costa Rica from the benefits of the Caribbean Basin Initiative (CBI), if the decision was not changed. Almost 50 per cent of Costa Rica's export at the time was destined to the US and its competitiveness was largely due to lower tariffs under the CBI scheme. Trying to avoid US reactions, in April 1995 the vice-president, Rodrigo Oreamuno, announced that a contract would be signed between RACSA and Millicom. According to the contract, RACSA would rent the equipment from Millicom and continue to serve its clients. RACSA would then get 34 per cent of the profits whereas 66 per cent would be left with Millicom (*La Nación* 18 April 1995).

This agreement infuriated the unions and even the President of ICE, Teófilo de la Torre, agreed that to allow for RACSA to compete with ICE (which by then was providing its own cellular services) was not in accordance with ICE's policy (*La Nación* 19 April 1995). The Unions threatened to paralyze the company, and on 9 May a general strike started. The result of the conflict was that on 17 May, the government broke off negotiations both with Millicom and the unions, and instructed ICE to provide cellular services to Millicom's subscribers.

The US government did not block Costa Rica from the CBI or use the Hickenlooper amendment to withhold funds from the multilateral development banks. However in February 1996, Millicom presented a demand for compensation of US$400 million from the Costa Rican government, ICE and RACSA, to a district court in Washington, DC, a sum which would exceed the total agreed financing for the whole of SAP III. In the end the compensation demand did not come through.

Thus Figueres was under financial pressure as well as facing demands for improved telecommunication services. His political vision was unclear. But whereas Figueres himself did not have clear ideas about ICE, his appointee as ICE President did. In July 1995, Figueres exchanged Teófilo de la Torre – who had disagreed with the government's handling of the Millicom issue, and was skeptical towards privatization – for Roberto Dobles as President of ICE.

As an industrial engineer with a PhD in business administration, a former Minister of Science and Technology, and with no history with ICE, Dobles had completely different ideas about how to run the telecommunication sector than his predecessor did. His goal was essentially twofold. Firstly, he wanted to modernize the company and the sector in accordance with current practices elsewhere in the world. He regarded the European model, based on introducing private competition to the state-owned company, more appropriate than the Latin American model, which included selling the SOT within a framework of limited or no competition, since the latter essentially was chosen due to fiscal considerations and not concern for efficiency.[38]

Secondly, he wanted to reduce the now familiar tensions between ICE and the central government. One means was to replace *a priori* controls of ICE, which hindered the company in responding to challenges in a timely manner, with *a posteriori* controls. This would simplify the lengthy process of public bidding, which reduced ICE's flexibility.

In August 1996, Dobles sent a triple project related to ICE to the legislative assembly. It consisted of three law projects: one aimed at modernizing and strengthening ICE (the Law of Modernization and Strengthening of the Costa Rican Electricity Institute, LMFICE; ICE 1996a), a new telecommunication law aimed at liberalizing the telecommunication sector (ICE 1996b), and a new electricity law that would liberalize the electricity sector (ICE 1996c). Together they resembled the model of reform that was introduced in several European countries (especially the Scandinavian ones) in the mid- to late 1990s. In the telecommunication sector the aim was to strengthen the state-owned carrier and allow it to operate as a private company, while gradually allowing for competition.

LMFICE proposed to transform ICE into a 100 per cent state-owned company (Corporation ICE) with administrative, technical and financial independence. The aim was to allow it to compete efficiently with other companies in an open market. It would be exempt from many of the laws that previously had limited ICE's autonomy.[39] The General Auditors Office would be in charge of auditing, but this would be *a posteriori* control, and thus less of a barrier to a flexible operation of the company. Of the profits of Corporation ICE, 75 per cent would be reinvested, and no more than 25 per cent transferred to the state. The board would consist of nine members, appointed by the Governmental Council,[40] and two representatives of the workers.

Corporation ICE, consisting of ICE's existing subsidiaries RACSA, CRICSA (International Radiographic Company of Costa Rica), CNFL, and two branches that would be established to exploit electricity and telecommunication services respectively, would be allowed to enter into strategic alliances with private companies, and also divest any of its subsidiaries. In effect this would allow for a partial privatization of ICE's projects and functions.

In sum, the law attempted to exempt ICE from the laws established during the 1970s and 1980s that had tied ICE's hands and made it incapable of fulfilling its tasks in an efficient way. At the same time, it allowed for ICE's engagement with private enterprises that would allow it to become an actor in the international telecommunication market. Although the law would free ICE from the nitty-gritty controls of the Comptroller General, it would make it even more dependent on the current government as the whole board including the president would be appointed by the sitting government, except from two representatives of the workers. On the other hand, the divisions within the ICE board seen under the regime of the 'Law of ¾' would be overcome.

The other law proposal concerning the telecommunication sector was Anteproyecto Ley General de Telecomunicaciones (ICE 1996b), which proposed a gradual opening up of the telecommunication industry to competition. The law furthermore proposed the establishment of a financially and administratively independent regulatory body, the Regulatory Institute for Telecommunications (IRETEL) that would have the authority to intervene if someone failed to comply with the rule of obligatory interconnection, or charged unreasonable prices for it. It would also administer the radio spectrum, and regulate final prices.

This was the first proposal in Costa Rica for an opening up of the telecommunication sector to competition, and it was largely a result of the merging of the new public management ideas of Roberto Dobles and the long-standing troubled relationship between ICE and the central government. The proposal was discussed in a special mixed commission in the Legislative Assembly,[41] headed by former Minister of Planning, and fierce privatization opponent Ottón Sollís (*La Nación* 12 September 1996). He prepared an alternative project which was aimed to strengthen ICE without allowing it to make use of private capital, and without opening the telecommunication sector to competition. However the governmental proposal was also amended before it was sent to the plenary of the Legislative Assembly, and this amendment was motivated by the need to address the pressing internal debt problem rather than improving telecommunication services. In the end, the amendment sealed the fate of the proposal.

ICE and the Internal Debt Problem

After a cap had been put on external borrowing during the Arias presidency, the government had increasingly attempted to finance its deficits through borrowing from the Central Bank and issuing bonds that it required the AIs to buy. This not only put pressure on the finances of strong AIs such as ICE, by the mid-1990s, the accumulated internal debt started to become a problem for the central government. In 1996 the internal debt had reached US$3355 million and interest rate payment reached 5.8 per cent of GDP. While the external debt had decreased by 32 per cent over a 10-year time-span, the internal debt had increased by 1956 per cent within the same time period (see Figure 4.1).

By this point, alleviation of the mounting internal debt became the main argument for privatizing ICE. A group of high-level economists studied the problem of internal debt in 1996,[42] and concluded that the most urgent action to alleviate the problem was to sell the telecommunication system owned by ICE. Furthermore it recommended selling electric generation plants, the national liquor factory and three banks. This would arguably reduce the internal debt with US$2500 million. Six ex-presidents of the republics meeting in November to discuss the problem endorsed the conclusions. The only ex-president that disagreed was, not surprisingly, Rodrigo Carazo (*La Nación* 13 November 1996).

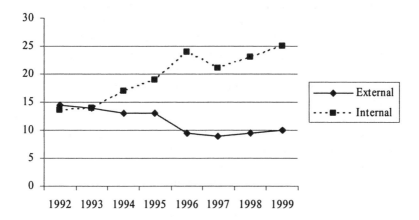

Source: Contraloría general de la República de Costa Rica, registro de la deuda pública.

Figure 4.1 Internal versus external debt in Costa Rica, % of GDP

This report was also the background for the move made by the government in January to connect the two issues: that of internal debt and the three ICE-proposals discussed in the commission in the Legislative Assembly. It proposed to accelerate the opening of the sector, so that the telecommunication market would open in 2000 and not in 2002 as the original Dobles project proposed. The income obtained from concessions to cellular operators and providers of Internet services was estimated to reduce the internal debt by at least 100 000 million colons (US$458 million). Moreover, it proposed to sell RACSA in order to generate further income.

The amendments made by the government provoked strong reactions among the deputies in the special mixed commission. The final project was voted down in the commission and the sudden proposal to sell RACSA clearly affected the deputies' attitudes. Thus the proposal was sent to the archives without even having been voted on in the plenary of the Legislative Assembly. In spite of having been the first country to suggest privatization of telecommunications in Latin America after Chile, by 1996 it had become clear that Costa Rica was a 'hard case' for privatization. This started to become clear also to the IFIs, who changed their strategy towards Costa Rica.

The IFIs Encounter a 'Hard Case'

The opponents of increasing private sector involvement in ICE often argued that the proposals to that end were the result of the pressure from the World Bank and the IMF. The truth was that whereas the IFIs had contributed to worsening the conditions for the operation of ICE over the course of the 1980s, they played only a marginal role in the development of proposals to reform it. They put pressure on Costa Rica to remedy its problematic fiscal situation. Moreover as discussed above, privatization of ICE was suggested as a solution to the internal debt problem that in the 1990s overshadowed the external debt problems and that also worried the IFIs. However the IFIs themselves never pushed directly for privatization of ICE. To understand why not, one has to take into account the internal politics of the IFIs, the competition between them, and also the fact that a degree of learning on the part of the IFIs occurred and made them more understanding of the Costa Rican situation.

In the Figueres period the general reforms aimed at modernizing the state virtually stalled. Figueres's strategy was to renegotiate the conditions for the adjustment program in order to ensure financial support with less reform. The World Bank granted six extensions of the effectiveness deadline from July 1994 to January 1995 (*Inforpress* 27 October 1994, *Reporte Politico* No. 99 November 1994).

However a review mission that visited Costa Rica in January 1995 concluded that the conditionalities had not been fulfilled satisfactorily, and in March 1995 SAL III (the World Bank component of SAP III) was canceled.[43] The IDB argued that Costa Rica had only fulfilled half of the conditionalities set as requisites for activating the loans, but nevertheless disbursed the first tranches of the Public Sector Adjustment Program as well as the Sector Investment Program.

In an attempt to rescue the remains of SAP III, Figueres entered into a 'patriotic pact' with ex-president Calderón a few days before he gave the annual speech to the Legislative Assembly on 1 May 1995. In June the same year, Figueres and Calderón entered into a new and more encompassing pact, where they agreed to end the state monopoly on current savings accounts, reform the pension regime, and put an end to subsidies to the private sector. A series of relatively small public institutes were mentioned as candidates for privatization. However only the President of the Central Bank advocated the privatization of ICE (*Reporte Politico* No. 105 June 1995) and it was not included in the agreement.

As a result of this pact, the avenues were again opened for conversations with the IDB for disbursements. In September 1995, the government was negotiating a disbursement of US$84 million from the IDB for which, among other issues, the separation of the electricity and telecommunication parts of ICE were conditionalities (*Reporte Político* No. 108 September 1995). Although it was widely acknowledged that the separation of ICE existed primarily on paper, and that several of the other conditionalities were not yet met, the project team recommended disbursement.

The more positive evaluation that the government got from the IDB than from the World Bank was partly due to the fact that there were different measures included in the programs. However there were also cases of different judgments of the same measures. For example, in contrast to the World Bank, the IDB saw the passing of the Law of SALES as a sufficient substitute for the Economic Democratization Law, although it contained no measure for downsizing the public sector or a regulatory framework for the services to be transferred to the private sector (IDB 1995). In general, the IDB did show a more lenient attitude, and put the desire to disburse loans before the desire to reform the Costa Rican economy. One reason for the different attitude by the IDB was that it had a large portfolio that had been held up, partly due to the governmental halt on spending by the autonomous institutions. In 1996, IDB had a loan portfolio of US$752 million that had not been disbursed. Of this, ICE accounted for US$389 million that was the remaining sum of the total US$576 million of approved loans for the electricity sector. [44]

The IFIs also recognized that to encourage telecommunication reform through pressure was a futile strategy. Thus the strategy was increasingly to provide 'technical cooperation' to enable the government itself to undertake reform. In the new IDB country assistance strategy it was argued that:

> Some areas in which the Bank should draw from its experience in other countries are concession arrangement for works contracting, sales of government assets, reconfiguration of strategic agencies like the ICE, restructuring of the State banking system, strengthening of prudential regulation, new regulatory frameworks for the financial system, securities markets, and insurance industry, and protection for private investment (IDB 1997).

By 1996, four new operations were under development, aimed at increasing private sector participation in investment and infrastructure sectors: three MIF technical cooperation projects and a loan (IDB 1997). But what was increasingly clear was that none of the IFIs would insist on privatization of ICE, and especially not include it as a loan conditionality.

World Bank and IDB representatives expressed three reasons for this in interviews. Firstly, putting privatization of ICE into the conditionalities was seen as a sure way to delay the approval of the project on the Costa Rican side or (if put as a conditionality for a later tranche) delaying the loan disbursement process. No IFI official with even the slightest concern for his or her career in the bank would want to lead a project that almost for certain would be delayed far beyond its planned timeframe.

Secondly, there was already a conditionality 'overload', particularly in SAP III, and adding more would further decrease the possibilities of getting it passed. As an example, the list of conditionalities for the disbursement of the first tranche of the sector investment loan by the IDB included 30 different points related to a wide variety of state institutions. In turn the disbursement of the first tranche of the public sector adjustment loan depended on satisfactory performance on a series of these points, in addition to eight further conditionalities.[45] The extremely complex program was characterized by one high-level IDB official as a 'conditionality hodgepodge' and she argued that part of the reason for the complex program was the relationship between the IDB and the World Bank:

> From a technical point of view, the conditions were very flawed. It was among the first sector adjustment loans we prepared, and we did not have much experience in it. A second problem was that we were a junior partner to the World Bank. There was competition between the two banks about who could put more conditionalities in there. On top of it, the government threw things in there that they wanted to do but they didn't have sufficient domestic support to do. The result was a hodgepodge of conditionalities. That made it extremely difficult for the government to comply with them. Each tranche had something like 30 conditionalities attached to them.[46]

The conclusion was that there was no room for further conditionalities. Finally, IFI officials showed increasing respect for the difference between Costa Rica and other countries regarding state-owned companies. Thus there was a process of 'mutual learning'. According to one mid-level World Bank official:

> We were talking to them about privatization [of ICE], and also about setting up an agency for independent control. But, you see, in Costa Rica, everything is different. They don't see the state as an evil thing that should be curtailed. So, our advice was to set up a regulatory institution. Although it is state-owned, it needs the regulation.[47]

In sum, it is hard to sustain an argument that the IFIs were behind the attempts to privatize ICE. The changing strategies of the IFIs contributed to increasing difficulties in obtaining funding for projects conducted by ICE. But the specific content of the reform attempts were largely a reflection of the ICE management's ideas and their struggles to regain autonomy from the political elites.

However parallel to the IFIs working with the governments, USAID attempted to work towards the private sector, as they did in Guatemala. That had a certain impact on the strategies of the following government that saw the main clash over telecommunication reform.

The Birth and Burial of 'Combo-ICE'

Figueres's successor, Miguel Angel Rodríguez, was also a businessman. However he had a more academic background, and he was viewed as a convinced neo-liberal, holding a PhD in economics from the University of California at Berkeley. He had also been the Minister of Planning (1968–69), the Minister of the Presidency (1970) and an economic advisor to president Calderón. Although his wealth and success as a businessman was often exaggerated, he was viewed as a typical representative of the private sector (Furlong 2000).

In the election campaign the candidate of the incumbent party, José Miguel Corrales (PLN), positioned himself as a fierce anti-privatization candidate, and committed to strengthening ICE. Rodríguez, on the other hand, was careful not to mention privatization of ICE, but he never opposed it, and most commentators agreed that his unspoken goal was to privatize.

Thus while the political project of the Figueres government was diffuse and its plans to reform ICE likewise, the Rodríguez government held a clearer neo-liberal profile without announcing publicly what the plan for ICE was. Rodríguez was also well aware that he needed support from more than the private sector if he were to avoid the same kind of stalemate that had occurred under Figueres. This was the background for the launching of the national consensus process (*proceso nacional de concertación*)[48] argued to be 'a gesture similar to that of "Pepe" Figueres when he abolished the military in 1948' (Presidencia de la República de Costa Rica 1998). Among the topics selected for discussion in this process was telecommunication reform, and in September 1998 the government sent a proposal for a new telecommunication law and a law to strengthen ICE to a special commission established within the framework of the consensus process. The commission included representatives from various sectors of the society: the unions, political parties, the private sector and NGOs. The intention was that the law proposal should first be discussed in the commission, then in a plenary session of the national consensus forum, and finally a proposal should be sent back to the government. However by 3 October, the deadline for submitting the reports from the commissions to the plenary, telecommunications was one of three topics on which no consensus was achieved.[49] In November the report from the telecommunication commission was sent to the government. However it was not a consensus document, as no agreement had been reached about whether to allow for competition in the telecommunication sector or not (*La Nación* various issues September–November 1998).

The new proposal for reforming ICE was sent to the Legislative Assembly on 17 January 1999. After having received the proposal from the commission in the consensus process, the government sent a revised version to the commission of governance in the Legislative Assembly (led by PUSC-deputy Vanessa Castro), which was already discussing changes to the electricity law. The governance commission reached an agreement about three law proposals that had several similarities with the Dobles project. Firstly, the General Law of the Telecommunication Sector would ensure a gradual opening up of the sector to competition towards the year 2002, and a new autonomous regulatory institution for the telecommunication sector, IRETEL, would be set up.[50] Secondly, the law of institutional strengthening of ICE would give it full administrative, technical and financial freedom and subject it to the regime of private companies.[51] The third element was a constitutional reform required for transforming ICE from an autonomous institution, to a public enterprise operating under a regime of private law.

There were differences between the PUSC and the PLN in the Legislative Assembly – they disagreed about the schedule for opening up the sector and whether it was necessary for an evaluation of the results after each step in the process; whether the constitutional changes should affect only ICE or also other autonomous institutions currently operating in monopoly; and about the destiny of ICE's profits.[52] The establishment of IRETEL also caused disagreement, but here it was the head of the Regulatory Authority for the Public Services (ARESEP), created in 1996 to replace SNE, Lionel Fonseca, that was the main opponent.

SNE, which dated back to 1928, had relatively limited powers. It could only regulate four public services: telecommunications, energy (only distribution), water and gasoline, and it was institutionally dependent on the Executive Power. In contrast, ARESEP regulated a wider set of services, it gave users the right to file complaints against for example tariff increases through public 'audiences', and it was autonomous from the Executive Power. In relation to ICE, ARESEP's powers were significantly extended compared to SNE. ARESEP was to set prices and tariffs and monitor the quality, quantity and regularity of the services. When the new reform proposal was brought to the Legislative Assembly, ARESEP had only functioned for just over two years and its director Lionel Fonseca had no desire to be replaced by a new institution.

Due to the conflicts, the process seemed to be stalled by mid-1999. In a move to avoid a lengthy process of discussion and approval of three different law proposals in the plenary, the President of the Assembly Carlos Vargas Pagan (PUSC) decided to merge the three projects into one, named the Law Project to Improve the Public Services of Electricity and Telecommunications and the State Participation, soon nicknamed 'Combo-

ICE' or 'Combo energetico'. A special commission was appointed to discuss Combo, and it reached an agreement on 21 December 1999.

Combo proposed to keep ICE as an autonomous institution, but that it should establish two subsidiaries, ICElec and ICEtel, with the status of stockholding companies. As in the Dobles project, ICE would further consist of RACSA, CRICSA and CNFL. ICE was to be given the right to establish new companies with up to 49 per cent participation of private capital for carrying out specific projects, and it was given full financial autonomy and could invest 100 per cent of its profits, but it was subject to pay regular income tax. ICE was also obliged to write off the 80 000 million colones (US$ 242 million) debt that the government had with the company.

A new section about the regulatory agency, this time named the Regulatory Authority for Telecommunications (ARETEL), was included in the new Combo. The new regulatory entity was given the task of ensuring the provision of universal access. ARETEL would have the power to regulate prices on fixed and international telephony, and on the services where competition had not entered into force. The new law introduced obligatory interconnection between parties and adopted the term 'essential resources' from the Guatemalan law. In the same vein as in the Guatemalan law, the Costa Rican one gave the different parties the right to freely negotiate interconnection, but with the possibility of calling upon ARETEL to intervene if no agreement was found. Competition was to be introduced in four steps, and every step in the market opening should be made dependent on an evaluation of the consequences of prior steps in the process.

Discussions continued in the Plenary Session of the Legislative Assembly during the first months of 2000. In order to be passed as a law, Combo had to be approved in two consecutive debates in the Legislative Assembly. On March 22 the Legislative Assembly approved Combo with some minor changes in the first debate.

This decision immediately provoked a massive public protest. On 14 March, the ICE unions had already started to protest against the possible acceptance of Combo, and they soon got broad public support. By 18 March they were accompanied by students of the University of Costa Rica. The demonstrations gained force and the final debates about the proposals occurred in a Legislative Assembly surrounded by demonstrators and security forces. After the approval of Combo, the students and ICE unions were joined by several other groups and the whole country was soon paralyzed by blockades of streets, bridges and ports, and strikes in various public institutions. On 24 March, the police reported 40 different demonstrations around the country, 52 students and teachers were arrested and an unknown number of demonstrators were hurt in the clashes with police and security forces. The day after, thousands of people marched on the streets of San José to protest against Combo. The demonstrations continued over the following days and one person died from the injuries he sustained in an attempt to defend a blockade. Two students occupied the ICE headquarters where they went on a hunger strike. Personnel at the main hospitals also joined the demonstrations and suspended all services except for emergency cover. By early April, the workers threatened a general strike. The complete chaos that the country found itself in, forced the government to back down and agree to a proposal by the social sectors to suspend Combo for 150 days and set down a new mixed commission (Comisión Especial Mixta) to reach a consensus on the future of ICE and the telecommunication and electricity sectors. It had representatives from the political parties, private sector chambers, the government and various social organizations.[53] On 19 April, the SALA IV issued a resolution that found various aspects of the Combo process unconstitutional, and by this, Combo was essentially dead.

In short, the ICE unions, supported by students and a large part of the general public, managed to reject a proposal for private sector participation in telecommunications and electricity that most of the political establishment, the private sector and the international institutions were for. As will be discussed in the following, there were three main reasons for this. Firstly, ICE's general strength; its workers were highly able technicians, and the unions had in addition a clear understanding of political strategy. Secondly, the private sector in Costa Rica was much weaker in terms of both economic clout and organization than its Guatemalan counterpart. However a third reason probably contributed equally significantly to tilting the balance against the reforms, namely the 'soft power' strategies of the US which were aimed at strengthening the Costa Rican private sector, but which provoked quite different reactions in Costa Rica than in its neighboring countries.

The Private Sector and 'Soft Power' Strategies of the US

The private sector in Costa Rica has never been able to match its Guatemalan counterpart in terms of economic strength and organization. It also played a much less important role in the development of privatization proposals. Indeed whereas the private sector in Guatemala pushed for privatization of Guatel from the early 1980s, UCCAEP and the Chamber of Commerce hardly knew about the 1988 privatization proposal in Costa Rica.[54] The UCCAEP was consulted about the Dobles project, but was highly critical of it. It argued that it left ICE in a too strong position, as a hybrid structure with no less monopoly powers than it had had before.[55]

UCCAEP's lack of direct involvement in the elaboration of proposals to reform ICE does not reflect the fact that there were no private actors in Costa

Rica which were interested in participating in the telecommunication sector, or that the private sector was pleased with the manner in which ICE operated. However the private sector was still not a strong coherent actor, and had not elaborated a firm platform that could enable it to develop policy proposals.

There also emerged a more ideologically based group aligned with businesses which made some attempts at influencing at the level of ideas, similar to CEES in Guatemala. The National Association for Economic Growth (ANFE) was formed the same year as CEES (1958) and it had many features in common with it. It was founded to promote liberal economic ideas, such as free trade, free markets, private enterprise and a reduced role for the government (Wilson 1998, p. 7). ANFE also had close relations to the Mont Pellerin Society, and with Manuel Ayau and CEES in Guatemala.

The strategies of ANFE were similar to those of CEES. From its start until the early 1990s, ANFE members divulged their ideas through a weekly column in the largest daily newspaper, *La Nación*, attempting to alter the general public's idea of the state. In 1975, ANFE associates founded a private university, Universidad de Centroamérica. Moreover ANFE associates were among the founders of the research institution Academia de Centroamérica in 1969. ANFE also refrained from establishing a political party, but was generally associated with PUSC.[56]

However ANFE gave the liberal ideas a less radical interpretation than its sister organization in Guatemala. Therefore ANFE also had fewer conflicts with the international financial institutions, but was also less eager to privatize ICE. Moreover, ANFE had much less influence on policy making.[57]

The weakness of the private sector in Costa Rica, in terms of both organization and ability to formulate policy, was well recognized by USAID from the 1980s. When the relationship between Costa Rica and the IFIs became increasingly troubled in the 1980s, it was funding from USAID that tided Costa Rica over (see Table 4.2). By the mid-1980s, Costa Rica became the second-largest recipient of aid from the US government in Central America, receiving 27 per cent of the total aid, only exceeded by El Salvador (Salom Echeverría 1992).

A main aim of USAID was to promote private sector development. Between 1982 and 1985, three programs were initiated for this purpose. Among the activities under these programs was the establishment of an export promotion center, the Costa Rica Coalition for Development Initiatives (CINDE), and a program to liquidate CODESA (Sojo 1992).

USAID attempted to promote private sector development in Costa Rica through two strategies: Firstly, it pushed for privatization of the CODESA enterprises, and secondly, it set up parallel institutions to the governmental ones which in turn would take over their functions. This is what later gave rise to the expression the 'parallel state' launched by Chile's ex-ambassador to Costa Rica and Oscar Arias's close advisor, John Biehl.

Viewed in hindsight, the latter part of the strategy was the most successful. Most of CODESA's assets were in the end sold to private investors with the assistance of USAID. However CODESA was already a 'ripe fruit'. Moreover USAID did not manage to privatize its largest holdings (most notably the national liquor factory, FANAL, and the oil company, RECOPE.[58]

The most important impact of the USAID strategy was to strengthen the private sector as a political actor. In the early 1980s, a group of prominent Costa Rican industrialists began to lobby the United States for some form of direct aid to promote a change in the development model towards exports. These groups established what Mary Clark has named a 'transnational alliance' between USAID officials, Costa Rican private sector leaders and state technocrats, which quickly assumed leadership in defining an export-led growth plan at the beginning of the Monge administration (Clark 1997). The centerpiece of this alliance was CINDE, which starting in January 1983, evolved into a center for development and elaboration of political proposals for strengthening of the private sector, supported by series of well-known businessmen and politicians. According to Clark: 'with the exception of the exchange rate modifications, all other important changes related to nontraditional exports originated with CINDE' (Clark 1997, p. 86).

The only direct impact of CINDE's work on the telecommunication sector in the early period was the attraction of Millicom, for which CINDE took much of the credit.[59] However the establishment and strengthening of CINDE would later make a significant impact on the debate of telecommunication reform.

When the Dobles project was discussed in the Legislative Assembly in Costa Rica, the privatization process was already well under way in El Salvador, and CIEN worked with Pablo Spiller to establish a similar framework for Guatemala as for El Salvador. CINDE's idea was to try and bring in experiences from the neighboring countries to establish a liberal telecommunication framework also in Costa Rica. In April 1997, CINDE arranged a seminar in cooperation with the Secretariat for Economic Integration in Central America (SIECA), funded by USAID in order to put focus on the benefits of an open telecommunication market. Here among others Juan José Daboub, the President of Antel in El Salvador, Alfredo Mena Lagos, and Pablo Spiller were invited to share their experiences and emphasize the urgency of a reform of the sector (*La Nación* 6 April 1997). However Spiller's ideas gained little support in Costa Rica. It was only representatives of CINDE who paid much attention to them.

As this was at the end of Figueres's presidency, CINDE started to contact the teams of the potential presidential candidates, Miguel Angel Rodríguez

(PUSC) and José Miguel Corrales (PLN) in order to ensure that telecommunication reform would be on the agenda of the government entering power in 1998.[60]

With resources from, among others, SIECA, which now primarily had funds from the USAID program Pro-Alca intended to prepare Latin American countries for the proposed Free Trade Area of the Americas (FTAA; ALCA in Spanish), CINDE had initiated research on business satisfaction with communications in Costa Rica, and concluded that it was an urgent area for action. CINDE also brought in Alvin Toffler to write a report on the importance of telecommunications for the development of Costa Rica (Toffler, n.d.).

CINDE's strategy was primarily to convince the Costa Rican population as well as the government of the virtues of opening up the sector to competition. However the efforts had unforeseen consequences.

When the Rodríguez government took power, CINDE's Ricardo Monge was appointed to lead the work of preparing a telecommunication law, and the plan that the government presented to the consensus process on 25 September 1998 was basically the result of the work of CINDE.

The main effect of the new proposal was to alienate the ICE unions. The unions reacted strongly against the content of the proposal and against a report prepared by CINDE as background material. In order to improve the relationship with the unions, the government appointed a respected telecommunication engineer with 15 years of experience in ICE as its representative in the telecommunication commission of the national consensus process. He managed to reach a partial agreement with the unions about a gradual opening of the sector, but failed in crafting a complete consensus and some reservations were included in the final report.[61]

However the fragile peace between the government and the unions broke down completely when the government presented its proposal for a new general law of telecommunications to the Legislative Assembly in January 1999. Far from reflecting the agreements from the consensus process, the project was a mix between these and the CINDE proposal. It included a gradual opening of the sector and the establishment of a new regulatory agency as agreed to in the consensus process, but it also had strong elements of the Guatemalan and Salvadoran laws, that is with respect to settlement of interconnection prices and management of the radio spectrum. Indeed, when the governmental team, headed by Monge, presented the project to the international business community in Miami in February 1999, it argued that the law had essentially two sources of inspiration: the national consensus process and 'new regulatory framework and best international practices in opening up the telecommunications market'.[62]

The hybrid nature of the law proposal made the project close to unintelligible for many telecommunication experts. As argued by one governmental advisor:

> The government accepted the agreements from the consensus process, but at this moment, it had already a telecommunication project written by CINDE. CINDE pressured the government and said: look, here is the project. Thus they start this exercise of transferring the agreements of the national consensus process into the CINDE project. The result was a hybrid that nobody understood. [The government] copied the model from Guatemala and El Salvador, but it had not understood the context. Because in Guatemala and El Salvador, they not only privatized but also introduced full competition. What resulted was a law project that in the end had no coherence.[63]

In a similar vein, a high-level legal advisor to the ICE management argued:

> At this moment, the following happened: CINDE unilaterally edited a law project, without taking us into account. They brought in this Uruguayan consultant Pablo Spiller. The experiences from Guatemala and El Salvador were a hallucination for all of Central America. Spiller came, participated in conferences, and explained the model. But here he did not have much of an audience. Here they hated Spiller. But CINDE copied the law of El Salvador and Guatemala. Cut and paste.[64]

Soon after the proposal had been presented to the Legislative Assembly, the unions started to complain that the governmental proposal included only superficial elements from the consensus agreements. According to a high-level governmental advisor:

> The unions are not stupid, not at all. When they saw this project, they said this is not what we agreed on. The government says: yes, it has a gradual opening of the sector; this is what we agreed on. But it was not the same, not exactly the same. From this moment, if we speak of a conjuncture, it is the point when the unions see that their political opportunity has come.[65]

This political opportunity, created in part by the adverse reactions to the USAID strategies, was eagerly seized by the unions, as will be discussed below. The legacy of CINDE's actions was that they constributed to the 'hybridization' of the project, which in the eyes of many telecommunication experts reduced its quality. However most importantly, CINDE's actions decreased the legitimacy of the proposal by making it look as if it was imposed from outside. Moreover it had an adverse impact on the climate for cooperation with the unions, who were already well prepared to fight against any further privatization attempt.

The Backlash: a Fruit of the Unions' Strategies

The unions of ICE had been working against privatization and liberalization since the Ecotel proposal in 1988 and the concession given to Millicom soon after. In comparison to the unions in the neighboring countries, the ICE workers had both superior technical skills and a longer experience in struggling against privatization. In 1987, the Organized Labor Front (FOL) was established to unify all the unions in ICE to fight privatization. It was first established as an ad hoc group, but later became an organization with its own judicial status.

The project that the unions put together was based on different sets of ideas and impulses, some more ideological than others. At the core of the project was a struggle for greater institutional autonomy for ICE in order to allow it to regain its previous position. Securing autonomy of ICE from the government was viewed as necessary in order for it also to gain autonomy from private sector elites, as these increasingly dominated the governments. ICE's autonomy in turn was viewed as necessary both in order to secure an equitable development in Costa Rica, and as a means to secure the unions' own position. There was also a more ideological element in the opposition, based on a general rejection of neo-liberal globalization. Finally, there was a group that looked at the issues from a more technical point of view, and that could accept a very limited market opening. However it was the most ideologically based opposition that dominated the choice of strategy.

One may point to three main parts of the strategy of the unions: (1) to use their technical knowledge to develop alternative proposals to the privatization proposals; (2) to embed the debate about ICE in a 'national development discourse'; and (3) to forge broad alliances in civil society.

The unions worked according to a principle that there should always be an alternative to the governmental strategy available.[66] The union leaders traveled to Europe and other Latin American countries with funds from, among others, the Friedrich Egbert Foundation, and they continuously improved their capacity to develop proposals. The high degree of continuation in the leadership of the unions also contributed to the high level of skills. Four union leaders led the opposition throughout the 15 years of struggle against privatization,[67] and few if any knew the details of the telecommunication and electricity sectors and the nature of the proposals as well as them. Thus the union leaders gained respect for their technical knowledge and they were often brought in as experts to the Legislative Assembly.

The ICE unions consistently emphasized ICE's apolitical and developmental nature. They argued that the main intention of their proposals was to maintain ICE as a well-respected social institution and a symbol of the Costa Rican developmental state. ICE's clients should not be customers, but citizens with a basic right to electricity and telecommunication services.

Related to this was the effort to depoliticize the institution and increase its autonomy, which had also been an important feature of previous proposals. FOL's argument against the Dobles project was primarily that it would decrease the autonomy of the institution: 'One increases the political interference of the sitting Executive Power in the management of ICE, decreasing ICE's autonomy of governance and administration which is indispensable for achieving its mandated goals. It contradicts the principal objective of giving back the autonomy of ICE in order to flexibilize its management and strengthen it' (FOL 1996, p. 4).

The unions moreover played into the anti neo-liberal sentiments by consistently labeling the government's proposal 'privatization'. Although no proposal after Ecotel included outright sale of ICE, the unions insisted that opening up for private participation in the subsidiaries of ICE or the possibility to enter into strategic alliances with private companies would in effect lead to privatization. Furthermore liberalization would lead to a privatization of the sector in the sense that it would be operated according to business principles and not according to a public service logic.

While technical arguments were efficient in order to mobilize workers and could be used in arguments with parts of the private sector, a developmental and partly nationalist discourse was more efficient for mobilizing the general population. A cornerstone of this strategy was the establishment of the Committee for the Defense of Constitutionality (CDC) (later Council for the Defense of Institutionality – CDI) in April 1996, which became a main producer of a nationalist ICE discourse. It was soon to be called 'the political arm of the unions' and it could count on the participation of various prominent people, among them ex-president Rodrigo Carazo Odio, and his son Ombudsman Rodrigo Carazo Zeledón. Carazo Odio argued that behind all the 'technical opinions and foundations, the complex plot of companies, subsidiaries, managements, commissions, methods of procurement, financing and taxes or the organizations involved in the projects, there is a unifying ideology... the exchange of a national development institution for a company run by profit concerns to serve the rich and powerful' (CDI 1996, p. 2).

The unions had already established close links with the old Communist Party, which in the early 1990s re-emerged with a less orthodox ideology under the name of the Democratic Force (FD). Several of the FD leaders had a background in ICE, and anti-privatization became one of its main issues. In the consensus process, FOL had officially only two representatives. However another union leader, Fabio Chavez, was elected as the representative for FD and yet another, Ricardo Segura, for CDI. Moreover the representative for women's organizations was also a member of FOL. Thus through alliances, the unions managed to fill a majority of the positions in the telecommunication commission of the consensus process.

The nationalist–developmentalist and anti neo-liberal rhetoric was strengthened significantly as wider groups of the civil society were mobilized. It became customary to sing the hymn to ICE along with the national hymn at meetings, and highly nationalist slogans were developed to be used in the demonstrations. The nationalist–developmentalist discourse secured the unions extensive support among the Costa Ricans that were increasingly tired of repeated attempts to market-orient state institutions. Opinion polls showed clearly a majority against general privatization and against Combo-ICE (see Figure 4.2).

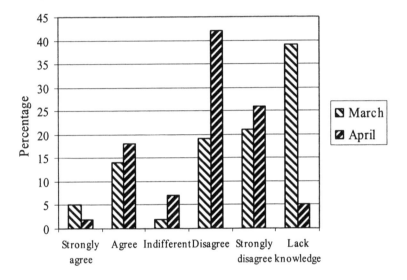

Source: Author's elaboration based on data from Institute of Social Population Studies
(IDESPO).

Figure 4.2 Opinion about Combo-ICE March–April 2000

When the conflict sharpened, FOL, which by this point had changed its name to FIT (Internal Workers Front), also created alliances with a series of other organizations: environmental organizations, the church, organizations of indigenous peoples, women's organizations and students' organizations. It was particularly the students' organizations that came to play a main role in the protests against Combo. An anti neo-liberalism movement had been created particularly at the University of Costa Rica, and the social science department became a center for organization of many of the activities in the anti-Combo campaign. The small secretariat established here included one person normally working for the National Association of Telecommunication Technicians (ANTECC), but who was now working full time with the students on an ANTECC salary.

The creation of areas of support in civil society was a clear and conscious strategy from FOL/FIT.[68] It involved the creation of alliances with several different sectors, a process that was strengthened at the outset of the consensus process.

> The ideological fight started 15 years ago, but the action started in December last year. We accepted a work plan internally in the institutions, between the workers of ICE and other social actors. We understood that we would never win this war by ourselves. We had to win it with the people.[69]

Although the anti neo-liberal ideology was clear in the rhetoric, it is also clear that the motivation of the unions was not only to restore the Costa Rican welfare state. An additional purpose was clearly to ensure their own job security.

Furthermore the unions had their own businesses to take care of. Many of the union leaders ran their own companies that provided services to ICE. In 1996, 13 of the aforementioned SALES had been established to operate specific services, such as number information and maintenance, providing extra income for the ICE workers (*La Nación* 21 February 1996). In a more open telecommunication market, the services that SALES provided would be open for competition, and therefore their position would be threatened.

Thus it was a mix between general political and economic motives and more particular economic motives that formed the basis of the project of the unions. By creating alliances with various organizations in the civil society, the unions strengthened their positions. They also created their own 'constituency' changing the bargaining game with representatives of the private sector and the government, as they could point to the commitment they had to the other social groups in order to reject proposals for moderate opening.

At the end of the day it was the actors that had grown out of the state led development project, namely the ICE management and its unions, that were the main actors behind the reforms. However they pursued different goals and the institution that resulted from the US's political project of the 1980s, namely CINDE, also influenced the government's ideas and strategies. CINDE's effect on the situation was primarily to spur opposition from the unions and make their nationalist discourse more credible.

Conclusion

The Costa Rican state that developed in the late nineteenth century differed significantly from the Guatemalan one, and the project within which the establishment of ICE formed a part was equally different. ICE formed an important part of the post-war developmental project of the political elites emerging around the social democratic party, PLN. In this context private sector elites were formed, and they developed in a 'parasitic' relation to the state. Thus in the case of Costa Rica, we can not speak of state capture; there was rather a symbiosis between private sector and political elites.

Over the course of the post-war period, ICE developed as a more and more autonomous institution, and it became an arena for the formation of a new political elite. This left the executive with little control over it, and much of the politics of the telecommunication reform in Costs Rica must be understood against the background of the power struggle between the executive and ICE.

However over the course of the 1980s and 1990s, the relationship between the Costa Rican political institutions and the private sector changed, and the private sector was in the process of establishing itself as an independent political force, supported by the IFIs, but primarily the USAID. In the telecommunication reform process it emerged as a significant political actor with the ability to provide policy proposals.

In spite of its influence on private sector organizations, one cannot escape the conclusion that the impact of the IFIs on the telecommunication reform process was marginal. This contrasts sharply with the role given to the IFIs in the discourse of the opponents of market-oriented telecommunication reform in Costa Rica, namely the ICE unions and their supporters within the civil society. It also contrasts sharply with the role of the IFIs in the case of Honduras.

NOTES

1. This had been formed by Figueres and José Arévalo in Guatemala the year before. It expressed strong commitments to economic nationalism and planned to topple several dictators with close ties to the US in the region. Nevertheless due to its opposition to the Communist alliance, neither the US nor Somoza of Nicaragua intervened in spite of their opposition to the Caribbean Legion (Cerdas Cruz 1992).
2. Article 188 states: 'The autonomous institutions of the State enjoy independence of governance and administration, and their directors are responsible for their management'.
3. This included Haya de la Torre and his nationalist, anti-imperialist, Aprismo movement, Roosevelt's New Deal political ideas, Edward Bernstein, John Maynard Keynes and Ludwig von Mises.
4. Member/supporter of the PLN.

5. Ley Constitutiva y Otras disposiciones Relativas al Instituto Costarricense de Electricidad, Julio de 1987.
6. ICE never had a monopoly on the production and distribution of electricity.
7. Interviews with current and former ICE staff.
8. Honduras received in the same period US$153.8 million. Guatemala received US$238 million, of which US$54.7 million was grants donated by the USAID in the period 1955-58. In 1964, Costa Rica had a GDP;Capital ratio of US$384, Guatemala US$300 and Honduras US$202.
9. Loan No. 346-CR, effective 10 October, 1963, for electricity and telecommunication development, Loan No. 632-CR, effective 20 October, 1966, including US$6.5 million for telecommunication development, Loan No. 801-CR, effective 2 June, 1967, including US$17.5 million for telecommunications development.
10. Interview, former ICE manager, 24 November 2000.
11. Interview, Rodolfo Cerdas Cruz, 28 September 2000.
12. Before 1977–78, 69 per cent of the members of the board of the Chamber of Industry belonged to the PLN, but by 1978, the support had dropped to 44 per cent
13. It consists of the Finance Minister, who serves as President, the Minster of Planning and National Economy and the President of the Central Bank (Jiménez C 1992).
14. Few reliable numbers exist for the early period, but by 2000, ICE accounted for 18.6 per cent of the total external debt.
15. Loan No. 1532-CR, effective 9 March, 1979, of US$10.6 million to finance the fifth and final part of ICE's development project.
16. World Bank (1986b), 3.
17. World Bank (1986b), p. 17.
18. Law No. 7134/89.
19. Board of Directors of ICE, 25 April 1988.
20. In the energy sector, the proposal was to permit private participation in small generation projects.
21. ICE, Reunión de Asuntos de Telecomunicaciones, July 1987, No. 17-87.
22. Directive Council of ICE, No. 1019, 1987.
23. Directive Council of ICE, No. 1019, 1987.
24. Interview, Antonio Cañas, 23 November 2000.
25. Interview, Antonio Cañas, 23 November 2000.
26. Acta. No 12, Comision Especial (Exp. 11.444) Assamblea Legislativa.
27. IFC started to fund telecommunication projects in Central America towards the end of the 1980s, and Millicom was the favored recipient. In 1995, it issued a $20 million loan to Telemóvil SA in El Salvador, owned 55 per cent by Millicom and 15 per cent by IFC.
28. Letter to Hernán Fournier from Carlos Vargas Pagán, Minister of Planning and Political Economy, 18 October 1991, DM-2034-91).
29. This constituted approximately 10 per cent of the total bandwidth available for exploitation for mobile telephony.
30. Exactly how this transfer happened and the legality of it was also questioned during the hearing in the Legislative Assembly. See Acta No. 14, Expediente No. 11.444.
31. The full name was: 'Special commission to investigate the area of telecommunications of ICE, including RACSA, in relation to communications via satellite, facsimile, analogue telephony, cellular, etc., as well as actuation of the hierarchies of the two institutions.'
32. *La Nación* 11 May 1995, *La Nación* 22 May 1995.
33. Costa Rica's agreement signified a reduction of the external debt from US$4500 million to US$3348 million and of annual payments from US$145 million to US$35 million. However in reality Costa Rica had only paid US$ 4–5 million annually after the debt moratorium.
34. World Bank (1992c).
35. Interview, Thelmo Vargas, 24 November 2000.
36. Eduardo Lizano, in Acta No. 95, Comisión de Asuntos Haciendarios, 2 March 1994.
37. 'The Hickenlooper amendment' (US Code 22, Foreign Relations and Intercourse, Ch. 32, Subsection III, Part 1, Section 2370) says: '... The President shall suspend assistance to the

government of any country to which assistance is provided under this chapter or any other Act when the government of such country or any government agency or subdivision within such country on or after January 1, 1962 – (A) has nationalized or expropriated or seized ownership or control of property owned by any United States citizen or by any corporation, partnership, or association not less than 50 per cent beneficially owned by United States citizens, or (B) has taken steps to repudiate or nullify existing contracts or agreements with any United States citizen or any corporation, partnership, or association not less than 50 per cent beneficially owned by United States citizens.'

38. Interview, Roberto Dobles, 26 September 2000.
39. Among these are Law N° 6955 para el Equilibrio Financiero del Sector Público and its reforms, Law No. 4646 and 5507 about Juntas Directivas and Presidencias Ejecutivas, Law No. 6821 of the Creation of the Budgetary Authority and its reforms, Law Law No. 7010 that creates the Department of Public Credit and in general all the regulations that establish limits of expenses for state institutions.
40. The Governmental Council (Consejo de Gobierno) is a body consisting of the President of the Republic and the ministers. It has five specific tasks, of which one is to appoint directors of the Autonomous Institutions (Art. 147, The Political Constitution of the Republic of Costa Rica).
41. The expression 'mixed commission' is used about commissions where 'external advisors' can participate. This may mean different experts, but also for example interest group representatives.
42. These were former president of the Central Bank, Eduardo Lizano, the economist of the Central American Academy and with close links to PUSC, Ronulfo Jiménez, ex-minister of Finance, Federico Vargas, the banker Oscar Rodgriguez and lawyer Marco Vinicio Tristán
43. The main issues that the World Bank found unacceptable were the unstable macroeconomic conditions and that the Economic Democratization Law had not been voted on in the Legislative Assembly. Furthermore the Government had not been able to provide precise data on the number of positions that had been eliminated from the public sector, and the numbers it provided showed that there was substantial deviation from the agreed 25 000.
44. Later the Figueres government canceled one of the remaining three IDB credit lines under SAP III in order to reorder its loan portfolio.
45. Contrato de Prestamo entre la República de Costa Rica y el Banco Interamericano de Desarollo (Programa Sectorial de Inversiones), 27 de marzo de 1993, Préstamo No. 742/OC-CR, Resolución No. DE-41/94, and Contrato de Prestamo entre la República de Costa Rica y el Banco Interamericano de Desarrollo (Programa de Ajuste del Sector Público), 13 de enero de 1993, Préstamo No. 739/OC-CR, Resolucón No. DE-293/93.
46. Interview, high-level IDB official, 13 February 1998.
47. Interview, mid-level World Bank official, 21 September 1999.
48. 'Concertación' may be translated as 'harmonization', 'reconciliation' or 'consensus'.
49. The others were reforms of the national insurance institute and unemployment compensation. *La Nación* 3 October, 1998.
50. Proyecto Ley general de Telecommunicaciónes, Exp. No. 12.694.
51. Proyecto de Ley de Fortalecimiento y Transformación del ICE, Comisión Especial ICE, Ex. No. 12753.
52. PUSC wanted a set schedule as had been included in the CINDE proposal, whereas PLN demanded evaluations of the consequences of the opening in each step. PLN wanted the constitutional changes only to affect ICE. Furthermore PUSC wanted parts of the profits to be transferred to the state Treasury, while PLN wanted them to be reinvested in ICE.
53. The composition was as follows: Eliseo Vargas, Walter Céspedes, Vanessa Castro and Carlos Vargas (PUSC), Guido Alberto Monge, Rafael Arias and Alex Sibaja/Guillermo Constenla (PLN), Eugenio Pignataro (UCCAEP), Ronulfo Jiménez (the government), María Pilar Ureña and William Vargas (the Catholic church), Rolando Portilla (environmental NGOs), Eva Carazo (the student movement) and Ricardo Segura, Fabio Chavez and Jorge Arguedas (FIT).

54. Interviews, UCCAEP representatives, 20 November 2000 and 29 November 2000. This contrasts with the union representatives who recalled the process very well.
55. Letter from Samuel Yankelewitz, President of UCCAEP to Ottón Sollís, with analysis of the LMFICE, 10 February 1997.
56. More recently PLN members also have entered. In 1995, a young ANFE associate, Otto Guevara, established the Libertarian Party.
57. The general influence of ANFE is debated. Arias Sánchez argues that it was one of the most influential groups in the country (Arias Sánchez 1971, p. 79). Wilson (1998, p. 71) argues that this view is significantly overstated.
58. As argued by former Vice-President of CODESA, and Vice-General Auditor, Jorge Corrales: 'That was how CODESA was; unmanageable and corrupt. The change came during the Monge period with the help from the AID. But it was easy. CODESA did not represent anything for anybody. Nobody cried for CODESA. But when we started to talk about the liquor factory it was different', interview, 4 October 2000.
59. Interview, Fernando Naranjo, Minister of Foreign Affairs in the Arias administration, 6 October 2000.
60. Interview, high-level governmental advisor, 13 September 2000.
61. Informe final de la Comisión para la Concertación Nacional, 1998, Presidencia de la República de Costa Rica.
62. Seminar on Costa Rica's new telecommunications legal framework, February 17, 1999, Hotel intercontinental Miami.
63. Interview, high-level governmental advisor, 13 September 2000.
64. Interview, ICE-advisor, 25 September 2000.
65. Interview, ICE-advisor, 13 September 2000.
66. Interview, union leader, 8 September 2000.
67. Jorge Arguedas and Dennis Cabezas of ANTECC, Fabio Chavez of Syndicate Association of ICE (ASDICE) and Ricardo Seguro of SIICE.
68. Interview, union leader, 10 October 2000.
69. Interview, union leader, 27 November 2000.

5. Honduras: Privatization in the Ritual Aid Dance

At first glance, the case of Honduras conforms closely with the popular thesis that privatization is imposed by external forces. Since the mid-1990s, the IFIs have pressured for reform of the Honduran telecommunication sector, including privatization (or capitalization) of the state-owned telecommunication company, Hondutel. Honduras had good reasons for following their advice as its debt to GDP ratio was among the highest in the Western Hemisphere, and significantly higher than those of the neighboring countries (see Table 1.1). Nevertheless, although privatization of Hondutel was on the agenda for many years, the actual privatization was not carried out. The privatization process was delayed several years, and when it finally was implemented in October 2000, the government turned down the only offer, which came from Telmex. The end result was a partial telecommunication reform with elements from the ideas of the World Bank's telecommunication experts, but affected by having been a part of the ritual aid dance for many years.

The main puzzle that emerges in the case of Honduras is why it failed to privatize in spite of such strong pressure from the IFIs. The argument I make here is that it was largely due to the IFIs' inability to link up with a domestic political actor that promoted the same kind of project. There were domestic groups that supported privatization, and the local private sector was more open about its intentions to participate in the privatization of Hondutel than it was in the case of Guatemala. However largely due to the involvement of the IFIs, there were fewer strategies available for them to purchase the company than had been the case in Guatemala.

In the first part of this chapter I trace the development of the Honduran state and discuss the political project in which telecommunications and infrastructure were embedded from the state consolidation process (1876–48) to the military governments of the 1970s and democratization in the late 1980s. In the second part, I discuss the process of reform from the first private mobile concession to the comprehensive new telecommunication legislation and attempts to privatize Hondutel.

TELECOMMUNICATIONS AND THE BASIS FOR STATE POWER

From Liberal Rule to the Banana Republic (1876–1948)

The period from 1876 to 1948 is often called the phase of state consolidation in Honduras (Posas and Del Cid 1983). The first liberal ruler, President Marco Aurelio Soto, was brought in from Guatemala, where he had worked for Barrios. In Honduras he introduced reforms to consolidate the state machinery and implemented economic policies designed to modernize the country based on the same liberal ideology as that of Barrios. Aurelio Soto also restructured the national postal services, and created a telegraph network to integrate different parts of the country.

However whereas Barrios in Guatemala promoted policies favoring the emergence of export agriculture (especially coffee and bananas), Soto's main focus was to attract foreign investment. Himself a miner, he created favorable conditions for the establishment of mining exports, through concessions to foreign companies.

Aurelio Soto had only partial success with achieving his main goals: to establish an export sector and to unify the country (Posas and Del Cid 1983). Due to a weakly developed infrastructure and a geography that made inter-regional communication difficult, he did not manage to integrate the economy. His success was also hampered by the heavy burden of the debt that had been acquired to build the inter-oceanic railway by General Medina between 1867 and 1870. Although the money was lost in corruption and the railway was never completed, it left Honduras ineligible for further foreign loans; and without credit and infrastructure, Soto's modernization policy was jeopardized.[1]

Soto's policy was continued by the two following presidents, Luis Bográn (1873–91) and Policarpio Bonilla (1894–99). In the 1890s, the two parties that are still dominating Honduran politics, the National Party and the Liberal Party, emerged. The coalitions on which they were based had been established already in the 1970s. However in the early years they were more accurately defined as armed factions under *caudillos* seeking control of the government through force, than as parties (Stokes 1950). In the 1890s this began to change, although it would still take a few years until they were formal parties.[2] The ideological difference between the two parties has never been significant, but the Nationalists were generally more skeptical of foreign influence and later also of state participation in the economy.

After the 1890s, presidents were generally selected from one of the two parties by vote. However in spite of semi-democratic elections, political instability continued, and 159 incidents of organized political violence as a means to conquer the presidency were registered.

A recurrent phenomenon was that presidential elections failed to give an absolute majority to one candidate, parliament rejected the elected candidate, political chaos occurred, and either the elected or an alternative candidate took power by force, often aided by troops from neighboring countries.

In the first two decades of the twentieth century, foreign-owned banana companies became a major political force in Honduras. Banana production in Honduras started in 1899 when the Vaccarro brothers, the owners of the most important North American trade companies in Honduras, started a plantation on the north coast. In 1902, another North American, William Streich, obtained a concession of 5000 hectares for banana production. His plantations were later taken over by an Arab immigrant Samuel Zamurray, who with financial aid from the United Fruit Company (UFCO) established Cuyamel Fruit Company (later to become the main competitor to the UFCO in Honduras.) The banana companies also took over as the main source of external finance. Among the main creditors of the government were the Cuyamel Fruit Company, the Vaccarro Brothers & Company and its two banks: Banco Atlántida and Banco del Comercio (Posas and Del Cid 1983).

However President Francisco Bertrand (1913–19) tried to curb the power of the banana companies and employ them for national purposes. He introduced a new export tax, and placed obligations on the banana companies to construct infrastructure and develop the municipalities where they operated. He attempted to modify the system of wholesale firing of the staff with any change of administration by keeping the most competent officials.

This policy was reversed by Bertrand's successor, Rafael López Gutierrez (1919–23), who reintroduced the wholesale firing of administrations and made the use of public resources for private purposes standard procedure (Stokes 1950). López Guitierrez also changed the policy towards the banana companies, who became important political actors and implementers of public policy during his period.

In the 1920s, banana export became the most important export item, and it transformed the initially scarcely populated areas in the North. In these areas the banana companies became virtual state substitutes. They constructed infrastructure, and established banks, schools and public buildings. There were even cases where the banana companies received parts of the municipal tax income in return for their services (Posas and Del Cid 1983).

The UFCO increased its presence in Honduras between 1905 and 1920, first through acquiring shares in the Vaccarro brothers' company and Cuyamel. It established various 'company towns' where it provided all public services and infrastructure. During the López Gutierrez regime it obtained a 60-years concession for the development of railroads and docks, and a monopoly concession to operate the telegraph and telephone services through its subsidiary TRT.

After the Nationalist general Tiburcio Carías won the 1923 elections and the parliament rejected the result, a new civil war broke out. The war had serious costs for the state and long-term consequences for the state finances. It ended in the ascent to power of Nationalist Paz Baracona, who governed through a period of relative stability between 1925 and 1929. The Paz Baracona government benefited from increased income from banana exports in the 1920s which translated into increased income for the state. Nevertheless he was primarily occupied with the establishment of public order and made few attempts to establish new infrastructure or any other developmentalist projects.

The start of the depression led to a fiscal crisis that close to paralyzed the Honduran state and led to new political turmoil. President Mejía Colínderes (1929–33) attempted to stabilize the fiscal situation by replacing the silver peso with a national currency, the lempira. Nevertheless the state was vulnerable to a new armed uprising. In the presidential elections in 1932, a second victory by Tiburcio Carías led to the familiar post-election civil war. This time Carías managed to win back the power which he kept until 1948.

Carías's long dictatorship was characterized by relative peace and stability. This was partially due to his brutal strategy of oppressing his enemies that has been summarized in three words '*encierro, destierro y entierro*' (imprisonment, exile and burial) (Posas and Del Cid 1983, p. 106). However it was also due to alliances with the banana companies. Carías owed his final ascent to power to support from the UFCO, whereas Cuyamel supported his competitor Manuel Bonilla. Part of the support for the government was through provision of loans. The UFCO became the most important lender, but Cuyamel also provided significant financing for the government. The UFCO further ensured the loyalty of lower-level governmental officials through generous payment. The great majority of the public officials at the north coast received salaries from the banana companies that were twice what the government paid (Posas and Del Cid 1983, p. 67). The UFCO thus established a network of local associates, a system in which the distinction between public and private was close to non-existent (Posas and Del Cid 1983, p. 72).

However the relationship between the banana companies and Carías was far from completely harmonious. There were frequent conflicts and attempts by the government to control the banana companies. Thus as argued by Rachel Sieder, the more lasting impact the banana companies had on the system was to perpetuate and strengthen the clientilism that had already marked the system. In this period the politics of favors became a defining feature of the political system (Sieder 1995).

It was an alliance between the fruit companies, the US State Department and competing Honduran elites that finally put an end to the Carías dictatorship. They viewed his rule as a threat to the country's fragile political consensus, and an obstacle to modernization as Carías initiated close to nothing in the way of development and modernization (Schulz and Sundloff Schulz 1994, p. 18).

In sum, *caudillismo*, civil war and dependence on banana companies were the determining factors for development of the state until the 1930s. This led to both a weak state and a weak private sector. Administrative capacity was curbed by the fact that a lion's share of the budget was war expenses and at the ascendance of a new president the whole administration was replaced (Stokes 1950). However as argued by Posas and Del Cid: 'In a formation in which the dominant social sectors have not achieved to establish a solid economic base, the control of the state activity becomes one of the primary sources of wealth and privileges of the political groups that encounter each other on the political arena' (1983, p. 37). Therefore the private sector and the state evolved in a more symbiotic relationship than that found in Guatemala.

Honduras also placed a strong emphasis on attracting foreign investment. Thus while the Honduran private sector was focused on the state, it was foreigners that developed the export sectors. Moreover the government's political projects were rather focused on defeating political enemies than developing an infrastructural state apparatus or developmental projects. Thus when Keynesianism and developmentalism rose on the international scene, there were few local groups to bring it to the national agenda.

A Civil Developmentalist Interlude (1948–54)

The campaign bringing down the Carías government brought Juan Manuel Gálvez to power in 1948. He had been the lawyer of both the Cuyamel Fruit Company and the United Fruit Company, and he was viewed as loyal to Carías under whose government he had been the Minister of War. Nevertheless he introduced a period of democratization, state expansion and increasing governmental participation in the economy. Under Gálvez the state undertook investments necessary for agro-industrial diversification, and initiated technical services for agricultural development.[3] Gálvez also undertook investments in infrastructure, particularly the road system.

For these projects, the government received increasing foreign aid and loans. With support from the US government the agricultural, health and education sectors were developed. The support for administrative strengthening also encompassed the military, which received extensive training and support from the US under a convention of defense against the

Guatemalan Arbenz regime (Ropp 1974). As a consequence the total governmental debt almost tripled and the component of external aid increased almost nine-fold.

During the Gálvez administration the Honduran government started to receive significant support from the IMF. On the recommendation from an IMF mission in 1950, a Central Bank, National Development Bank, Superior Council of Economic Planning (CONUPLANE) and a Ministry of Economics and Commerce were established (Morris 1984). The IMF mission also contributed to the formulation and implementation of a new income tax that allowed the government to capture more of the profits from the banana companies.

Of great significance for state development, Gálvez reformed the spoils system. William Stokes wrote in 1950 that: 'The politicians of Honduras have carried the idea of spoils to its logical ends and have concluded that the struggle for the government must be decided on a winner-take-all basis' (Stokes 1950, p. 192). However Gálvez managed to reform this by introducing reforms to the civil code.

An important effect of the democratic opening was to further the strengthening of opposition movements within the two traditional parties and the labor movement. In this period the chain of *caudillos* was broken in the National Party and Ramón Villeda Morales renewed the Liberal Party's ability to mobilize politically (Posas and Del Cid 1983, pp. 142–46).

In sum, in this period state expansion and modernization was undertaken by a government which although allowing for increased political participation, was never able to extend its support basis significantly in the manner that happened in Costa Rica. However it also did not cause US suspiciousness as in Guatemala. Therefore what finally led to its downfall was rather internal opposition, and as in Guatemala, the result was a new and strengthened role for the military.

Telecommunications and the Civil–Military Governments (1954–72)

The 1954 elections proved to be consequential for the future of Honduran politics. The elections were won by the Liberals, but the Congress would not let the candidate take power. In the political chaos that followed, the former Vice-President Julio Lozano took over, but he enjoyed little legitimacy and was increasingly authoritarian.

The Honduran military had been strengthened during the 1950s, partly because of aid from the US government. Between 1950 and 1969, 391 officers and 689 soldiers were trained through the US training programs (Ropp 1974). In the chaotic post-electoral situation, the Honduran Armed Forces ousted Lozano in a coup on 21 October 1956 and established a military junta which governed the country for 14 months and supervised free elections that gave the Liberals a landslide victory in 1957. Before leaving power, the armed forces negotiated the institution of several key provisions to be placed in the constitution. These formally guaranteed the military a future political role and ensured its institutional insulation from further partisan interference (Ruhl 1996, p. 36).

The new constitution of 1957 also formally sanctioned state intervention in the economy and the establishment of AIs, on the model of the neighboring countries. Several new institutions, among them the National Electricity Institute (ENEE), were established. Liberal Ramón Villeda Morales won the 1957 elections, and continued the process of state expansion. He has been compared in style and ideology with Figueres in Costa Rica and like him he was influenced by the ideas of Peruvian Haya de la Torre (Posas and Del Cid 1983). Between 1958 and 1963, a national Institute for Water and Sewerage (SAANA) was established with funds from USAID and IDB, a National Social Security Instiute (IHSS) was created and a thorough reform of the municipalities were conducted. Most importantly for the development in the 1960s, the National Agrarian Institute (INA) was established in 1961. Villeda Morales also promoted industrialization under the Central American Common Market scheme by introducing the Law of Industrial Strengthening. This led to the expansion of the production of other goods, such as coffee, woods, cotton and meat.

However his government did not coexist comfortably with the military, as it promoted several reforms curbing its power. The Liberal candidate to the 1963 elections infuriated the military by promising that if elected he would terminate the autonomy of the armed forces. As a result, the military launched a preemptive coup in March 1963, bringing General Oswaldo López Arellano to power. This established the military as the most powerful political player in Honduras (Ruhl 1996).

From 1963 to 1969 the country was ruled by a civil–military alliance between López Arellano and National Party boss Ricardo Zúniga Agustinus, in which the former held the formal title of Chief of State (Morris 1984). A series of new public institutions was established during this '*pacto*' government – particularly institutions occupied with national planning, influenced by the World Bank and the Alliance for Progress (1961).

The Mexico office of ECLA became an important intellectual leader in the process of state expansion, related largely to the process of Central American integration.[4] Under a development plan elaborated by the Mexico office of ECLA (1965–69), extensive public investment was made and between 1966 and 1971, the number of employees of the state increased from 28 164 to 35 692 persons.

As a consequence of the new policies public expenses and foreign debt increased. However the development plan contributed more to the consolidation of the spoils system than to development of national industry and infrastructure. As argued by Posas and Del Cid: 'In Zúñiga Agustinus the spoils system, the profound characteristics of Honduran political life, and the "quasi" private use of public funds, had encountered a mastermind' (1983, p. 201).

This contributed to increasing opposition from popular sectors. The strike settlement following the great banana strike in 1954 had brought formal establishment of trade unions in Honduras. Due to resentment against the *pacto* government, an alliance was created between labor organizations and the progressive private sector with its basis in San Pedro Sula, represented by the Chamber of Commerce and Industry of Cortés (CCIC), a form of alliance unthinkable in neighboring Guatemala.

Understanding this, one has to understand the roots of the relative weakness of the Honduran private sector. The traditional explanation is that a national bourgeoisie failed to develop because of the economic structure. As opposed to Guatemala and Costa Rica, Honduras came to depend on mining and the banana industry, dominated by foreign companies who established a virtual enclave economy (Vega-Carballo 1989; Vilas 1995, p. 72–3).[5] Thus there were no strong national elites upon which the formation of a national private sector could be based.

Moreover the small private sector was split along geographical, ethnic and sector lines in a manner not experienced in for example Guatemala. Honduras has two large cities, Tegucigalpa in the Central Valley and San Pedro Sula situated on the north coast, the former recognized as being the political capital of Honduras, whereas the latter is the industrial capital. It was the north coast business community that established the relatively progressive CCIC. In 1966 an umbrella organization, the Honduran Council for Private Enterprise (COHEP), was established, encompassing the various regional organizations, and it managed to bring a common vision to industry and commerce (Euraque 1992). Nevertheless there has continued to be a certain degree of bifurcation between organizations based in Tegucigalpa, and those based on the north coast (Crosby 1985).

A third factor that historically has contributed to the political weakness of the private sector in Honduras is the fact that much of the industry in San Pedro Sula was established by immigrants from Palestine, Lebanon and Syria. These immigrants invested in various local industries and formed partnerships with the foreign-owned banana companies. But, whereas their wealth grew, they suffered from racism and political exclusion for many decades. Although they gained influence in the CCIC, and certain individuals gained significant political prestige, they suffered from discrimination in political circles (Euraque 1992). Although currently the *arabes* are completely integrated into Honduran society at all levels, historically it contributed to a weakening of the traditional political role of the private sector (Marín-Guzmán 2000).

As a response to the opposition's protests, López Arellano started to employ repressive strategies, also towards the private sector. That included imprisonment of Jaime Rosenthal Oliva, a prominent representative of San Pedro Sula's business community and the owner of *Tiempo*, a newspaper that had been highly critical of the '*pacto* regime'.

However after the fraudulent election of 1968 and the defeat of the Honduran military in the 1969 'Soccer War' against El Salvador, resentment against the *pacto* government increased. Pressure from the opposing alliance convinced López Arellano to make way for a bipartisan government led by a civilian (the '*pactito*' government (1971–72)). However the new government was unable to conduct any of the reforms proposed. It became mired in the usual factionalism and corruption and failed to enact anticipated social reforms. Consequently López Arellano deposed it in 1972, and in its place he created a military regime. This coup set the stage for a ten-year long period of military regime, but it also set the stage for the military reformism that came to mark the early 1970s in Honduras and that expanded the Honduran state.

In sum, it was not so much competing elites as foreign companies that reduced the state's ability to centralize power. The foreign companies took on many state functions and opposed taxes and other forms of state control. The result was that the Honduran state was largely irrelevant in large parts of the country. Its basis of power was primarily clientilist practices and the charisma of *caudillos*. In the attempts to centralize power, it was not the autonomous institutions that emerged as independent state actors as in the case of Costa Rica, but the military. As we shall see, the military also became important in the development of telecommunication infrastructure in Honduras.

Military Reformism and the Establishment of Hondutel (1972–76)

The new López Arellano government elaborated a National Development Plan and started an ambitious process to strengthen the state, promote development and create conditions for industrialization. The reform that has gained most attention in the literature is the agrarian reform. Although it achieved its goals only to a limited extent, it is by many argued to be one of the main factors enabling Honduras to avoid the political uprisings that the neighboring countries experienced in the 1980s.[6] The reforms had started before the Soccer War, but was strengthened by Decree No. 8 that gave landless farmers the right (subject to the approval of INA) to temporarily occupy national and *ejido* (common) land, and forced the rental of idle privately owned land to INA for allocation to landless beneficiaries. This reform was backed both by the US embassy and the World Bank.

Further reforms created a centralized agency for the administration of the country's vital forest preserves, and in 1974 a semi-autonomous state development agency which would provide state guarantees to promote private investment (the National Investment Corporation – CONADI) (Rosenberg 1986). CONADI participated in mixed enterprises in a variety of sectors: forestry, sugar, textiles, food, cement, paper, and so on.

The military reformism in Honduras was influenced significantly by the Peruvian and Panamanian military reformist projects (Rouquié 1973). Increasing popular participation and redistributive economic measures were important elements. The justification for including development as one of the tasks of the military was that order was seen as contingent on progress, and definitions of national security were extended to include national socio-economic development. López Arellano also introduced a certain 'populist openness' to the military institution as an attempt to gain political support (Salomón 1992, p. 22). However as noted by Sieder (1995, pp. 112–13) the Honduran reformist project was to a larger extent built on traditions of *caudillismo*, clientilism and patronage politics which were intrinsic to the development of the political system in Honduras.

Clientilism became the principal mechanism through which the discourse and practice of military reformism were articulated. Thus 'between 1972 and 1978, patron–client relationships were restructured, recreated and selectively extended in an attempt to incorporate emergent social actors on the terms of those controlling the balance of power within the reformist state, providing the latter with a limited but nonetheless significant degree of legitimacy' (Sieder 1995, p. 113).

By 1975 the reformist project was in trouble and López's authority was seriously undermined. Unexpected economic difficulties occasioned by the tripling of world oil prices in 1973, costly damages to north coast banana production during Hurricane Fifi in 1974, rising private sector discontent with the expanding role of the public sector and open hostility to the reform efforts from neighboring governments contributed to the problems. In early 1975, López was forced to relinquish his command of the armed forces to Colonel Juan Melgar Castro, and later the same year he was ousted from the presidency through an internal coup. The coup came immediately after the 'bananagate affair', linking López to a bribe by the UFCO in order to avoid the announced US$1 tax per exported box of bananas.[7]

The ascent of Melgar Castro marked the change from military reformism to a military government inspired by the 'national security doctrine', as in Guatemala. However Melgar Castro also had a development program. It differed from that of the former government by de-emphasizing social reform, and by emphasizing the development of infrastructure and the nationalization of property and functions previously held by banana companies. The banana companies' concessions to operate railways, docks and telecommunications were terminated and a series of new autonomous institutions were established to fulfill their functions. Among these were the Honduran Telecommunication Enterprise, Hondutel, established in 1976 (Decree No. 341) as an autonomous institution, but with administrative links to the Ministry of Communications, Public Works and Transport (República de Honduras 1977).

President Melgar's tenure lasted for three years. Although he continued some of López' reforms, it was a period in which military hardliners gained the upper hand and military factionalism flourished. In 1978, Paz García overthrew him in another internal revolt. By this point the military had become less of a reformist force and increasingly repressive.

Paz García was characterized as an army officer 'possessing few strong ideas on any subject' (Rosenberg 1986, p. 12). He soon acquired the nickname 'Incapaz García' (incapable García), and under his government the country experienced rampant corruption, increased public sector spending and alienation of most parts of the private sector, even those that previously had supported the government.

Another legacy of the military governments of the 1970s was a galloping foreign debt. This was caused by agrarian reform in the first period (1972–75), and in the second period (1975–78) major infrastructure investments. Between 1973 and 1978, public expenses increased annually by 26 per cent. Approximately 16.6 per cent of this increase was externally financed, and the primary source of financing was mixed credits from the IFIs. At the beginning of the 1970s the foreign debt was US$93.5 million, and in order to fulfill the financial obligations established in the National Plan for Development (1973–78) it grew sixfold by 1979, reaching a total of US$602 million (Vinelli 1986). In the same period, interest rates increased. The proportion of debt with an interest rate of 7 per cent or higher increased from 19.6 per cent to 28.3 per cent between 1973 and 1978 (Posas and Del Cid 1983).

In summary, the military in Honduras attempted to gain public support by the extension of services to the population, based on developmentalist ideas common to the Latin American militaries at the time. However it also based its power on a continuity of clientilist practices. Hondutel played a role in both respects, extending services but also serving as a conduit for patronage. The result of the project was an expansion of the Honduran state, and increasing antagonism between the state and the private sector. Yet the network of clientilist practices was too dense for any confrontation between private sector groups and the military-dominated states to occur.

The US Air-Stripe State (1978–86)

Developments in Honduras in the 1980s may be summarized under three main headlines: return to democracy, a serious economic crisis, and increasing dominance of security concerns and US priorities in policy making. As has been treated at length elsewhere,[8] in this period Honduras allowed its territory to be used as a staging ground for the operations of the US-supported anti-Sandinista military forces (Contras) in Nicaragua, and as a consequence the dependency of the Honduran government on the United States increased.

Electoral democracy was reintroduced in 1980, when the Paz government allowed for elections of a constituent assembly due to the combined pressure from national popular sectors, the private sector and an increasing fear of radicalization of the opposition. The Liberal candidate Roberto Suazo Córdova gained the presidency; Paz stayed on as Chief of State in the interim government and forced the presidential candidates of both traditional parties to agree to a military veto over Cabinet appointments, exclusive military control over security policy and no investigations into military corruption or charges of human rights violations. In fact the armed forces grew even stronger under the new regime (Ruhl 1996). President Suazo based his support structure primarily on the chief of the armed forces General Gustavo Alvarez Martínez, US Ambassador John D. Negroponte, and a small part of the private business sector, headed by the Miguel Facussé family (Molina 1986). In the 1980s the president was commonly regarded as the junior partner in this alliance (Schulz and Sundloff Schulz 1994).[9]

In 1984, General Alvarez was ousted and replaced by General Walter López Reyes. He started to drive harder bargains with the US over Honduras's position in US foreign policy towards Central America, and introduced a somewhat more open political style (Ruhl 1996). Nevertheless throughout the 1980s many of the political decisions in Honduras were de facto made through negotiations between the civilian government and either (or both) the US Embassy or the Chief of the Armed Forces. As important as the formal dominance by the military, was its more informal control. Thus Rosenberg (1995) argues that 'leading Honduran civilian decision makers are reticent to confront the military directly because that would almost necessarily imply their own greater responsibility' (1995, p. 82). What was at stake in the 1990s was not only to push the military back to the barracks, but also to 'demilitarize' civilian elites. As we will see, one of the areas in which the civilian elites had little desire to take responsibility, was the economy and the issue of state reform.

Whereas the 1980s in Latin America have gone into history as the decade of the roll-back of the state, in Honduras the expansion gained new pace in the 1980s. The establishment of AIs slowed down, but the public sector participation in the economy continued to grow. The increased participation took two forms. Firstly, there was an increase in the direct participation in economic activity. The public sector value-added as a proportion of gross domestic product was 18 percent in the early 1980s and reached 23 percent by the end of the decade. Public sector consumption as percentage of general consumption also rose, while public sector investment fell. Secondly, the regulatory frameworks for private sector activities became increasingly detailed and encompassing, although they were still highly unstable (World Bank 1992d).

However the investment corporation CONADI experienced severe problems, and by 1981 it was effectively bankrupt. Between 1975 and 1980, CONADI authorized 102 million lempiras (US$51 million) in direct loans and 208 million (US$104 million) in loan guarantees to industrialists at a ratio of 8.08 lempiras for every lempira of private capital invested. To finance its operations, it borrowed heavily on international capital markets, where its dealings were underwritten by the Honduran government. However the CONADI operations were known for inefficiency and corruption, lending rules were often violated and advice was ignored. According to a World Bank report, only 5 per cent of the funded companies were financially sound, and of the 34 companies that had absorbed 94 per cent of the loans, 16 were bankrupt. In some cases the companies involved were non-existent (World Bank 1992d).

The AIs were generally under military control, and Hondutel more so than others. It provided free services to the armed forces and it functioned as a source of jobs and income for them and their families.[10] Whereas in Guatemala it was a general rule that military governments appointed military managers of Guatel, in Honduras there was no exception to the rule of military managers even with civilian governments until 1994. The position as a manager of Hondutel was seen as one carrying a high degree of prestige, and to obtain it was considered a 'reward'. Between 1978 and 1994, there were 12 managers of Hondutel, and none of them had any particular knowledge of the telecommunication sector, but ran it as a national security institution.[11]

State expansion and military dominance happened in the shadows of a deep economic crisis. GDP had increased with an average of 8.8 per cent throughout the 1970s, but during the first five years of the 1980s it fell to an average of 1 per cent annual increase. In terms of GDP per capita, it fell by 3.4 per cent. This was primarily caused by a fall in exports and the level of investments. Whereas exports had increased by 9.8 per cent on average during the 1970s, in the first half of the 1980s, they increased by on average 0.70 per cent. The comparable numbers for internal capital formation were 10 per cent (average increase in the 1970s) and 2.3 per cent (average increase 1980–1985). Although the exports recuperated partially from 1985 to 1988 (due primarily to increasing international prices of coffee) macroeconomic indicators continued to deteriorate. By 1989, the fiscal deficit had arrived at 13 per cent of GDP (Noé Pino 1992).

The multilateral institutions contributed 48 per cent of the total influx of capital (US$623 million) between 1980 and 1985. The decade started with an Agreement of Extended Service signed with the IMF in 1979. It included conditionalities demanding reductions on current expenses of the central government, increasing tax burdens and increasing public investments. Due to failure to meet conditionalities, only 50 per cent of the 47.6 million agreed upon was disbursed, and the program was suspended in 1981. In 1982, two new agreements were signed with the IMF for a total of US$100 million: one 'stand-by' agreement of $77 million, and one compensatory credit of US$23 million. This also had several conditionalities attached, among them reduction of the fiscal deficit, limitation of the increase in current expenses and the strengthening of the position of current accounts of the decentralized institutions. In the same way as the previous program, it failed to be completed and was suspended in 1983. The Honduran government failed to reach any further agreement with the IMF during the 1980s. In 1983, Honduras obtained a loan to alleviate the financial disequilibrium with the World Bank for an amount of US$100 million, including $45 million as balance of payment support, and the rest for the agricultural sector. However Honduras failed to meet the conditionalities, and the loan was suspended. Moreover from 1983, Honduras maintained an undeclared moratorium on commercial debt.

The third major IFI, the IDB had been a significant actor in Honduras in the 1960s and 1970s, financing first projects related to the Alliance for Progress, and later reforms under the military National Development Plan. Among the projects funded were CONADI and the hydroelectric project of the Cajón Dam. The debt contracted to construct this dam constituted 50 per cent of the total public external debt in the early 1980s and most of it was with the IDB (Ordóñez Baca 1999). However as the 1980s proceeded, the financial situation of the IDB was such that it could contribute little to Honduras's grave financial crisis and had little means and willingness to set conditions.

Nonetheless foreign financing both voluntary (loans and grants) and involuntary (arrears) as a percentage of the fiscal deficit increased from 24 per cent in 1984 to about 76 per cent in 1990 (World Bank 1992e). The main reason for this was the politically motivated financial support from the

USAID. The aid from the US government increased from a modest US$16.2 million in 1978, to US$231.1 million in 1986. In the same period the share of military aid increased from 20 per cent to 38 per cent (Lapper 1985, p. 86–7).

According to USAID officials, there was considerable internal disagreement with respect to the policy towards Honduras in this period. Some argued that political concerns should not allow Honduras to continue its devastating economic policy, particularly the seriously overvalued exchange rate. However the US strategic concerns in the region remained of higher importance than economic policy, and the US support continued until the end of the decade.[12]

In summary, during the 1980s, Honduran politics were dominated by US security concerns. The military continued its stronghold on the state and increased its infrastructural power. The role of the state in the economy also increased significantly, primarily through CONADI. Thus while it is impossible to speak of a state independent from the military, what nevertheless emerged was a state with a certain autonomy from private sector elites and a limited capacity to direct the economy. US security concerns allowed Honduras to avoid serious financial repercussions, in spite of its severely destructive economic policy. However this would change significantly as the 1980s were coming to an end and US security concerns shifted.

THE PROCESS OF REFORM

The 'Soft' (and not so 'Soft') Power Strategies of the USAID

The beginning of the end of the Central American conflicts caused a change of strategies of the USAID in the region. This meant that Honduras's strategic location no longer protected it from pressure to reform its economic policy. Increasing focus was placed on reform of the state, export orientation of the economy, and strengthening of the export oriented segments of the private sector.

However the USAID pressure had little impact until the government of José Azcona (1986–90) took power. Azcona proved less resistant to North American pressure than his predecessor, Suazo Córdova, and starting in the mid-1980s Honduran economic policy would become highly influenced by the USAID. In 1985 USAID had conditioned further support on the emission of a Decree allowing for privatization of CONADI, much in the same manner as it had done with CODESA in Costa Rica. Decree No. 161 was issued in September 1985, authorizing CONADI to elaborate a 'plan for the transference of the companies in the portfolio of the Corporation to the private sector'. In a convention signed between President Azcona Hoyo and the USAID in 1986, he committed to privatizing 12 to 15 of the companies of CONADI within a time frame of 30 months (Posas 1995). In 1987, Azcona signed an Economic Stabilization Agreement with the USAID, and subsequently he enacted a series of laws to encourage exports, particularly non-traditional exports (Noé Pino 1990). Thus, in many ways USAID acted as a virtual 'shadow government' with parallel bureaus corresponding to Honduran ministries and agencies influencing key areas of policy making (Schulz and Sundloff Schulz 1994, pp. 199–200).

However there were frequent conflicts between Azcona and the international agencies, particularly the USAID. In spite of the agreements signed, the government resisted many of the policies agreed to, particularly the introduction of privatization policies and devaluation of the currency.

Also the relationship between the private sector and the USAID was problematic. Vice-President and prominent businessman Jaime Rosenthal had masterminded the 1986 economic plan which by the local press had been called 'Reaganomics for Honduras'. However Rosenthal had also expressed several critical viewpoints against the government and USAID through his newspaper *Tiempo*, arguing that the USAID resources were wasted through corruption and graft. Consequently, he was excluded from participating in the economic plan of 1987, and he eventually resigned from his position as a vice-president.

Other parts of the private sector denounced the USAID due to its economic policies. The USAID worked to encourage the establishment of a Honduran free trade zone, development of *maquiladora* industry, and export diversification. These strategies did not resonate well with the whole private sector. The private sector feared that encouraging growth in the export sector would require resources which in turn would have to be extracted from other sectors. Tension increased between the export sectors that potentially would benefit and those who feared they would have to pay for the party (Crosby 1985). Thus the traditional private sector organizations in Honduras were skeptical, and the only organization that supported it was the CCIC. In order to increase support for its policies, USAID supported both financially and organizationally the creation of a series of new organizations to serve functions presumed to be non-existent in the older organizations. Five new organizations were established in Honduras by the USAID,[13] and only one of the traditional organizations (National Industrial Association – ANI) received more than token financing from USAID (Crosby 1985). The leaders of the new groups were younger and less well-connected members of the private sector, and although there was little outright hostility between the traditional and new private sector groups, their establishment contributed to 'something of a diluting effect on the capacity of the private sector organizations' (Crosby 1985, p. 18).

With regards to privatization, Azcona did indeed privatize ten of the 15 CONADI companies that he had agreed to with the USAID (Posas 1985). However the agreements did not mention Hondutel or any other infrastructure companies as potential candidates for privatization.

The final blow to the relationship between Azcona and the USAID came right before the new presidential election in 1989. Azcona publicly rejected the IMF-AID economic prescription for Honduras only a couple of weeks before the elections (13 November 1989). Furthermore he charged that a suspension of US$70 million from the USAID was politically motivated. By deepening the country's economic crisis, he alleged, the USAID was undercutting the Liberal campaign and thus helping the competitor for office, Rafael Callejas (Schulz and Sundloff Schulz 1994).

Predictably Azcona lost the election, and the entering of Callejas was greeted by the international community as optimistically as Ascona had been. However the end results were equally disappointing.

International Pressure and Reluctant Reforms by the Last Caudillo

Although Azcona signed the first structural adjustment loan (SAL I) with the World Bank in 1988, worth $50 million, structural adjustment did not really start in Honduras until the entering of the Callejas government in 1990. The conditionalities for SAL I included monetary measures, reduction of the fiscal deficit and liberalization of prices and markets. However Azcona failed to implement many of the conditionalities and in 1987 Honduras began to incur arrears with the IFIs. As a consequence, in 1989 the disbursement of the second tranche of SAL was suspended and the same year Honduras was declared ineligible for further aid by the World Bank, the IDB and the IMF (World Bank 1992e).[14]

The entering of the Callejas government in 1990 therefore represented a great new hope for the IFIs. Not only was Callejas a favorite of the United States, he was viewed as personally holding neo-liberal ideas, along with a series of his members of government. This was the group that came to be called the Honduran 'Chicago Boys' including Minister of Finance Benjamin Villanueva, President of the Central Bank Ricardo Maduro, and Minister of Economy Ramón Medina Luna (Posas 1995). Callejas also seemed to invoke the confidence required to continue the privatization process, and he had a personal charisma and gift for public speech which gave him respect even among his enemies. However it would soon become clear that political goals and personal economic benefit were more important motivating factors for him than developmental goals.

Callejas took over a troubled economy, a fiscal deficit of 7.4 per cent of GDP and arrears with the IFIs of US$250 million. His solution to it was to start a process of structural adjustment. The first phase of structural adjustment started with the Law of Structural Adjustment of the Economy (Decreto 18-90 popularly called the '*paquetazo*') that was passed soon after Callejas's inauguration in March 1990. This opened the way for an agreement with IDB, IMF and the World Bank, with bridging finance from Mexico, Venezuela and the United States, complemented with a long-term loan from Japan. By September 1990, Callejas signed the second structural adjustment loan (SAL II) with the World Bank for US$90 million to be disbursed in three tranches. This was followed by two sector adjustment loans from the IDB (an agricultural sector loan of US$60 million, signed in November 1990, and an electricity sector adjustment loan of US$50 million), and a sector adjustment loan financed with IDA funds (petroleum sector adjustment loan of US$50 million). In June 1991 the IMF opened a credit line of US$1.8 billion to be disbursed over the next three years, depending on continued adjustment.

The loans came with a complex set of conditionalities. For the disbursement of the first tranche of the World Bank SAL II only, 18 conditionalities had to be fulfilled. With respect to telecommunications, the disbursement of the first tranche required increased charges for telecommunication services. Consequently in September 1990 the prices of national telephony increased by 100 per cent and international telephony increased by 200 per cent (*Reporte Político* No. 53 September 1990; *Inforpress* 20 September 1990). However many of these were already in place with the passage of the *paquetazo* and they may therefore be called pro forma conditionalities.

A second phase of the adjustment started in March 1992, with the passage of the Law of Modernization and Development of the Agricultural Sector. An ESAF for US$58.5 million was reached with the IMF in July 1992 as a support for the adjustment policy that the government had introduced in 1990. Although privatization of Hondutel was not included in this agreement, it was discussed and, according to high-level officials, the basis of the privatization program that would be initiated later was laid out in the 1992 ESAF.

The first two and a half years of the Callejas government was a period of a certain economic recovery and reduction of fiscal deficit. Fiscal deficit fell to 5.9 per cent in 1990, 2.2 per cent in 1991 and then 3.4 per cent in 1992. Growth recovered gradually, and reached 6.2 per cent in 1993 (IDB 1998). There were, however, serious social problems partly caused by the economic crisis and partly by the program intended to alleviate it. The percentage of Hondurans living below the poverty line increased from 68 per cent in 1989 to 73 per cent in 1991 (Noé Pino 1992). In 1993 new problems started. During the last 18 months of the Callejas government, the fiscal deficit rose to about 10 per cent of GDP, and as a result of this, the enhanced structural adjustment facility (ESAF) agreement was suspended (UNAT 1998).

Nevertheless the Callejas government did take some actions with regards to privatization. Callejas appointed a liquidating board in charge of privatizing the remaining CONADI companies and by December 1993, 36 of the companies of CONADI had been privatized. Callejas also started a process of privatization of public services, among them some of the services of the EENE, the IHSS and the Honduran Agricultural Market Institute.

However accusations of corruption and favoritism soon emerged. Most of the companies were sold at a price significantly below market prices and many of them to groups or persons with close relations to the government or to the military (see following section). One of the most criticized processes was the privatization of the governmentally owned cement factory INCHESA. In 1991, the government opened a bidding procedure to sell CONADI's share in INCHESA, and among the main bidders was businessman and former vice-president Jaime Rosenthal. However the company was sold at a favorable price and under highly non-transparent conditions to the Military Pensions Institute (IPM).[15] This process deeply affected the public's faith in the government's intentions with privatization, and it also alienated parts of the private sector, particularly of course Jaime Rosenthal.

Callejas also took the first initiative to start a process of privatizing Hondutel. On 23 January 1993, he asked Congress to study 'the adequate legislation to privatize Hondutel and with its revenue finance a new educational system which could give us the Honduran that we need' (*El Heraldo* 26 January 1993, quoted in Posas 1995, p. 9). However in spite of an intense initial debate, little happened afterwards.

Callejas furthermore issued a bid for a concession to operate the cellular system. The process in which this happened had several similarities with the process occurring in Guatemala. It was characterized by unclear concession criteria, corruption charges and canceling of bidding processes.[16] In 1995, at the fourth attempt, Celtel managed to get the concession. By this time all possible competitors had lost patience and withdrawn. But as this was the end of the Callejas government, they did not feel comfortable about the state of affairs and awaited the entering of the new president to start operations.

Finally, Celtel managed to get a very favorable agreement with the government.[17] Initially the government wanted to give a concession for both the A and the B band to Celtel, but this was found unconstitutional. Rather, Celtel managed to get an agreement in which it only operated the A band, but where the Congress committed to not give a concession to operate the B band. Thus neither Hondutel nor any other company was allowed to exploit cellular services and consequently Celtel remained as a monopoly.

What was lacking was a political project which included a vision for the telecommunication sector. Hondutel was primarily viewed as a source of income, spoils and patronage. Callejas looked on Hondutel and many other state institutions more or less as his own property, and he would have sold off Hondutel to personal contacts if he had had the opportunity. As expressed by one of his telecommunication advisors:

> Callejas personally was close to selling Hondutel to the Americans. I was in a meeting with Callejas and a representative from the American embassy, and they were discussing the sale of the company. The American said that they had supported various presidential candidates in the region, among them Violetta Chamorro and Callejas, and now they were collecting their rewards. But I said to Callejas, you can't just sell Hondutel like that, it is against the constitution.[18]

Thus although privatization of Hondutel was discussed during the government of Callejas, it was primarily as a means of improving the fiscal situation, and as a business opportunity for the government. The process of expanding the telephone network with 110 000 lines in the urban areas of Honduras in 1991 was conducted according to a logic of favoritism, but not only within Honduras. Siemens originally gained the concession in competition with AT&T. However Hondutel planned to finance the project by issuing bonds through the Caribbean Basin Project Financing Authority (CARIFA), and by the end of 1992 Hondutel and Siemens waited for acceptance by the CARIFA board. The decision was postponed due to pressure from AT&T, and when the CARIFA board finally accepted the project it was on the condition that AT&T got a supply contract of equal size as Siemens. That meant that instead of 110 000 lines, 220 000 lines would be installed and that Hondutel's debt would be increased correspondingly.[19] Allegations against the CARIFA board for giving in to pressure from AT&T due to economic nationalism were soon matched with charges of corruption against Siemens. In either case, the story added to the scruffy reputation that Honduras had acquired as a destination for telecommunication investments, and it made Hondutel increasingly vulnerable to pressure from the IFIs, since the expansion process had virtually bankrupted it. However Hondutel also underwent deep changes from the inside. The most important was the gradual withdrawal of the military from the main positions.

The Demilitarization of Hondutel and the Military as Businessmen

By the early 1990s, it started to become clear that the process of demilitarization and democratization that Honduras was undergoing, would lead the military to lose control over state institutions, among them Hondutel. This led the military to pursue two strategies. The first reaction could be understood as being based on an acceptance of the situation. Rather than attempting to maintain control over the state, some groups within the armed forces attempted to gain control over the market. The main instrument for gaining such control was the Military Pensions Institute (IPM). The IPM had invested in several of the CONADI enterprises, and it was clear that it was also interested in purchasing a share of Hondutel (Brenes and Casas 1998). The manager of the IPM, Hector Fonseca, declared to the press that although the IPM alone would not be able to buy Hondutel, it could do so in partnership with other social security institutes such as the Institute for Retirement and Pensions of the Public Employees (INJUPEM) (Posas 1995). Thus some parts of the military favored privatization for particular economic reasons.

However other parts of the military, including chief of the armed forces Alonso Discua, resisted privatization of Hondutel because it would weaken the military's control over it. The military enjoyed extensive benefits as a result of being in control over telecommunications. The physical integration of military communication systems and Hondutel's infrastructure had not been broken, and the military still benefited from free access to communication services. The newspaper *El Heraldo* reported for example that in 1993, the military made free calls worth 18 million lempiras, and in 1994 the number had increased to 20.4 million lempiras (*Inforpress* 11 May 1995).

Furthermore there were still many incidents showing that the military looked upon Hondutel as its own private company. One example was when the only telephone line of the community of Tatumble was moved to the house of the Chief of the Armed Forces in the area in order to 'give him a more pleasurable Christmas'. As a consequence, the more than 3000 inhabitants of the community were left without access to a telephone (*Tiempo* 3–4 June 1990, quoted in Salomón et al. 1996, p. 181). Hondutel was also frequently involved in overpaying for services. One such case was when Hondutel moved from a building where it paid 22 000 lempiras monthly to a similar one rented for 60 000 monthly from the IPM in order to favor the military (*Tiempo* 24 January 1992).

Putting an end to the military's involvement in politics and control over the state was the main goal of President Carlos Roberto Reina of the Liberal Party who took office in 1994. He came to power under the banner of a 'moral revolution', and his main goals were to combat corruption and end military dominance over Honduran political and economic life. During the 1980s he had been a leader of the social-democratic branch of the Liberal Party (M-LIDER) and he had been persecuted by the military during the repressive governments of the early 1980s. In his inauguration speech he declared that his goal was to 'do whatever it takes to reduce the room for action of the Honduran armed forces in the politics of the state and the productive activities'. One of his first actions upon taking office was to abolish the decades-long military draft and convoke a National Reconciliation Council, where the relationship between civilian and military elites were among the most important topics (*Reporte Político* No. 108 September 1995). Furthermore he appointed civilians to head public institutions traditionally dominated by the military: the merchant marine, the National Directorate of Migration Policy and the National Geographic Institute (Isacson 1997).

As a part of his campaign to demilitarize politics, Reina took a series of actions to get the process of privatization of Hondutel going. In February 1994 he announced that he had started talks with the militaries in order to privatize Hondutel, and in March he declared that he had made the decision to privatize (Posas 1995). In a letter to the people in May 1994, he announced that he had established a commission to privatize Hondutel, something he saw as a historical step towards a pact between the people and the armed forces (*El Heraldo* 11 May 1994).

Subsequently, Rothschild was hired as the investment bank, a job for which it was promised US$1 million plus 1.98 per cent of the privatization proceeds. It formed a consortium of Squire Sanders & Dempsey and Price Waterhouse to undertake a review of the company (Proyecto de Privatización, Resolución No. CCP-01-96). The conclusion from the Rothschild group's first review of the company was that the total assets of the company were worth US$800 million. At this point the intention was to sell 47 per cent, thus the government expected to receive US$372 million for the transaction, and President Reina declared optimistically that there would be at least 200 companies in the world that would be interested in purchasing Hondutel.[20]

Reina also appointed the first civilian in the position as a Hondutel manager, Mario Maldonado. However he was a retired colonel, a former a veteran of the reformist branch of the armed forces, and by no means a believer in the free market.[21] He was chosen for the position due to his long-term relations with Reina, as a reward for his support in Reina's election campaign, and as a 'bridge' to the military. But although claiming that he was appointed to conduct the privatization process, he was seen as an obstacle to privatization. In January 1996, he was removed and replaced with a previous official of the commission for state modernization.[22] This was a further step towards the military's loss of control over the institution.

In sum, the military was split in respect of how to handle the pressure for reducing its role in the state. It was not able to unify around a common strategy to deal with the pressure for privatizing the company nor with the pressure to demilitarize it. Also many non-military telecommunication experts within Hondutel were ambivalent with respect to further military dominance. On the one hand, military dominance meant continuation of clientilistic practices and free services to the military.[23] On the other hand, it meant a higher degree of stability than what was seen in public institutions operating at the will of the politicians.[24] What was clearly lacking was a public sector agency with the ability to influence the agenda by providing content to a possible reform process.

However Reina's eagerness to get the military out of the economy eventually also increased the political influence of the private sector. This would have serious consequences for the nature and speed of telecommunication reform in the period to follow.

The World Bank, the Private Sector and the Half-Way Telecommunication Reform

Reina did not only inherit a militarized state apparatus from Callejas, but also a huge foreign debt. When he took office in 1994 the foreign debt represented 113 per cent of GDP and 30 per cent of the government's revenues went to servicing it. Reina started to negotiate with the IFIs and by January, the ESAF had been restored (*Reporte Político* No. 112 March 1996). This also made possible negotiations with the MDBs for restructuring the debt, in accordance with Reina's general policy of only contracting conventional debt and converting as much of the commercial as possible.

Following this, the third structural adjustment program – an encompassing public sector modernization program – was initiated (Public Sector Modernization Adjustment Program – PSMAP) (see Table 5.1). That would channel a total of US$210 million to Honduras, and included conditionalities for maintaining macro-economic stability and obliging the government to reform the telecommunications, civil aviation and electricity sectors (World Bank 1996c).

With respect to telecommunications, the conditionalities were as follows. For the presentation of the project to the respective boards of the World Bank and the IDB and the consequent disbursement of the first tranche of the loan, the passage of a new framework law for the telecommunication sector, including amendments to the organic law of Hondutel, were required. For the disbursement of the second tranche, it was required that the regulations of the framework law for the telecommunication sector were issued and put into effect, that a new regulatory authority Conatel had received a budget and started its operations, and that bidding documents to solicit bids for private partners in Hondutel had been issued. Finally, for the disbursement of the third tranche, it was a requirement that a new subsidiary was established by Hondutel, controlled and partly owned by private capital, and that it was operating in the Tegucigalpa and San Pedro Sula regions. This meant that the process of capitalization of Hondutel had been concluded. The conditionalities of the two programs were crossing. Moreover the disbursement of the first tranche was dependent on an agreement with the IMF which was reached in 1996.

Table 5.1 Public Sector Modernization Adjustment Program, Honduras,
*   sources of funds (million US$)*

Source	Type	Total funds	Tranche 1	Tranche 2	Tranche 3
IDA	Concessional	55	20	20	15
IDB	Concessional	155	199	30	25
IDB/ World Bank	Technical assistance credit	9.6			

Source: World Bank (1995c).

However by the signing of the agreement, the new telecommunication law had already been adopted, and the conditionality was thus only pro forma. The new telecommunication law was adopted in 1995 (Ley Marco del Sector de Telecomunicaciones) as the first of its kind in Central America.[25] This gave the state the main responsibility for regulation and supervision of the telecommunication sector, through the National Telecommunication Commission (CONATEL), that was to establish tariffs, issue concessions for the utilization of the radio spectrum, and resolve conflicts over interconnection. The law further established a system of limited competition, but a transitory regime of exclusivity (article 26). Furthermore, the law gave a concession to Hondutel of operation for 25 years, that it could utilize directly or through establishment of subsidiaries in alliances with private international telecommunication companies. As a transitory regime, Hondutel was given a period of exclusivity of ten years on all national and international telecommunication services. The model that was outlined in the new law resembled in other words the traditional model of Latin American privatization (Raventós 1997).

Fulfillment of the conditionalities for the disbursement of further tranches revealed itself to be much more difficult. The new telecommunication law was intended to be only one part of a comprehensive plan for restructuring the sector. The other main legal change intended was the Law to Restructure Hondutel, which would facilitate the process of issuing bids for the company, as required by the conditioniality for disbursement of the second tranche of the PSMAP. The Law to Restructure Hondutel was sent to Congress in May 1995 and it described the process of restructuring Hondutel from an autonomous state institution to a company under private law – Compañia Hondureña de Teléfonos SA (Honducom SA) and the process of selling stocks to the private sector. However when the Congress voted for the two laws, only the telecommunication law passed. As a consequence, there would be no law to regulate the processes of privatizing the company. The half-way reform in fact left the new regulatory institution with the task of regulating both a public monopoly (Hondutel) and a private one (Celtel).

The explanation for the lack of endorsement of the Law to Restructure Hondutel is found in the relationship between the government, the military and private sector elites. In order to fulfill his main goal of limiting the role of the military, Reina needed the support from the private sector. He therefore appointed Guillermo Bueso, the owner of one of Honduras's largest banks, Banco Atlántida, as the Minister of the Presidency. He also appointed Mario Agüero – a former USAID official and a confidant of Guillermo Bueso – as the Executive Secretary for the Privatization Commission, established as a dependency of the Ministry of Finance. Some observers argued that Reina left the private sector to run the country basically as its own business in exchange for support for dealing with the military. An IFI official for example characterized the role of Guillermo Bueso as follows: 'Bueso had a very important position. He basically ran the show out of his own office. There were meetings in his boardroom at the Banco Atlántida, where he is the director. You can say he mixed the private and the public role a little bit.' [26]

However the private sector was far from unified with regards to privatization, and the differences within the private sector cut right across the Liberal Party. While private sector Liberal Party members such as Jaime Rosenthal warmly supported privatization of Hondutel, the Liberal Party President of Congress, Carlos Flores Facussé, opposed it. Flores had had presidential aspirations and ran a campaign to weaken the president, by publishing letters in the press accusing the government of passivity (*Reporte Político* No. 95 July 1994). Attempting to pass a package to reduce the fiscal deficit, Reina negotiated with both factions, but managed in the end only to win back Flores Facussé's support. This ensured the possibility of getting the fiscal packages passed in the Congress, but most observers concluded from the concessions that Reina had to give to Flores, that he had effectively lost leadership of the party. Furthermore he lost the possibilities to get the complete privatization package passed.

The Privatization Decrees

The coming to power of the Liberal Party's candidate Carlos Flores Facussé in February 1998 was not a good omen for the privatization process. As shown above, during the Reina period Flores had used his position as the President of Congress to obstruct the privatization of Hondutel (*La Prensa*, 18 October 1995). Flores had also run for president in 1989, but then he enjoyed little popularity even within the liberal circles. According to Schulz and Sundloff Schulz: 'He was often perceived as arrogant and unscrupulous. He was a *turco* (Arab), married to a gringa,[27] and his name (flowers) did not inspire confidence in this machismo-oriented society. To make matters worse, the Facussé family was deeply involved in the CONADI scandal' (1994, p. 270).

In the internal campaign in the Liberal Party, Flores had won over the main proponent of privatization of Hondutel, Jaime Rosenthal, who headed a competing faction (*Reporte Político* No. 116 June 1996). Although not formally disagreeing with his predecessor with respect to privatization policies, Flores lacked Reina's main motivation for pursuing it: the desire to send the military firmly back to its barracks. Flores showed soon after his inauguration that he rather put priority on financial issues, and one of them was to lower the US$152 million fiscal deficit he inherited from Reina (*Reporte Político* No. 138 June 1998).

Nevertheless, when he took office in February 1998, Flores decided to review the privatization process. In October 1998 a legislative decree was passed that regulated the process of capitalization of Hondutel. The decree also demanded that an ad hoc commission was established composed of the Minister of Finance, the Minister of Public Works, Transport and Housing (SOPTRAVI) and the Manager of Hondutel, in order to oversee the process and ensure transparency. The privatization secretariat, already established and funded by the World Bank, would act as the executive body of the ad hoc commission.

The decree further gave Conatel the mandate to give a 25-year concession to Hondutel with monopoly on several services until 24 December 2005. Thus due to the delays in the process, the actual monopoly period had been shortened from ten to seven years. Moreover value-added services and basic infrastructure (*servicios portadores*) were opened to competition. New in the 1998 decree was also that Hondutel was given the concession to operate a PCS band, but not in exclusivity. It should start to offer PCS services as soon as the capitalization process was completed.

To the decrees originally sent from the government, the Congress added that every step in the privatization process had to be approved of by Congress. That meant that the concession contract signed between Conatel and Hondutel and the bidding documents should be approved by Congress, and that the international auction should be notified to Congress prior to its realization.

According to the decree, the new company (here called Cohdetel) should find a strategic investor to purchase 50 per cent of the stocks. After this, it could sell 4 per cent of the stocks to public pension funds, the Hondutel workers, users and schools (*colegios profesionales*) at the same price per stock as the strategic investor had paid.

The decree also outlined in detail how the process of selling the stocks of the company should take place, and it specified the conditions for participating in the auction; the strategic investor should be an operator of telecommunications, with at least a million lines in service, annual income from telecommunications of at least US$1250 million, at least five years' experience from telecommunications, and comply with all further legal and ethical requirements. This effectively excluded local investors from participating. According to the decree, Cohdetel was obliged to install at least two public phones in all communities with 500 or more inhabitants within a time frame of five years.

With this decree in place, the government was all set for starting the process of privatizing Hondutel. However in November 1998 Hurricane Mitch struck Honduras and left approximately 6000 people dead; 70 per cent of the agricultural crop was lost, and a large part of the country's infrastructure was ruined.[28] The telecommunication sector was among the least affected, and although the official estimate of the losses in the telecommunication sector was set at US$48 million (Gobierno de Honduras 1999), many contested this figure and Conatel concluded that only a few of Hondutel's buildings had been affected whereas the basic infrastructure was intact (Conatel 2001).

Nevertheless Mitch made the government change its development priorities in many respects. In May 1999, a new decree was sent to congress with the purpose of guaranteeing success in the choice of strategic investor, modernization and extension of telecommunication services in the country, but also that the proceeds contributed to the Project of National Reconstruction. In order to ensure this, 51 per cent of the stocks of the new stockholding company, this time named Cohondetel SA should be sold and the strategic partner was allowed to participate in consortia with other investors as long as the telecommunication operator was in a majority position.

Thus the new decree opened a small window for the participation of local groups. Furthermore the decree removed all obligations to expand rural infrastructure from the privatized company as soon as the exclusivity period was over, but obliged the state to designate at least 10 million lempiras annually to expansion of the rural network when the period of exclusivity of the private company was over.

The new decree also involved both a further opening of the sector to competition and limiting competition. The exclusivity period was still set to last until 24 December 2005 and therefore was yet another year shorter than originally intended. Furthermore the B band was to be auctioned separately after the capitalization process was undertaken, thus ensuring in the end three competing companies on the mobile market: the winner of the B band, Cohondetel (having got a PCS band in the package) and Celtel. On the other hand, Cohondetel was given monopoly on basic infrastructure (*servicios portadores*), which limited competition.

In sum, the new decree aimed at making Hondutel a more attractive investment by increasing the percentage of the stocks to be sold to the private investor, by increasing the exclusivity rights, and by reducing the obligations to expand the rural network. In many respects, the decree adapted the privatization framework to the precarious fiscal situation. However in other respects it adapted it to suit the interests of the local private sector, that was by this point openly announcing its interest in participating in the process, and that had launched an intense lobbying campaign in Congress to have the decree amended (*La Prensa* 15 May 1999). The local private sector would also turn out to have some impact on the process of privatization, but in a quite different manner than in Guatemala.

The Attempted Privatization of Hondutel

After all the postponements, in the spring of 1999 the capitalization process was finally relaunched. This time it was a part of a larger package of reforms, many of which had been under way for years, but that were now promoted with greater urgency because of Mitch. The main aim of the package was to attract foreign investments to telecommunications, ports, airports and the tourist business. An ad hoc commission was established in accordance with the privatization decree, and the privatization commission, headed by Mario Agüero, was to assist it. Furthermore, Rothschild conducted a new evaluation of the value of the company, estimating that the assets of the company were worth US$600 million. In addition to this the new company would have to invest approximately US$500 million in 16 000 public phones and 320 000 fixed lines in order to achieve a telephone density of 10 per 100 inhabitants by 2005. The minimum price of 51 per cent of the stocks was set to US$300 million.

After the passage of the new decree in May 1999, the Minister of Finance Gabriela Núñez announced that the capitalization would take place by the end of 1999. However as in Guatemala, the process suffered a series of postponements. The negotiation of an agreement with the union Sitratelh upheld the process for some weeks. Furthermore, a few potential buyers – notably France Telecom, Telmex and Telefónica de España – had expressed their interest in participating, but asked for postponement of the pre-qualification process due to involvement in other privatization processes (*La Prensa* 9 October 2001). Moreover Celtel did its best to postpone the process. Since concessioning of the B band was made dependent on the capitalization of Hondutel, Celtel had every incentive to avoid it.

When finally the first phase of the qualification process was closed in February 2000, seven companies had pre-qualified for bidding for Hondutel and thereby automatically also for gaining a concession to the B band.[29] To participate in the second qualification phase the interested companies had to purchase the right to get access to all Hondutel information for US$20 000. The three companies that did this – Telmex, Telefónica and France Telecom – also started negotiations over the details of the contract with the ad hoc commission. Finally, on 16 October 2000 the auction of Hondutel took place. However only Telmex made a bid and it was only US$106 million, merely a third of the price that the ad hoc commission had expected. It took the commission only four hours to decide upon rejection of the offer.

Secretary of the Privatization Commission, Agüero, pointed to three reasons for the lack of offers for Hondutel. Firstly, the number of interested companies had been exaggerated. Many of the companies had participated in the pre-qualification process in order to bid for the B band and not to participate in the capitalization process. Secondly, the monopoly rights could no longer compensate for the many obligations placed on the new owners, both in terms of investments and in terms of obligations towards labor. Thirdly, taking into account the investment requirements, the minimum price was too high.[30]

Less official sources argued that the government did not want Mexican investors. Moreover the negative reputation that Honduras had internationally with respect to the transparency of the bidding processes made the international companies less interested.[31]

In sum, Honduras had got no more than a half-way reform. And although there were talks about making new attempts at opening bids, the prospects worsened over the course of the following year due to decreasing interest by the main international telecommunication companies for investing in developing countries' telecommunication companies.

The process in Honduras illustrates both the limitation of conditionalities and the failure of the IFIs to transfer knowledge if there arc no counterparts with the ability and desire to be carriers of the new knowledge in the national context. In the following I will seek an answer to why neither pressure through conditionalities nor transfer of knowledge seemed to work in the intended manner in Honduras.

The Limitation of Conditionalities

The continuous postponements of the privatization of Hondutel occurred in spite of repeated threats from the IFIs to hold back funds if privatization was not implemented. Not only was privatization of Hondutel a conditionality for the disbursement of the third tranche of the PSMAP, it was also a conditionality for various IMF agreements. In this section I will ask how this could happen. As shown above, Honduras entered the 1990s in a critical financial situation. Between 1994 and 1998, Honduras's external debt position improved somewhat. Between 1994 and 1998 the Debt:GDP ratio fell from 111 per cent of GDP to 74 per cent, largely due to an agreement with the Paris Club. Nevertheless Honduras was one of the most heavily indebted countries in the Western Hemisphere (see Figure 5.1).

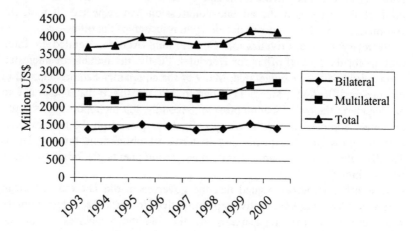

Source: Author's elaboration based on Memoria de Labores, Secretaria de Finanzas, Honduras, various issues.

Figure 5.1 Development of Honduras's external debt

Hondutel also faced increasing problems finding funds for investments. Due to the way the government handled the issue of capitalization an offer from IFC to invest in 20–25 per cent of the stocks, made in the mid-1990s, was also withdrawn. Moreover Mitch made Honduras even more dependent on international finance in order to pay for the estimated US$4 billion cost of reconstruction.[32] In the immediate aftermath of Mitch Honduras received disbursements worth US$506 million, but it was promised much more dependent on fulfillment of conditionalities (Secretaria de Finanzas 2000).

New debt rescheduling had been under way when Mitch struck in the autumn of 1998. The Honduran government had reached an agreement with the IMF for a Letter of Intent, and aimed for a new ESAF. This would also open the way for negotiations for restructuring of the US$1200 million debt with the Paris Club (*Reporte Político* No. 141 September 1998). Among the main conditionalities for this was privatization of Hondutel.

Moreover in March 1999, a US$200 million loan from the Poverty Reduction and Growth Facility (PRGF) of the IMF was approved for which privatization of Hondutel was a clear conditionality.

Finally, privatization of Hondutel was made a conditionality for the entering of Honduras into the Heavily Indebted Poor Countries Initiative (HIPC) in the autumn of 1999. Honduras had by then a total foreign debt of around US$4000 million, and with the entering into HIPC, up to 40 per cent was expected to be written off if all the stages of the HIPC process were completed.[33] On December 8 Honduras was declared eligible for HIPC, and it was to be reviewed for passage of the decision point that would take it to stage two of the HIPC process in June 2000. This decision point was conditional on: '(i) satisfactory progress under the new three-year PRGF arrangement; (ii) progress on key structural reforms, *particularly the privatization of the telecommunication company, Hondutel*; and (iii) satisfactory progress toward the completion of the Poverty Reduction Strategy Paper' (IMF 1999, p. 27, emphasis added). Privatization of Hondutel was seen as particularly important to the IFIs, not only because it was viewed as a necessary reform, but also because the government had dragged its feet for so long on this issue, and needed to demonstrate its willingness to reform through privatizing Hondutel. According to some IFI officials, it had come to be seen as a pivotal case, and put other reforms in the background.[34]

Thus the possible financial benefits for Honduras from privatizing Hondutel increased significantly, and so did the repercussions from failing to do so. Hondutel had become a test case on the government's willingness to pursue structural reform. Nevertheless Honduras did not speed up the process of selling the company. What can explain this failure to follow the recommended policy when there were such great financial repercussions from failing to do so? In order to understand this, we have to look at the interaction between the IFIs and the various domestic actors.

Firstly, the failure to comply on the part of the Honduran government can be understood as a series of instances of 'involuntary defections'. The congressional amendment requiring the government to seek Congress's approval for every step in the privatization process, limited the government's room for action significantly and contributed to many of the delays that hindered the government in fulfilling conditionalities. Due to their apolitical character, the IFIs are formally constrained from negotiating with Congress and have to relate primarily to the government. It is the government that signs contracts with the IFIs and it is the government that meets with the IFI missions from Washington, DC. However although the president in Honduras is powerful, that primarily means that no law proposal he is against will be passed; it does not mean that all the proposals he is in favor of will be passed. The stalemate this creates was expressed as follows by an IFI official based in Tegucigalpa:

> I do not know why we continue working this way. We make a deal with the executive power. The mission comes from Washington, puts the papers on the table: 'sign it here.' It returns happily to Washington, but nothing happens afterwards. The problem is that we have to involve the congress. This is a terrain that is strictly political, but we lack the ability to negotiate. We have to generate a different culture of negotiation, other skills, political concepts, a different paradigm of reform.[35]

The fear of Congress's reactions also contributed to the IFIs attempting to increase the perceived value of the company in order for Congress not to charge that the government was giving it away. In 1995, Price Waterhouse undertook an audit of the company from which it concluded that Hondutel was indeed no attractive investment. A note that circulated in March 1995 concluded that:

> Hondutel is currently mismanaged, highly leveraged and undergoing an over ambitious program of expansion which will likely lead the company to a potentially high risk situation ... Hondutel is becoming less and less attractive to potential investors, particularly foreign investors who understand the telecommunication business and would be acutely aware of the weaknesses of the enterprise.[36]

Among the further weaknesses listed were a debt schedule which cash flows could not compensate for, overstaffing, inaccurate accounting and distorted tariff structures. Furthermore, it is argued: 'Honduras today lacks a solid regulatory structure for its telecommunications sector and is not in a position to offer a reliable and clearly defined legal framework for foreign investment.' The conclusion was that one should lower the expectations about the price of the company.

The World Bank feared that a too-low price estimation would lead to opposition from Congress to the whole privatization process, and it argued that Price Waterhouse's evaluation was based on a series of outdated premises, particularly those related to investments and debt.[37] The World

Bank thus warned Rothschild that: 'The Government is concerned that a very pessimistic valuation of Hondutel may have a serious political impact in Congress, specially because of the recent events in El Salvador, where Congress turned down the privatization bill for similar reasons.'[38] In the end, the attempts to avoid causing reactions in the Congress contributed to the exaggerated expectations for the price to be obtained for the company. In turn this may have contributed to the lack of interest in buying it.

But while the IFIs were formally constrained from reaching across the two levels of the game, the local actors were not. Thus there were several examples that sub-level national actors attempted to use the IFIs to favor their positions. The most remarkable was the move made by Sitratelh to make the World Bank pressure the government to continue the process. The unions had ensured themselves a nice deal in the case that Hondutel would be privatized: they would be entitled to 2 per cent of the stocks in the company, 100 per cent of the benefits (for example pensions) they were entitled to while Hondutel was state-owned, and an annual bonus of 7000 lempiras for at least 20 years.[39] As the unions would get none of the extra benefits if privatization was not carried out, when the process seemed stalled in 1998, Sitratelh went to the World Bank to ask it to put pressure on the government in order to speed up the privatization process. As explained by one Sitratelh leader:

> When the whole process was stalled, after Mitch, we went to talk to the World Bank, the representative of the World Bank here, and we said: 'Señor, do something, pressure the government.' We told him that we wanted this to happen. We asked this person, a very accessible person. He said: 'It is not possible that the workers pressure for the process to move on!' And the whole world says this; that it is the government that pressures the workers. It is incredible! And finally they started and pressured again. [40]

A second reason for the IFIs' failure to use financial threats in order to secure compliance was that the threats might have lacked credibility. In spite of not having privatized Hondutel, Honduras passed the decision point for the HIPC in July 2000 and could thus start the second phase on the road towards debt relief. The justification for adjusting the criteria was that Honduras had made satisfactory overall progress. According to an IMF press release: 'Honduras has made substantial progress in implementing economic reforms over the past decade ... Honduras has also made a strong structural reform effort in recent years, including public sector modernization and financial liberalization' (IMF 2000, p. 1). This meant that Honduras would likely face a US$900 million cut in external debt.

With respect to the PSMAP, the conditionalities were also gradually waived. The second tranche of the PSMAP was originally dependent on the issuing of bids for capitalization of Hondutel. However due to the financial crisis following Mitch, the World Bank disbursed the second tranche with a waiver three weeks after the hurricane struck. In 1999, discussions about the disbursement of the third tranche of the PSMAP were undertaken and the main issue for discussion was privatization of Hondutel and reforms of the electricity sector. Although disbursement without capitalization of Hondutel was clearly not in accordance with the agreement, there was considerable eagerness to disburse in the World Bank. In the autumn of 1999, one high-level World Bank official guessed that the disbursement would be made in mid-2000 irrespective of whether Honduras had fulfilled all the conditionalities.[41] Finally, it was disbursed in mid-2001 – still without the privatization conditionality having been complied with.

Part of the reason for the World Bank's 'soft' disbursement practice may be found internally. When President Wolfensohn entered the World Bank, he conducted a review of the ongoing lending programs, and the Honduran PSMAP was given an award for being a comprehensive, 'new generation approach' to public sector modernization. This was in line with the new focus on state reform outlined for example in the World Bank report *The State in a Changing World* (World Bank 1997). Thus for the officials that worked on it, there was significant prestige involved in getting the program implemented and the funds disbursed.[42] Referring to the delays occurring in 1997–98, a World Bank official concluded: 'To be honest with you, we could not leave, even if the Hondurans didn't fulfill their targets. We had prepared the loan since 1994. We couldn't leave'.[43]

Moreover although the World Bank and the IDB at times postponed disbursements, they never cut off the contact with the Hondurans completely. As one World Bank official said upon being asked about whether it was frustrating to work with Honduras, experiencing such slow progress in terms of reforms: 'Yes, but there is so much demand here, we cannot stop working with Honduras.'[44]

A third reason for the inefficiency of the IFIs in pushing reform was that several IFI representatives were skeptical of the need for and efficiency of conditionalities. The processes of policy reform and the movement of funds were seen to some extent as separate processes. As expressed by one IDB official:

> What has never been clear to me is why the privatization of telecommunications in Honduras should require a 150 million dollar loan as an inducement. The telephone company was so unpopular anyway. The government could just have approached an investment bank and let them take care of it. To my understanding, relating Hondutel to the 150 million dollar loan, it is more actually, it is more like 210 all together, was rather a convenient way to move a lot of money into Honduras to repay the loans they already had. It was neither necessary nor efficient.[45]

Fourthly and finally, although there was general agreement among the IFI officials that something had to be done with the telecommunication sector, many of them showed little enthusiasm for privatization. As expressed by one Tegucigalpa-based official:

> We come to slim the state in a country where there is hardly a state. It is tiny, very weak. Instead of strengthening the state, we come to disarm it, where it hardly exists. There is no state, there is no sense of the common good, there is no community, no sense of the public. And we come to discredit the public. Some day, the people will understand it, and they are going to kill us.[46]

Thus understanding the Honduran reaction to the attempt to pressure them to privatize the telecommunication company must be understood with reference both to the source of the pressure and the object of it. While the Hondurans' motivation for conducting reform was questionable, also many IFI officials lacked the conviction or incentives to place strong pressure on the Hondurans. Moreover the nature of the 'two-level game' was such that compliance was hard to secure.

However it was not only the strategy of imposing changes through conditionalities that failed. Attempts at transferring knowledge or the creation of a domestic political group supporting telecommunication privatization also failed.

The Transfer and Transformation of Knowledge and the Sources of an Obsolete Reform

Whereas the IFIs had limited success with respect to pressuring the government to privatize, they were initially far more successful with respect to setting the agenda for telecommunication reform through the adoption of a new telecommunication legislation.

The work with the new telecommunication law started in the last years of the Callejas government. When the debate about telecommunication reform started in Honduras, the World Bank had already elaborated a detailed proposal. According to one high-level Honduran telecommunication expert: 'It was a done deal. When we started to discuss what to do to face challenges in the telecommunication sector, I was told, "we already have a draft from the World Bank.' There was nothing more to do.' [47]

The main initiative and the main ideas for the telecommunication legislation came from the World Bank's telecommunication expert, Eloy Vidal. Vidal wanted to ensure competition, but also to allow for exception to this in the cases where there were limitations in the radio spectrum or where the Government backed accelerated investment in order to extend services for the population. The argument for granting exclusivity was that it would be necessary in order to attract foreign investors to the sector and that it would mean more money for the Treasury. Moreover he argued that a five to ten-years exclusivity period was customary in Latin America, and that investors were used to it.[48]

The process of implementing the law and privatizing the company turned out to be much more prolonged than foreseen. In the process, the privatization framework that had been state-of-the-art in the mid-1990s, became more and more obsolete. By then, the name of the game was competition, not monopoly. Most large international telecommunication companies had switched strategy and were looking for possibilities for entering into markets as competitors to the incumbent carrier, not for possibilities for investing in old state-owned telecommunication companies. And where they wanted to invest, they would rather accept competition from day one, than take on responsibilities, for example extending services to rural areas. In spite of this, there was little willingness to change the requirements. In order to understand, there is again a need to take into account the dynamics between the IFIs and the domestic actors.

The power center of the privatization process was the Privatization Commission and its secretariat, headed by Mario Agüero, funded by the World Bank which also financed the investment bank (Rothschild). Rothschild and the World Bank largely agreed on the framework: Rothschild pushed for the bundling of assets and a long exclusivity period in order to maximize the fiscal revenue, whereas the World Bank expert favored exclusivity as a trade-off for obligations placed on the new company. Thus although they had different reasons for favoring privatization, the result was that there was little room for change.

The position of the privatization triangle – World Bank, privatization secretariat and investment bank – remained unchallenged, largely due to the lack of flexibility of the Honduran political system. As everybody knew that any change in the legislation would mean a prolonged negotiation process with a very uncertain outcome, not even the most eager proponents of market orientation of the Honduran economy dared utter such a proposal in fear of obstructing the fragile process.[49]

Thus the IFIs had some influence on the process due to its ideational power. As in the other countries, the IFIs did attempt to create local institutions with the capacity to formulate policy. Hondutel was generally known as being the company with the lowest level of expertise of the Central American telecommunication companies (with the exception of the Nicaraguan), and did not have the same kind of ability in terms of agenda setting as for example ICE. Furthermore Honduras had neither active, capable universities to give policy advice, nor active think-tanks.

In order to compensate for this, the USAID established the Unit for

Analysis of Economic Policy (UDAPE) in the mid-1990s on the model of a similar institution in Bolivia that had been key to a major policy reform.[50] After reorganization in 1997, in which the United Nations Development Program (UNDP), the World Bank and the IDB were added to the list of donors, the name was changed (to the Unit for Technical Analysis – UNAT). It received funding both for carrying out specific tasks and for increasing the technical capacity of the personnel. However UNAT was from the start a deeply political institution. In 1997, it changed from being a dependency of the Ministry of Finance, to being placed directly under the Ministry of the Presidency. This gave it more direct influence on the governmental policies, but it also increased its political nature. Thus although UNAT elaborated some policies related to the telecommunication sector after Mitch (Gobierno de Honduras 1999), it never played a major role in telecommunication reform.

The establishment of and support for Conatel initially had more impact on the domestic ability to formulate telecommunication reform. It was initially able to recruit a series of well-qualified people (mostly from Hondutel) and gained a reputation for a high degree of capacity. However the stalled reform process meant that few opportunities for telecommunication engineers were created in Honduras. For example after eight years of close to no investments in the sector in Honduras (it invested for example only US$12 million in 2000), equipment providers started to move their offices elsewhere in the region This had an effect on recruitment to the extent that only four students a year chose telecommunication engineering as a career at the university (Conatel 2001).

As a consequence, after the prolonged process of reform, there was a dearth of expertise in the country and few institutions that could provide good policy advice for the government and the national congress and contribute to a possible 'update' of the law.

Conclusion

After the failed privatization attempt, privatization of Hondutel was postponed to 2005, and there may be doubts that it will ever occur. In April 2003, Conatel awarded a PCS license to Megatel-Emce (a Swedish– Honduran consortium). Thus Celtel's monopoly was eventually challenged.

In spite of this, the conclusion that Honduras has experienced a slow, partial and largely unfinished reform process remains. The main reasons for this that I have pointed to are, firstly, the lack of domestic actors with a strong motivation to pursue privatization and liberalization of the telecommunication. Some private sector groups were interested in purchasing the company, and a small group even favored privatization for ideological reasons. However they were not significant enough to provide a strong force backing privatization. Secondly, there was a scarcity of institutions with the necessary expertise that could promote ideas supporting a market orientation of the economy.

This also limited the influence of the IFIs. The alliance made between Rothschild, the World Bank and the Privatization Secretariat may be identified as the main force behind the reforms, but they failed in enrolling significant domestic groups into their project. This also limited the success of the use of the other means of influence that IFIs had: the use of conditionalities and transfer of knowledge.

At the end of the day therefore some historical patterns seemed to re-emerge in the process to reform the telecommunication sector in Honduras. For a government in a state as dependent on foreign resources as the Honduran one is, it is difficult not to pay attention to the demands of foreign actors, be it banana companies or international financial institutions. Nevertheless the outcome of political processes is primarily dependent upon the domestic political game, in which competition between different elites plays an important part. In a country with such scarce resources, as observed by Posas and Del Cid (1983), the control of the state activity had become one of the primary sources of wealth and privileges. This remained true also when the state activities were about to be transferred to the private sector.

Thus the government played its game on two levels, and the domestic one got most attention. With regards to the handling of the demands from the IFIs, the strategy to resist foreign intrusion in colonial times seems to have been followed also here: '*obedezco pero no cumplo*' (I obey but I don't comply).

NOTES

1. Due to failure to pay the debt, it also led the British to shell a Honduran port in 1872 (Krasner 1999).
2. As the groups and coalitions forming the parties were changing, the dating of their establishment depends on what definition one uses. Stokes (1950) dates the Liberal Party establishment to 1891 and the formal establishment of the National Party to 1923.
3. Servicio Técnico Interamericano de Cooperación Agrícola.
4. Interview, Victor Urquidi, former director of the Mexico office of ECLA, 18 June 2000.
5. They used mostly imported material for the production, and they established few links to local businesses. There are some exceptions to this, for example the close relationship between San Pedro Sula's business community and Cuyamel's (later UFCO's) Sam Zamurray 'the banana man' (Euraque 1992).
6. See for example Sieder (1995) for a review of the arguments. The literature emphasizes two main links between the land reform and lack of insurgency. One is that it had a co-optive and counter-revolutionary impact on *campesino* movements, and that it was important symbolically because it demonstrated the reformist potential of the Honduran government

(Ruhl 1984). The other is that the reform process transformed the clientilist networks enabling it to absorb popular movements.

7. The scandal called 'bananagate' started when Eli Black, Chairman of United Brands, committed suicide by jumping out of his window in Manhattan. The investigation revealed that United Brands had paid a Honduran official US$1.25 million as the initial installment of a US$2.25 million bribe to gain relief from an export tax on bananas. There were allegations that López Arrellano himself had been involved. However López's involvement has never been proven.

8. See Schulz and Sundloff Schulz (1994), Peckenham and Street (1985), Lapper (1985).

9. According to a poll, a majority of Honduras perceived this to be the real power relations in Honduras as late as 1995. The majority was of the opinion that the American ambassador was the most powerful person in the country, followed by the Chief of the Armed Forces with the president as number three (*El Heraldo* Honduras, 13 September 1995).

10. Interviews with ex-Hondutel workers.

11. Interview with Mario Maldonado Muñóz, ex-general and Hondutel manager 1994–96, 24 November 1999.

12. Interview with former USAID officials in Honduras.

13. FIDE (Foundation for Business Research and Development), Feproexah (Federatio of Agricultural Producers and Exporters of Honduras), Gemah (Managers, Businessmen and Administrators of Honduras), the Honduran-American Chamber of Commerce, and a tiny organization called Fudeh (National Development Association of Honduras). In addition, the Anexhon (Association of Honduran Exporters) benefited considerably from USAID encouragement and Financing.

14. By December, external arrears to all creditors amounted to about 15.5 per cent of GDP.

15. The shares were sold at a price of 110.6 lempiras (US$20.4 million), with 40 million lempiras (US$8.4 million) paid up front. The remainder of the sum was according to the agreement to be paid by the transfer of foreign debts. However a year after, the IPM had not paid the debt. The liquidating board signed an agreement with the IPM to pay the remaining 70.6 million lempiras (US$12 million) over 15 years with an interest rate of 7 per cent, at a point when the bank rate was 24 per cent (Posas 1995; Brenes and Casas 1998, pp. 5–9; *Inforpress* 12 July 1991).

16. This section is based primarily on interviews with private sector representatives, former members of the Hondutel management, and external advisors.

17. Celtel paid US$5 million for the concession. In addition it was to pay 8 per cent of the gross income to the government, and a fee of US$7 per line in operation up to 28 000 lines which was the development target. Initially, the government intended to oblige Celtel to invest 5 per cent of the profits in rural areas, but this was not enforced. There is moreover a system where the holders of the mobile phones pay the additional costs of completing the call in the mobile network (receiving party pays), thus increasing the charges of mobile telephony. On the other hand, Celtel is entitled to 23 cents of the 30 cents that fixed telephony subscribers are charged for calling to a mobile phone. Thus Celtel is able to profit both from the fixed telephone subscribers and from the mobile telephone subscribers. Indeed, the main source of income for Celtel is, according to Comtelca, the share of the revenue from fixed-to-mobile calls. Interview with Comtelca's general manager.

18. Interview, senior telecommunication expert, 29 August 2001.

19. Fax from Siemens to IMF, 6 November 1995.

20. There are several anecdotes illustrating Reina's limited understanding of the telecommunication business. One of his former aides told the following story: 'When Reina got to power he called me to get advice. In the first meeting, I presented some plans to him that we had been working on how to develop the sector. Reina liked the plans, and he said, you should present them to the board [of Hondutel]. However he said, Hondutel is going to be sold to the Englishmen. I asked, who? He said, to Rothschild [laughter]. It was a done deal, you see. All Reina knew was that Rothschild would make some money from it' (Interview, senior telecommunication expert, 29 August 2001).

21. He was the leader of the National Agrarian Institute during the second part of the Arellano López regime (1972–75) when he was leading the land reform campaign.
22. Interview with author, 24 November, 1999.
23. This is primarily based on interviews. Some documentation of the clientilistic practices of Hondutel personnel exist in Salomón et al. (1996).
24. This is based on various interviews with high- and medium-level managers and ex-managers of Hondutel.
25. It was approved of on October 1995 and entered into effect in December (Decree 185-95, published in *La Gaceta* 5 December 1995.
26. Interview, IFI official, 25 November 1999.
27. Slang for US citizen.
28. The total number of deaths in Central America was approximately 11 000.
29. These were Telmex, France Telecom, Videsh Snahcar Nigam Limited from India, Avantel from Mexico, Entel from Chile, Global Crossing from the United States and Telefónica Internacional de España.
30. Interview, Mario Agüero, 4 September 2001.
31. This was partly due to the difficult process of concessioning the A band in the mid-1990s and the Siemens/AT&T corruption scandal.
32. This was the official number that the government used. It was twice as much as the costs that were estimated in a workshop where input from all the ministries were discussed and analyzed in cooperation between the government and the donor community.
33. Honduras failed to qualify in the initial round of admission to the HIPC starting in 1996. However after Mitch, discussions were opened again. This was partly because Honduras's situation had been aggravated, and partly because the criteria for eligibility for HIPC changed in September 1999. The new criteria lowered the debt:GDP ratios and debt:export value ratios required to be eligible.
34. Interviews, IMF and World Bank officials.
35. Interview, 4 September 2001.
36. Status report on Hondutel, restricted distribution, March 1995, sent from Price Waterhouse to the USAID mission in Honduras.
37. The World Bank argued that Price Waterhouse's estimation of required investments (US$225 million in new infrastructure within a 3 year time frame) were exaggerated and that US$40 million would suffice. Furthermore Price Waterhouse had assumed that the new company take over US$158 million of Hondutel's debt, whereas the rest of the debt (about US$68) million was Paris Club debt which would remain in the government because the government would have a better chance for rescheduling this debt and obtaining a discount than would a new company. The World Bank argued that any new company would renegotiate the conditions of the current debt, which was that it had to be repaid over a four-year period with an interest of near 27 per cent.
38. Internal communication, World Bank-IDB.
39. This was the final agreement achieved after Sitratelh, among other measures, had gone on strike when the first privatization decree had been passed in Congress. The reason was that the Hondutel workers had been lumped together with other groups to fight for 4 per cent of the stocks, whereas they argued that they were entitled to 2 per cent by themselves.
40. Interview, technical advisor, Sitratelh, 5 September 2001.
41. Interview, high-level official, 24 September 1999.
42. Interviews, World Bank officials, February 1998 and October 1999.
43. Interview, 9 February 1998.
44. Interview, 25 November 1999.
45. Interview, 30 August 2001.
46. Interview, 4 September 2001.
47. Interview, 29 August 2001.
48. Various internal communication notes, World Bank-IDB October 1995.
49. Interview, private sector leader, 24 November 1999.
50. Interview, USAID consultant, 3 December 1999.

6. Comparisons and Conclusions: Privatization, Development and Legitimacy

Privatization, deregulation and re-regulation of the telecommunication sector have brought changes at many levels to the Central American countries. In this final chapter I will first compare the cases and conclude with regard to the question of why the different countries adopted or rejected reforms aimed at market-orienting the respective telecommunication sectors. Related to that, I discuss the role of the IFIs. Furthermore I will discuss whether we see the emergence of a regulatory state in Central America by comparing the regulatory frameworks that have resulted from the reforms (or the lack of such). Subsequently I turn to the question of why privatization remains so unpopular in Central America, focusing first on outcomes in terms of price, availability and quality of services, but also on how the privatization processes have affected the legitimacy of the state, the regime and the political elites.

THE SOURCES OF REFORM

Private Sector Strategies and Competing Elites

The cases discussed above show one thing clearly: politicians have not adopted telecommunication reforms, including privatization and regulatory reforms, purely in order to ensure a more efficient production of services. There may be many motives, including fiscal motives and a desire to improve the relationship with foreign creditors.

However where privatization has been pursued there have in addition been political motives. Privatization has been a means to weaken or strengthen either private sector elites, military elites or state elites.

The state-owned telecommunication companies were not only companies. As shown above, they have been important institutions in nation and state building. The states that they have contributed to building have ranged from coercive military dictatorships (as in Guatemala) to welfare states (as may

169

describe several aspects of the Costa Rican state). Moreover they have evolved as institutions and political actors whether they have been controlled by the military (as in Honduras) or developed as separate sub-cultures (as in Costa Rica). Thus they have also become parties in political elite competition, and weakening or strengthening them has been an important motivation for privatization. In Honduras for example, President Carlos Roberto Reina wanted to privatize Hondutel in order to weaken the military. In Costa Rica, many reform proposals emerged out of the power contest between ICE and the central government.

However equally important have been attempts to weaken or strengthen the private sector elites. Throughout the case studies, the private sector has been identified as a main force behind the reforms. The local private sector has contributed with policy ideas (as was the case with the development of the Telecommunication Law in Guatemala), it has put pressure on the government to divest the SOT, or to open the sector to private investments in order to secure rents from it. The governments have reacted differently to private sector pressure depending on the state in question; in Guatemala which I have called a captured state, private sector pressure has been of great impact. Thus privatization attempts that were intended to weaken domestic private sector elites (during the government of Vinicio Cerezo) failed, whereas the form of privatization that was finally conducted generously benefited parts of the private sector elites. In Costa Rica and Honduras although the private sector were eager proponents of privatization, they were not able to dictate policy to the same extent as in Guatemala.

Policy diffusion, policy learning and policy emulation have been discussed as important mechanisms for understanding the global drive towards privatization and regulatory reform. However the lesson that can be drawn from this comparative case study is that such mechanisms can not fully explain the outcomes in the different cases. Although diffusion, learning and emulation are important, and ideas and knowledge travel across borders, we also see that ideas are rejected and/or adapted to the interests of local political and economic elites. One example is the ideas of Pablo Spiller that were embraced by the private sector-dominated Guatemalan government, and the liberal think-tanks that were its advisers, whereas the group that attempted to introduce them to Costa Rica got little support. At the same time, in Guatemala the liberal Spiller model was adapted to suit the government's fiscal concerns and private sector aims of becoming players in the local telecommunication industry.

Rather than a homogenization of economic policies and processes, we see the emergence of various hybrid models (Christensen and Lægreid 2001). These are persistent features of policy making and economic organization, rather than features of former models that are in the process of being eliminated. Using the concept of 'hybridity' means that we do not attempt to pass judgments about the degree to which some models 'fit' with an ideal. Rather, the goal is to understand the origins of different elements of a form of policy. These may be well suited or not so well suited to overcome the specific issues that have hampered transformative processes in specific contexts.

What forms such hybrids take, depend on the constellation of political and economic elites and the relationships between them. Changes in the global telecommunication industry changed the equation with regard to possible benefits from gaining control over the telecommunication industry. The primary effect was that it made private sector groups more interested in gaining a share in the business. While some groups connected to the private sector had been interested in privatization for a long time for ideological reasons (as was the case with CEES in Guatemala), they attained little influence until other private sector groups saw it as a business opportunity.

A further lesson to be drawn is that political and legal institutions are not unimportant, but the degree to which they define the rules of the game varies across the cases. In a highly institutionalized democracy such as Costa Rica, institutions have defined who were the legitimate political players (that included business, unions and other parts of the civil society), and the limits of action (defined in the constitution). In contrast, in the case of Guatemala, formal institutional rules and legal procedures have constituted some challenges to the reformers, but not much more than what good lawyers could take care of.

In sum, the most important element in an explanation for why privatization has been adopted in some countries and not in others and why the specific regulatory models differ across countries, I have found to be the strategies of competing elites, particularly the private sector elites. The strength of different elites (private sector, state elites and military elites) depends on the development of the state in question, its degree of autonomy and legitimacy.

This means that the commonly held opinion that privatization policies are attributable to the pressure from international financial institutions, must be modified. However it should not be rejected outright. In the following, I will discuss the influence of the IFIs.

The Role of the International Financial Institutions

This study largely confirms the conclusions of the literature referred to in Chapter 1: that the attempts by IFIs to forge policy change through the use of conditionalities are largely inefficient. In the cases above, the IFIs were active to different extents. In the case of Honduras, privatization of telecommunications was a conditionality, not only for a structural adjustment program, but also for various agreements with the IMF, and finally for large-scale debt reduction under the HIPC initiative. In spite of this, although a new legislative framework for the telecommunication sector was adopted, the company was never privatized. In Guatemala, the government initially attempted to get support from the World Bank for privatization of telecommunications, but the World Bank refused. When privatization of telecommunications finally appeared as a conditionality for an IDB loan, the deal was already done. In Costa Rica, none of the IFIs risked including privatization of telecommunications as a conditionality for a loan, for fear of getting involved in a protracted disbursement process.

The reasons for lack of efficiency of conditionality are many. We have seen incidents of involuntary defection (as in the case of Honduras and Costa Rica) and a lack of credibility on the part of the IFIs (as in the case of Honduras). The IFIs have lacked credibility because they have repeatedly shown that although a lack of fulfillment of conditionalities would mean a temporary cut-off from support, new funds would soon be offered. Furthermore not even the IFI officials have always been convinced of the virtues of pressuring the governments through the use of conditionalities.

Related to the argument about learning above, the study also gives little support for the thesis that the IFIs are effective 'teachers' of policy. Their efficiency as teachers has been shown to depend on the prior attitudes of the 'pupils'. The national policy makers choose what consultants they want to hire (as was the case when the El Salvadoran and Guatemalan policy makers picked Spiller as a consultant over others with alternative ideas). Moreover while in some cases the IFIs may give some ideas credibility over others, in other cases the very association of some ideas with the IFIs may reduce their credibility. This was the case in such different instances as the Guatemalan Liberals' rejection of proposals to privatize electricity because they were associated with the World Bank, and the Costa Rican opposition's rejection of the government's privatization proposal because it was associated with the USAID and the IFIs.

A further element that weakens the effect of 'teaching' by the IFIs is the fact that they constantly change their ideas. In much of the critical literature, the IFIs are viewed as homogenous institutions that persistently have advocated neo-liberalism. However scrutinizing their ideas and policies in a longer time perspective, it appears that they continuously change ideas about what are the best policies. As argued by an experienced Honduran politician:

In Latin America, [the IFIs] were the great supporters of the politics of import substitution. They were thinking in terms of economic nationalism; that the state should control the organizations, the grand enterprises, the basic telecommunications, mines and all that. Afterwards they changed their attitude. And many of the people that came here, they came to preach something, and soon they came back and preached the contrary. Thus the most important effect of their policies is that they have created a great confusion. I remember the times of MacNamara in the World Bank – then the issue was the poorest of the poor. The same in the IDB, the same in what they call the non-financial organizations, such as CEPAL. CEPAL was pursuing very nationalistic policies until a few years ago. And then they changed everything fundamentally. Thus as an economist and politician, one does not understand how to go on.[1]

Arguing that the IFIs have limited influence based on relational and ideational power, does not mean that they have not had influence over national policy making. Their strongest influence has been through weakening some elites and strengthening others. There are two mechanisms through which that has happened. Firstly, cutting off funds from the SOTs and other state institutions starting in the mid-1980s, significantly weakened the SOTs. Subsequently it weakened the groups that had evolved around the state institutions over the course of the post-war period. As seen primarily in the case of Costa Rica, the changing policy of the IFIs weakened ICE both as a service provider and as a political actor. Furthermore it ensured stronger executive control over it, a matter that may have contributed to improved checks and balances, but also to increased politicization.

Secondly, the IFIs and the USAID strengthened private sector groups as political actors. This happened through conscious strategies of strengthening the organizational and policy making capacity of private sector groups, and strengthening private sector-dominated think-tanks and policy institutions. Although not always successful, this contributed to the creation of a constituency for the market-oriented reforms.

The process of transformation of reform that occurred along with the transfer of knowledge produced a series of hybrid telecommunication models; hybrids between internationally circulating ideas about the proper telecommunication frameworks, and interests and ideas of competing domestic elites. In the following, I will discuss the nature of these resulting reforms and the degree to which they constitute a regulatory state in the telecommunication sector. I will also discuss the outcome of the reforms in terms of a few indicators of telecommunication sector performance.

THE OUTCOME OF REFORMS

Telecommunication Models in Central America Compared: Towards a Regulatory State?

In order to describe the different reforms and their outcome, in this section I will broaden the perspective a bit and also include El Salvador and Nicaragua. There were three different international models that were the starting point for reforms in Central America: a traditional Latin American telecommunication reform model in Nicaragua and Honduras, a 'European-style' telecommunication reform in Costa Rica and a radically competitive model discussed in Guatemala and El Salvador. They differ along three main dimensions: (1) degree of privatization, (2) degree of competition, and (3) the existence of an independent regulatory agency (IRA). However during the process of implementation the models were transformed into national hybrids.

The Guatemalan/El Salvadoran model is the most competitive one. In both countries, operation was privatized through divestiture of the state-owned company, and radio frequencies were handed over to the private sector through the sale of 'Use Entitlements', signifying that they were almost to be considered private property. A separate regulatory agency was created and competition was intended to be introduced in all parts of the telecommunication services. In reality, the models have functioned differently in the two countries. In Guatemala, the regulatory agency, the SIT, was created as a dependency of the Ministry of Communications, whereas the El Salvadoran regulatory agency, the General Superintendent for Electricity and Telecommunications (SIGET), was given administrative and financial autonomy. Furthermore in El Salvador competition on fixed telephony was ensured from day one through an innovative system of dividing the fixed network in two. In Guatemala, Telgua used several different means to avoid competition both in mobile and fixed line telephony and was successful for a while. It pressured the regulatory agency, the SIT, to postpone auctions of personal communication service (PCS) bands, and obscured and postponed interconnection to competitors both on cellular and fixed services. In spite of Telgua's best efforts to avoid it, there gradually emerged significant competition on mobile services,[2] but there is still limited competition on fixed-line services.

The Honduran/Nicaraguan model is less competitive and the SOT remains in a stronger position than in the Guatemalan/Salvadoran model. The main feature is that the incumbent carrier is sold within a fixed monopoly period but often also with obligations to invest in expansion and improvement of the telecommunication infrastructure. Due to the failure of divesting Hondutel, in Honduras at the end of 2004 there was still a state-owned company operating with de facto monopoly on all services except mobile services. The radio spectrum is considered state property, but is to be utilized by private operators through concessions. The mobile monopoly was finally broken in 2004, but it is too early to see the consequences of that. The regulatory agency, Conatel, was originally organized as a 'de-concentrated' entity of the Ministry of Communications, Public Works and Transport with formal technical, administrative and budgetary independence. This independence was always more formal than real, as Conatel was budgetarily dependent on the Ministry of Finance, and three representatives on its board (the commissioners) were appointed by the president. A reform of 1997 further curbed the autonomy by moving Conatel to the Ministry of Governance, directly under the President of the Republic. In spite of this, Conatel has gained a reputation for operating with a degree of autonomy from the central government.

The Nicaraguan model has a lot in common with the Honduran model. The regulatory and operational functions were separated at an early stage (into Telcor regulating the sector and Enitel operating the sector). Moreover a cellular concession was early on given to a private operator, but repeated attempts to privatize the company failed due to various political problems until 2001 when 40 per cent of Enitel was sold to the Swedish–Honduran consortium Telia.[3] Although there are plans for increased competition, currently Enitel has a monopoly on fixed-line services, and the mobile market is divided between Bell South and Enitel.

At the end of the spectrum we find Costa Rica. After the constitutional court had found Combo-ICE unconstitutional, the Mixed Commission elaborated a plan to strengthen ICE through an ambitious investment plan that among other goals would enable ICE to cut down on the waiting lists for fixed and mobile telephony.[4] However the mixed commission did not reach agreement with regards to competition, and the private sector fiercely resisted the plan. In 2004, an agreement was reached about very limited opening for competition, first on private networks and internet services, and later (in 2007) on mobile services. The regulatory agency ARESEP is formally autonomous, but it often becomes the weaker part in relation to the state-owned company (ICE).

In sum, whether we see the development of a regulatory state in the telecommunication industry in Central America is still rather unclear. Although there are formally autonomous regulatory institutions established in many cases, their real autonomy is often challenged. However it is not always the case that it is challenged by representatives of transnational capital, as authors describing the current development as a transnationalization of the state would argue (Robinson 2003). Rather, both transnational elites and traditional national economic and political elites challenge the autonomy of the regulatory institutions.

Telecommunication reform may impact on the emergence of a regulatory state in yet another manner. A regulatory state is not only dependent on the existence of formally autonomous regulatory institutions. Its capacity to regulate also depends on its financial basis. Privatization was launched as a strategy for improving the state finances through extraction of the privatization proceeds. But what happened? We only have one case to draw lessons from here, namely Guatemala. In Guatemala, one of the main explicit intentions of the divestiture of Guatel/Telgua was to strengthen the state financially by reducing the fiscal deficit. This would contribute to making the large social investments needed after the end of the civil war (World Bank 2000). However that was far from what happened. The fact that Luca SA had made a deal with Telgua to pay for the company in tranches meant that the immediate effect on the fiscal deficit was minimal. In the end, Banco de Guatemala only received US$72 million, as US$120 million went to payment of the loan that Guatel had made with the Hamilton Bank, and another US$8 million was used to pay various debts that Guatel had with internal banks. The total dollar receipts received by the Bank of Guatemala in the telecommunication sector were for 1998, US$72 million from the first installation for Telgua, in 1999, US$32.7 million from Telefónica de España and US$33.4 million from Bell South for the purchase of frequencies, between 1999 and 2000, US$218 million from the second installment for Telgua. By the end of 2000, the Guatemalan state had received a total of US$416 million from investments in the telecommunication sector, which was much less than expected.[5]

However there were further effects of the sale. Before the final sale of Telgua, the banking sector in Guatemala had shown clear signs of instability. When the sale of Telgua was finally declared, the Central Bank recommended that part of the payment should be made in the local currency, quetzals, in order to avoid an increase in the demand for dollars, which in turn would cause a pressure on the exchange rate. This did not happen, and as US$136 million of the required downpayment by local investors was purchased in the domestic foreign exchange market, it generated pressure on the quetzal in late 1998. The Bank of Guatemala heavily supported the quetzal by selling more than US$688 million – more than the total proceeds from the privatization program (World Bank 2000). This led the President of the Central Bank to call the transaction 'the Financial Mitch',[6] leaving the Guatemalan banks with a severe shortage of foreign exchange. Thus the fiscal gains for the Guatemalan state from selling Telgua were meager, and it is difficult to argue that the state came out of the process strengthened. This could perhaps be forgiven if the provision of telecommunication services improved. But did it?

The Development of Telecommunication Services

There is a range of different measures of the success of a telecommunication reform. In the following I will only review a few in order to give a glimpse of the actual changes that occurred: (1) extension of services, (2) tariffs, and (3) quality in order to shed light on that.

Regarding extension of services, this is commonly measured in teledensity (number of lines in operation per 100 innhabitants). The conclusion that can be drawn from Central America is that the countries that have privatized have not experienced any major growth in number of fixed lines, but the number of cellular lines has boomed. Costa Rica has had higher growth rate in fixed lines between 1998 and 2002 than Guatemala and El Salvador although there has been no growth between 2000 and 2002.[7] Consequently Costa Rica still has a major lead compared to its neighboring countries regarding fixed line teledensity (see Figures 6.1 and 6.2).

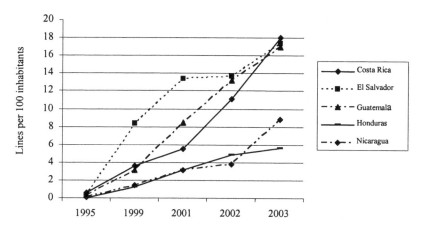

Source: Data from ARESEP, CONATEL, ITU, SIGET, SIT, and Telcor.

Figure 6.1 Mobile lines per 100 inhabitants

Development of mobile services shows a quite different pattern. In 1999 only one year after the respective mobile sectors had been opened for

competition in El Salvador, it surpassed Costa Rica in terms of the number of
lines in operation per inhabitant. By 2001 El Salvador had more than twice as
many mobile subscribers per inhabitant as Costa Rica. Moreover in both El
Salvador and Guatemala, the number of mobile subscribers had surpassed the
number of subscribers to fixed line services.[8] However after 2002, the
development slowed down in El Salvador, whereas growth continued in
Costa Rica and Guatemala. By 2003, the three countries were close to equal
with respect to numbers of cellular lines in operation per 100 inhabitants.
Honduras and Nicaragua shared the last place here also, although Nicaragua
experienced a rapid growth of mobile lines per 100 inhabitants after 2002.

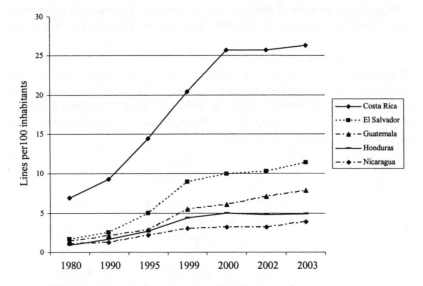

Source: Data from ARESEP, CONATEL, ITU, SIGET, SIT and Telcor

Figure 6.2 Fixed lines per 100 inhabitants

A further key aspect in the availability of services is whether they are
affordable to the majority of the population, here measured by the cheapest
prices offered by the dominant company.[9] With regards to fixed-line
telephony, three things have happened: Firstly, in the countries that have
privatized the prices of local calls have increased, whereas in the other
countries, they have dropped.[10] This reflects the rebalancing of tariffs that
normally takes place before a privatization. Note that Table 6.1 does not give
an entirely correct picture with regards to local telephony as El Salvador had
already rebalanced at this point. The number given for Guatemala is more

representative of what often happens related to a privatization process, although a similar process did not occur in Honduras in the process of preparing the company for sale. Local calls are most expensive in the country with a private monopoly, Nicaragua. Secondly, monthly subscription rates have increased in the countries that have privatized. Here a similar pattern emerges to the one we have seen on local calls; prices have increased most in Guatemala and El Salvador (again note that the main price increase occurred before 1998 in El Salvador), but also significantly in Nicaragua. There is a small increase in Honduras but a decline in Costa Rica.

Finally, with regards to international calls, prices have dropped significantly in three cases: El Salvador, Guatemala and Costa Rica. El Salvador can offer the cheapest international telephony in the region, but Costa Rica is not far behind Guatemala. Honduras and Nicaragua still remains expensive.

Table 6.1 Fixed-line tariffs in Central America, 1998–2003, US$[a]

	Monthly subscription		Minutes included[b] (local calls)		Per minute local		Per minute to USA	
	1998	2003	1998	2003	1998	2003	1998	2003
Costa Rica	4.3	3.65	150	0	0.030	0.012	1.06	0.45
El Salvador	6.8	8.2	0	0	0.060	0.023	0.8	0.22
Guatemala	0.7[c]	5.6	600	200	0.0009	0.026	--	0.40
Honduras	1.5	2.28	200	200	0.06	0.020	--	0.84
Nicaragua	6.4	12	--	25	0.11	0.30	--	1.0

Notes:
a. Cheapest price offered by main operator.
b. In monthly subscription
c. This is the number used by the ITU. In fact the price increase had occurred before 1998 (February 1997).

Source: Data from ARESEP, CONATEL, ITU, SIGET, SIT and Telcor.

Also with respect to cellular lines, there have been major tariff cuts in all countries. The most dramatic tariff cuts have occurred in El Salvador and Guatemala. However Costa Rica still offers the cheapest cellular services in the region. A third aspect of performance is efficiency, measured by the reduction of waiting lists and lines per employee. According to the ITU, privatization tends to reduce waiting lists and increase number of lines per employee. This holds for Central America if we compare El Salvador and Guatemala to Honduras (insufficient data is available on Nicaragua). In

Honduras, the waiting list for getting a phone line installed was more than ten years in 1996, and waiting lists were not reduced by 1999. There is also a more than ten-year wait for getting a cellular phone (Conatel 2001). In the same period, waiting lists were reduced in El Salvador from five years to seven months and in Guatemala from four to two years. Numbers are not available for the period after this, but there is reason to believe that waiting lists have decreased further. However ICE also reduced waiting lists in the same period, from ten to eight months for installation of a fixed line, and by 2003 the waiting list for cellular phones was finally eradicated (ITU 2000, Raventos 1997, ARESEP 2003). Nevertheless there were still 13 637 people on a waiting list to get a fixed line installed. With respect to efficiency, ICE still had more lines per employee than the privatized Telgua in 2000 (179 versus 147), but Telgua had experienced a more rapid increase. In 1995, Guatel had only 39 lines per employee, while ICE at the same point had 106 (ESA Consultores 2001).

Table 6.2 Cellular tariffs in Central America,1995–2003, US$*

	Monthly payment		Per minute	
	1995	2003	1995	2003
Costa Rica	16.7	6.4	0.19	0.07
El Salvador	35.8		0.35	0.12
Guatemala	27.1		0.33	
Honduras	n.a.	25	n.a.	0.25
Nicaragua	41.6	12	0.62	0.48

Note: *Lowest prices offered by main operator on monthly subsription basis.

Source: Data from ARESEP, CONATEL, ITU, SIGET, SIT and Telcor.

In sum, privatization and liberalization have brought unquestionable benefits only with respect to the density of mobile phones in central areas and tariffs on mobile services and international telephony. It is highly unlikely that El Salvador and Guatemala would have been able to leap forward on these indicators had it not been for the introduction of competition and the privatization of the state-owned companies in 1998. However of these two elements, it is competition that has been the most important. As we have seen, Nicaragua and Honduras also have private operators of mobile telephony, and Nicaragua has a private fixed-line company, a matter which has not saved them from sharing the last place in the ranking of the five countries, in terms of both density and tariffs.

A further conclusion that emerges from the comparison between the different countries is that privatization is not the only way to provide reasonable and extensive services. Guatemala and El Salvador still do not beat Costa Rica on most services. That does not mean that privatization has not been beneficial for them, only that a public company may also provide good service, if given satisfactory operating conditions. This conclusion also holds if we take into account the effect of GDP per capita. As shown by Raventós (2001), Costa Rica has a much higher teledensity than what we would expect from its income level, whereas the rest of Central America has roughly the average teledensity for their income level.

To the question posed in Chapter 1 of whether market-oriented reforms could be a way in which human agency could defeat the structural constraints that history had produced, we can therefore answer both yes and no. There is a certain degree of 'path dependence' as the countries that had the strongest private sector and weakest state also got the reform that left the state in the weakest position and gave most room for the private sector. However it will be for the future to judge whether under this model one will be able to provide reasonably priced telecommunication services for all. If that is the case, we may conclude that a transformation of one sector at least has occurred although underlying structures have changed little. However as will be discussed in the following, it is unlikely that cheap mobile bills will appease the public, which according to polls is deeply concerned about the lack of justice in the current political-economic model.

TELECOMMUNICATION PRIVATIZATION AND LEGITIMACY

Irrespective of the benefits that privatization has brought to Guatemala and El Salvador, privatization remains highly unpopular all over Central America. Although we have no polling data on the Central American public's view of the telecommunication reform processes in particular, we have data on their view of privatization in general. As mentioned in Chapter 1, in Guatemala 98 per cent of the population said that they were unsatisfied with the privatization of public services in 2004, which is the highest percentage in all of Latin America. In Honduras, the corresponding number was 80 per cent, in Nicaragua 79 per cent and El Salvador 78 per cent. (Due to the lack of privatizations in Costa Rica, the question about privatization has not been included in the Latinobarómetro survey there. However there was included a question of whether people were satisfied with the market economy in 2003, to which only 17 per cent of the Costa Ricans said yes.) In all countries, there is a clear downward tendency in the support for privatization. In 1998, 68 per

cent of the Guatemalans said they were satisfied with privatization, the
number dropped to 29 per cent in 2002, 16 per cent in 2003 and 2 per cent in
2004. A similar, although not as steep, curve is found in the other countries
(see Figure 6.3).

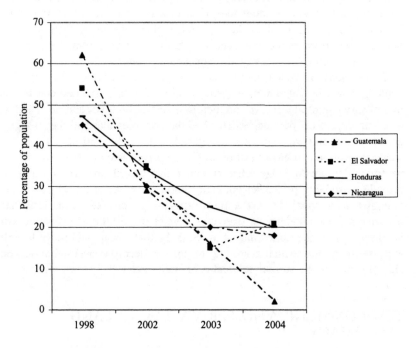

Note: The question changed slightly between 2003 and 2004. The numbers for 1998, 2002, and
2003 reflect the numbers of people answering 'I agree' or 'I strongly agree' to the
question: 'Do you agree that the privatizations have been beneficial for the country?' In
2004, the question had changed to: 'Many public services (water, electricity, etc.) have
been privatized. Taking into account the price and quality, are you today much more
satisfied, more satisfied, less satisfied or much less satisfied with the public services?'
and the numbers reflect the people choosing the first two categories.

Source: Data from Latinobarómetro.

Figure 6.3 Satisfaction with privatization in Central America

The preceding chapters have aimed to give a background for
understanding why this is the case. In the following I will discuss the
processes of reform related to the different concepts of legitimacy outlined in
Chapter 2.

Democratic Legitimacy: Transparency and Participation

One of the most persistent critiques against the privatization processes in Latin America has been that they were conducted behind closed doors, and have failed to include civil society and labor. In the analysis above, I have only given significant space to civil society and labor in the case of Costa Rica, where they indeed played an important role in the process of reform (or lack of such). The lack of inclusion in the other cases reflects the lack of influence they have had on the process of reform, which has been due both to a lack of responsiveness on the part of the political elites, but also to their lack of mobilization.

In Guatemala, the whole process of telecommunication reform was characterized by a lack of participation and transparency. Neither labor unions nor civil society groups participated to any significant extent in the process. However there were two attempts to include these groups. The first one was an attempt by the government to include popular sectors in the work with state modernization. As a consequence of increasing public opposition against privatization, the presidential commission for modernization of the state of the Arzù government invited various groups from the civil society and the political parties to participate in a series of meetings with the aim of informing, discussing and reaching a consensus on issues of importance in the state reform process (Presidencia de la República de Guatemala 1997, pp. 228–29). However as early as the first meeting (20 May), the differences between the parties surfaced. The main issue of disagreement was whether to include privatization in the discussions and among the most controversial issues was Guatel's destiny. Due to the disagreement over privatization, a series of political parties and civil society organizations withdrew from the process, and consequently, the process died.[11]

In stark contrast to the case of Costa Rica, in Guatemala, not even the unions of Guatel were included in the process. However the unions themselves must bear a great deal of responsibility for that. Initially the two labor unions of Guatel – Stelgua and Sindicato 22 de Febrero – were both fiercely opposed to the Telecommunication Law. In September, an assassination attempt was made on Victor Hugo Duran, the leader of the smallest and most militant union, Sindicato 22 de Febrero, an incident which he interpreted as a reaction to the repeated demonstrations against the governmental privatization plans.[12]

However over the course of the next year, the labor unions started to cooperate with the management. Although the union leaders argued that this was because they had gained a better understanding of the telecommunication business in Latin America,[13] it is clear that union leaders had received a generous private compensation. Moreover the leaders of the two unions were included as partners when the new stockholding company Telgua was established. Thus it was not only the privatization process that suffered from lack of transparency and participation, but also the unions themselves.

This stands in clear contrast to the case of Costa Rica, where the unions were among the most important participants in the elaboration of reform proposals. The political mobilization occurring surrounding the ICE process had a lasting impact on the Costa Rican political landscape. The social movement emerging as a response to Combo established the National Coordinator for Networking and Follow-Up (CONAES), a network of various organizations that has continued to mobilize against various market-oriented reforms.

The case of Honduras provides an interesting contrast to the cases above. In Honduras, the transparency of the process was ensured from the beginning. Bidding documents were posted on the website of Hondutel, and there were no surprise auctions (as in Guatemala). Moreover the processes did follow closely the democratic process. Indeed the cumbersome process of seeking endorsement by Congress for every step in the privatization process was among the main causes of delay. However the process cannot be characterized as participative. A main reason was the lack of interest by either the unions or other civil society groups. The unions did participate but they primarily pursued three goals: labor stability, bonuses for accepting to be rehired by the private company, and participation as stockholders. They were not interested in telecommunication reform issues. When representatives of the Friedrich Egbert Foundation attempted to enroll the unions in a more ideologically based opposition group, they met with little interest.[14] Thus what was lacking in Honduras was a general mobilization of the civil society. The privatization process was a reflection of that, not a cause of it.

Legal-Rational Legitimacy: the Rule of Law and Elite Consolidation

A second main critique of the privatization processes has been that they have primarily benefited a small elite, and operated at the edges of the rule of law. These factors are interlinked, because the elites have often ensured their own benefits through operating at the edges of, if not at odds with, the law. In Guatemala there is ground for both parts of the critique. In Chapter 3, I showed how the reforms have benefited the economic elite. The process's adherence to the rule of law could also be questioned, particularly the legal process that was used to prepare Guatel for sale, which bypassed the requirement of a 2:3 majority in congress for privatizing autonomous institutions. Moreover several accusations emerged about threats against representatives of foreign companies (particularly against Deutche Telekom) visiting Guatemala in order to review the possibilities for investing in Telgua. These threats allegedly came from groups close to the government's change-team, and resulted in favoring the local economic elite.

The failure of the PAN presidential candidate Oscar Berger to win the elections in 1999, may be interpreted as a sign of protest against the political elite's handling of privatization, as the Telgua case was an important issue in the election campaign. However the incoming President Alfonso Portillo of the FRG did not fare much better. In September 2000, he declared the privatization of Telgua illegal, and brought the case to court. However at the same time he initiated negotiations with Telmex, that was now the majority owner of Telgua. After a series of meetings with Mexican authorities and the owner of Telmex, Carlos Slim, the government withdrew its charges provided that Telgua paid its US$451.8 million debt to the Guatemalan government. Furthermore public attention soon switched to President Portillo's own dubious economic transactions, and public rage was directed at the entire political elite, not only the oligarchs traditionally joined together in the PAN.

The reform process in Honduras did not happen at the edges of the law as was the case in Guatemala. Nevertheless in the case of Honduras too, the local economic elites ensured themselves a part of the transaction that did occur, namely the concession given to Celtel. Apart from the international companies, both stockholders and management of Celtel had close links to the political elites. The General Manager of Celtel, Ramón Medina Luna, had been the first Minister of Economy in the Callejas government, and he was considered one of the Honduran Chicago Boys. By the time the bidding process for the A band was opened he had been replaced by businessman Carlos Chaín Chaín as Minister of Economy. He in turn formed a part of Luca SA, the group that bought Telgua in Guatemala (*Prensa Libre* 11 December 1998). Thus rather than strengthening either the private sector or the state, the process contributed to a continuation of the intimate relationships between the two.

In Costa Rica it is difficult to judge the extent to which privatization benefited traditional elites, as privatization was never implemented. Moreover in the cases where proposed policies have not been in accordance with the law, the constitutional court has ruled against them (as was the case with regards to the concession given to Millicom and the Combo proposal). What is interesting to observe is that a similar process of elite disgrace due to lack of adherence to legal and democratic rules related to the telecommunication sector occurred in Costa Rica as in Guatemala, in spite of no privatization taking place.

The first expression of resentment towards the elite was the creation and ascendance of a new political party, the Citizens Action Party (PAC) led by Ottón Sollís. Ottón Sollís was the only member of the traditional PLN elite that came out of the process with increased popularity and credibility. He had consistently argued against privatization and other neo-liberal reforms since he resigned from the Arias government. After the Combo fight was won, he established alliances with the unions, the university students and the other social movements, and declared his candidature for the 2002 elections. In the elections of February 2002 he managed to get 26 per cent of the votes, which made a second election round necessary for the first time in Costa Rican history. This could hardly be interpreted as anything else than discontent with the political elites that had dominated the country since the war.

The traditional elite suffered further blows two years later. In September 2004, it was revealed that Jean Philip Gallup, wife of ex-director of ICE, José Antonio Lobo, had received US$2.4 million from Alcatel for ensuring that the French company gained the contract for 400 000 cellular lines. Also the company Bosques de Olimpo, headed by another ex-director of ICE, Joaquín Alberto Fernández Alfaro, received US$1.2 million from Alcatel, and a smaller sum (US$50 000) had gone to the ex-ICE engineer Rodrígo Méndez Soto. When the case came up for the General Attorney, Lobo revealed that ex-president Miguel Ángel Rodríguez (1998–2000) had demanded 60 per cent of the Alcatel bribe. As a result of that he resigned from his short-lived career as the Secretary General of the Organization of American States (OAS) and was brought home to Costa Rica in handcuffs. A series of further corruption scandals continued to be revealed during the autumn of 2004. A third ex-director of ICE, Hernan Bravo, had received US$800 000 from Alcatel. Furthermore ex-president José Maria Figueres (1994–98), by then president of the prestigious World Economic Forum, was revealed to have received US$900 000 from Alcatel, allegedly for consulting services. At the same time, ex-president Rafael Ángel Calderón (1990–94) was accused of masterminding the distribution of a $9.2 million 'commission' connected to a $39.5 million contract with a Finnish medical supply company to update the nation's public hospital equipment. By October 2002, all three ex-presidents were detained: Rodríguez was under house arrest, whereas the other two were in prison (*La Nación* especial, 27 October 2004).

The revelations of the autumn of 2004 shed important light on the motives of the opponents of Combo. To the outside observer, it may appear as a puzzle that so many Costa Ricans would care so much for a phone company. It is hard to imagine masses of people going to the streets to defend AT&T,

Deutsche Telecom or Telefónica de España in their respective home countries. However what the Costa Ricans tried to defend was not the company as such, and certainly not as it had come to operate by the late 1990s, but rather to defend the Costa Rican state from the most detrimental effects of global economic competition, among which high-level systematic corruption is one.

It is difficult to draw implications for state legitimacy from the analysis of one policy process. However it is clear that the reform processes have contributed to the weakened legitimacy of the political elites. There is little that indicates that this has led to a weakened legitimacy of democracy. However if the state apparatus continue to be utilized as an instrument by the elites, the population is likely to increasingly challenge its legitimacy.

If the state is to continue to be legitimate within a liberalized economy, they will have to show that it is able to steer the economy in a just and equitable manner which benefits the population at large. The Central American elites have so far only partially proved that they will support a justly functioning state apparatus able to back autonomous agencies that not only regulate to facilitate the functioning of the capitalist economy, but also to make it benefit the population at large.

Concluding Remarks

When privatization was launched as a policy measure by the IFIs in the mid-1980s, a main hope was that it would be an efficient means not only for production of better services, but also to solve the problem of the capture of the state by specific groups. However over the almost 20 years that have passed, it has become obvious at the time of writing in 2005 that privatization has rather been a vehicle for elites to ensure themselves economic and political positions within the context of a globally liberalized economy. Through studying the forces behind the reforms and their beneficiaries, this book has attempted to shed light on the role of competing elites as well as the IFIs in shaping the new political economy of Central America.

The in-depth scrutiny of three similar processes in three contexts characterized by different relationships between state and economic elites, has allowed me to shed important light on the impact of the latter on the unfolding of privatization process. Studying the interaction between the IFIs and domestic elites has also given a more nuanced picture of the role of the IFIs than the customary image of the overwhelmingly powerful Washington institutions.

However such a research design also has its weaknesses. Firstly, by not studying other sectors in depth, there is a risk of overemphasizing the role of the local private sector elites, as telecommunications is a much more profitable enterprise than other sectors that have currently undergone market-oriented reforms. Secondly, the conclusions about the role of the IFIs are based on a study of long-term interaction between IFIs and domestic elites. That has included some crisis situations, but mostly normal day-to-day interaction. There is reason to believe that the dynamic between the IFIs and domestic elites is different when the former are brought in to solve urgent crisis situations.

Nevertheless the lessons that could be drawn from this case study should have some validity for donors, IFIs and other countries faced with reform processes. Firstly, regarding conditionalities, they are unlikely to ensure sustainability of reform, as the threat of cutting off funding that they are founded upon lacks credibility. They are rather a part of a perpetual process of lending, repaying, creation of new demand and lending again. The most detrimental effect of IFI activities, I would argue, is not that they contribute to the introduction and sustainability of market-oriented reform. They rather contribute to 'sustainability of reform' in a quite perverted sense: ensuring that reforms are sustained as an ever-returning and ever-present feature of the political agenda. As a result, the IFIs cannot be regarded external actors but rather as more or less permanent players within domestic politics in many countries. This means that they should be concerned about their own legitimacy and not only rest on the acceptance by the government of their presence.

Secondly, the IFIs and other donors should pay more careful attention to what political forces they do support with their policies. Although the IFIs and the USAID at times have consciously supported political groups through for example support for business organizations, often they have supported policies that have had the effect of strengthening domestic political groups. Moreover often we have seen that they have supported interest groups with the idea that they operate in a pluralistic system in which the state is the neutral arbiter of different interests. However such an image of reality has little relevance in a captured state such as the Guatemalan one, or a weak and dependent state such as the Honduran one. In such contexts the support of private sector groups may have quite unforeseen consequences – conesquences that the IFIs and other donors should pay much more attention to.

NOTES

1. Interview, Manuel Acosta Bonilla, former Honduran Minister of Economy (1972–75) and former Director of the Office of Modernization of the State (1990–94), 3 September 2001.
2. Four major players vie for market share: Comcel (Millicom-Luxembourg), Telefonica Guatemala (majority owned by Telefónica Móvil), Sercom (Telmex) and Bell South Guatemala.
3. The sale was challenged twice, firstly due to the alleged failure of Enitel to pay city taxes – an allegation that was disputed by the Supreme Court – and secondly due to the revelation of a systematic web of corruption. Nevertheless the government continued and sold 49 per cent of the remaining stocks to América Móvil, part of the Telmex empire.
4. The representatives agreed that one should permit that 100 per cent of ICE's profit were reinvested in development of electricity and telecommunications, remove the limits placed on investments, increase the amount that ICE was allowed to borrow, make the appointment of the board of directors independent of party politics, allow for participation of the civil society, and finally improve the procurement procedures with the goal of making purchases easier, but also ensuring justice among equipment providers.
5. Banco de Guatemala, Memória de Labores, various issues.
6. Lizardo Sosa, speech to the annual luncheon of American Chamber of Commerce (AmCham), Guatemala City, November 2000.
7. This conclusion discords with the general experience from Latin America, which is that the countries have experienced a high growth of fixed lines in the first four years after the privatization and that it thereafter slowed down (ITU 2000, pp.34–5). The explanation for the discord between the Central American experience and the experience of Latin America in general might be the different time periods in which the privatization occurred. Whereas many of the countries included in ITU's study privatized in the early to mid-1990s, Guatemala and El Salvador privatized in the late 1990s. When Guatemala and El Salvador privatized, the companies that entered the markets placed their main emphasis on extending the cellular network.
8. In Guatemala the respective figures were 712 625 fixed-line subscribers and 935 488 subscribers to cellular mobile services (data from SIT).
9. There are a series of difficulties involved in comparing telephone rates as they change frequently and come in different packages and it is therefore often difficult to 'unbundle' the price of distinct services.
10. In El Salvador, tariffs on calls to the United States per minute decreased from 80 US cents in 1998 to 48 in 1999 and to 18 in 2000. In Guatemala, the tariffs have decreased by approximately 75 per cent between 1998 and 2000
11. The parties were FRG and FDNG and the Unión del Centro Nacional (UCN). The civil society organizations were the Episcopal Conference, the San Carlos University, Unistragua, Expresiones Organizadas de Mujeres de la Sociedad Civil and the Association for the Advance of the Social Sciences (*Reporte Político* No. 128 June 1997).
12. Interview, Victor Hugo Durán, 15 November 1999.
13. Interview, Victor Hugo Durán, 15 November 1999.
14. Interview, Mario Posas, 1 September 2001.

Bibliography

Amador, José Luis (2000), *El ICE: Un símbolo, 50 años después ¿Por qué los costarricenses siguen queriendo al ICE?* Unpublished manuscript.

Amoore, Louise, Richard Dodgson, Barry K. Gills, Paul Langley, Don Marshall and Iain Watson (1997), 'Overturning "globalisation": resisting the teleological, Reclaiming the "Political"', *New Political Economy*, **2** (1), pp. 179–95.

Araya Soto, Gilberto (1988), 'Relación Gobierno Central – Empresas Públicas en Gosta Rica', in Nuria Cunill and Juan Martin (eds), *Relación Gobierno Central – Empresas Públicas en América Latina*, Caracas, Venezuela: ILPES/CLAD, pp. 211–22.

ARESEP (2003), 'Datos estadísticos del sistema a Diciembre 2003', San José, Costa Rica, Autoridad Reguladora de los Servicios Públicos, http://www.aresep.go.cr.

Arias Sánchez, Oscar (1971), *Grupos de Presión en Costa Rica*, San José, Costa Rica: Editorial Costa Rica.

Armeringer, Charles D. (1978), *Don Pepe: A Political Biography of José Figueres of Costa Rica*, Albuquerque, NM: University of New Mexico Press.

Armeringer, Charles D. (1982), *Democracy in Costa Rica*, New York: Praeger Publishers.

Arnbak, Jens C. (1997), 'Technology trends and the implications for telecom regulation', in William Melody (ed.), *Telecom Reform: Principles and Regulatory Practices*, Lyngby: Technical University of Denmark, pp. 67–96.

Ayau Cordón, Manuel F. (1992a), *Mis memorias y mis comentarios sobre la fundación de la Universidad Francisco Marroquín y sus antecedentes*, Guatemala: Editorial UFM - IDEA, Universidad en su casa.

Ayau Cordón, Manuel F. (1992b), *No tenemos que seguir siendo pobres para siempre*, Guatemala: Editorial Centro de Estudios Económico-Sociales.

Bach, Daniel (2003), 'Regionalisation through insecurity, violence and plunder', paper presented to the workshop 'States and Regions: Exploring the Interlinkages', 23–26 April, Noresund, Norway.

Banco de Guatemala, Memoria de labores (annual reports), various issues, Guatemala: Banco de Guatemala.

Barahona Montero, Manuel (1999), 'El Desarrollo Económico', in Juan Rafael Quesada Camacho, Daniel Masis Iverson, Manuel Barahona Montero, Tobías Meza Ocampo, Rafael Cuevas Molina and Jorge Rhenan Segura, *Costa Rica Contemporánea: raíces del estado de la nación*, San José, Costa Rica: Editorial de la Universidad de Costa Rica, pp. 97–149.

Barnett, Michael and Martha Finnemore (1999), 'The politics, power and pathologies of international organizations', *International Organization*, 53 (4), pp. 699–732.

Basañes, Federico, Evamaria Uribe and Robert Willig (1999), *Can Privatization Deliver? Infrastructure for Latin America*, Washington, DC and New York: Inter-American Development Bank/Johns Hopkins University Press.

Bates, Robert H. (1981), *Markets and States in Tropical Africa*, Berkeley, CA: University of California Press.

Belt, Juan A.B. (1999), 'Telecommunications reform to promote efficiency and private sector participation: the cases of El Salvador and Guatemala', Economist Working Paper Series, 10, June.

Berger, Susan A. (1992), *Political and Agrarian Development in Guatemala*, Boulder, CO: Westview Press.

Birch, Melissa H. and Jerry Haar (2000), 'Privatization in the Americas: the challenge of adjustment', in Melissa H. Birch and Jerry Haar (eds), *The Impact of Privatization in the Americas,* Miami, FL: North-South Center Press, pp. 1–11.

Bjørsvik, Bjarte (1993), *Neoliberalisme eller 'halvføydalisme'? Økonomisk politikk i Guatemala 1980–1992*, Bergen: Norges Handelshøyskole.

Black, George (1984), *Garrison Guatemala*, London: Zed Books.

Booth, John A. and Thomas Walker (1989), *Understanding Central America.* Boulder, CO, San Fransisco, CA and London: Westview Press.

Boron, Atilio A. (1995), *State, Capitalism, and Democracy in Latin America*, Boulder, CO and London: Lynne Rienner Publishers.

Bratton, Michael and Nicolas van de Walle (1997), *Democratic Experiments in Africa: Regime Transitions in Comparative Perspective*, Cambridge: Cambridge University Press.

Brenes, Arnold and Kevin Casas (1998), *Soldiers as Businessmen: The Economic Activities of Central America's Militaries*, San José, Costa Rica: Fundación Arias Para la Paz y El Progreso Humano.

Bulmer-Thomas, Victor (1987), *The Political Economy of Central America since 1920*, Cambridge: Cambridge University Press.

Bulmer-Thomas, Victor (1994), *The Economic History of Latin America since Independence*, Cambridge: Cambridge University Press.

Cabrera, Marco Vinicio (1997), *Desmonopolización vrs. Privatización: Su Contenido y Alcance*, Guatemala: Universidad de San Carlos de Guatemala, Facultad de Ciencias Económicas.

Calderón, César and Luis Servén (2004), *Trends in Infrastructure in Latin America, 1980–2001*, http://www.worldbank.org

Cameron, Maxwell A. (1998), 'Latin American autogolpes: dangerous undertows in the third wave of democratization', *Third World Quarterly*, **19** (2), pp. 219–39.

Carballo Q, Manuel (1992), 'El Partido Liberación Nacional: necesidad de nuevos contenidos y formas de acción política', in Juan Manuel Villasuso (ed.), *El Nuevo Rostro de Costa Rica*, Heredia, Costa Rica: CEDAL, pp. 313–22.

Casaus Arzú, Marta Elena (1992a), 'El retorno al poder de las elites familiares centroamericanas, 1979–1990', *Polémica*, **18**, Septiembre–Deciembre, pp. 51–62.

Casaus Arzú, Marta Elena (1992b), *Guatemala: Linaje y Racismo*, San José, Costa Rica: FLACSO.

Castelar Pinheiro, A. and Ben Ross Schneider (1995), 'The fiscal impact of privatization in Latin America', *Journal of Development Studies*, **31** (3), pp. 751–76.

Castiglioni, Rosanna (2000), 'Welfare state reform in Chile and Uruguay: cross-class coalitions, elite ideology, and veto players', paper prepared for delivery at the 22nd International Congress of the Latin American Studies Association, Miami, FL, 15–18 March.

Castro, Carlos (1995), 'The public sector and structural adjustment in Costa Rica (1983–1992)', in Trevor Evans, Carlos Castro and Jennifer Jones (eds), *Structural Adjustment and the Public Sector in Central America and the Caribbean*, Managua: CRIES, pp. 46–99.

CDI (1996), 'Conceptos del Consejo de Defensa de la Institucionalidad sobre los anteproyectos de transformación del ICE', unpublished document presented to the Legislative Assembly of Costa Rica (Exp. 12.753)

CEES (2000), 'Diez mandamientos para el nuevo gobierno', *Tópicos de Actualidad*, Enero de 2000.

Celarier, Michelle (1997), 'Privatization: A case study in corruption', *Journal of International Affairs*, **50** (2) pp. 531–43.

Cerdas Cruz, Rodolfo (1979), 'Del Estado Intervencionista al Estado Empresario', *Anuario de Estudios Sociales*, **15** (1), pp. 81–97.

Cerdas Cruz, Rodolfo (1992), 'Colonial heritage, external domination, and political systems in Central America', in Louis Goodman, William M.

LeoGrande and Johanna Mendelson Forman (eds), *Political Parties and Democracy in Central America*, Boulder, CO: Westview Press, pp. 17–31.

Cerezo, Vinicio (1987), 'Guatemala: El Programa de Reorganizacion Nacional', *Panorama Centroamericana*, **6** (nueva época) Abril–Junio, pp. 25–47.

Chong, Alberto and Florencio López-de-Silanes (2003), 'The truth about privatization in Latin America', Research Network Working Paper #R-486, October, Washington, DC: The Inter-American Development Bank.

Christensen, Tom and Per Lægreid (2001), *New Public Management: The Transformation of Ideas and Practice,* Aldershot: Ashgate Publishing.

CIEN (1999a), *Infrastructure in Guatemala: Infrastructure for the Third Millennium*, Guatemala: National Economics Research Center.

CIEN (1999b), *Communications in Guatemala: Infrastructure for the Third Millennium*, Guatemala: National Economics Research Center.

Clark, Mary (1997), 'Transnational alliances and development policy in Latin America: nontraditional export promotion in Costa Rica', *Latin America Research Review,* **32** (2), pp. 71–97.

Conatel (2001), 'Comentarios al documento Honduras: Informe Marco Sobre la Infraestructura', unpublished note, Tegucigalpa, August.

CONSECA (1979), *Políticas de Gobierno*, Guatemala: Consultoría en Economía y finanzas, Cta. Ltda.

Contraloría General de la Republica (2000), 'Registro de la Deuda Pública, Costa Rica', http:///www.cgr.go.cr/site3/deuda/deud_ind.html

COREC (1991), *Reforma del Estado en Costa Rica*, Comisión de Reforma del Estado Costarricense.

Cox, Robert W. (1981), 'Social forces, states, and world orders: beyond international relations theory', reprinted in Robert W. Cox with Timothy J. Sinclair (1996), *Approaches to World Order,* Cambridge: Cambridge University Press, 124–43.

Cox, Robert W. (1992), 'Towards a posthegemonic conceptualization of world order: reflections on the relevancy of Ibn Kaldhun', reprinted in Robert W. Cox with Timothy J. Sinclair (1996), *Approaches to World Order*, Cambridge: Cambridge University Press, pp. 144–73.

Cox, Robert W. (1999), 'Civil society at the turn of the millennium: prospects for an alternative world order', *Review of International Studies*, **25** (1), pp. 3–28.

Cox, Robert W. and Harold K. Jacobson (1973), *The Anatomy of Influence: Decision Making in International Organization*, New Haven and London: Yale University Press.

Crosby, Benjamin L. (1985), 'Divided we Stand, Divided we fall: Public-private sector relations in Central America', Occasional Papers Series

#10, Latin American and Caribbean Center, Miami, FL: Florida International University.

Davis, Harold E. (1963), *Latin American Social Thought: The History of Its Development Since Independence, with Selected Readings*, Washington, DC: University Press of Washington, DC.

De Molina, Ana Ordóñez (1999), 'Dimensión Económica y Social de las Finanzas Públicas', in Ana O. De Molina, A. Estevez Clavería and C. R. De León (eds), *Política Fiscal, Finazas Públicas y Estructura Tributaria en Guatemala Periodo 1990–1998: Análisis Específico del Impuesto sobre la Renta*, Guatemala: Universidad de San Carlos de Guatemala, Facultad de Ciencias Económicas. Departamento de Estudio de Problemas Nacionales, pp. 1–27.

De Witt, R. Peter, Jr. (1977), *The Inter-American Development Bank and Political Influence: With Special Reference to Costa Rica*, New York and London: Praeger Publishers.

Del Valle, José Cecilio (1963 [1821]), 'America', in Harold Eugene Davis (ed.), *Latin American Social Thought: The History of Its Development Since Independence, with Selected Readings,* Washington, DC: University Press, pp. 81–92.

Denton, Charles (1969), *La Política del Desarrollo en Costa Rica*, San José, Costa Rica: Editora Novedades de Costa Rica, S.A.

Dosal, Paul J. (1993), *Doing Business with the Dictators: A Political History of United Fruit in Guatemala, 1899–1944*, Wilmington, DE: Scholarly Resources.

Dosal, Paul J. (1995), *Power in Transition. The Rise of Guatemala's Industrial Oligarchy, 1971–1994*, Westport, CT: Prager.

Dunkerley, James (1991), 'Guatemala since 1930', in Leslie Bethell (ed.), *Central America since Independence,* Cambridge: Cambridge University Press, pp. 119–90.

Dunkerley, James (1994), *The Pacification of Central America. Political Change in the Isthmus, 1978–1993*, New York and London: Verso.

Edelman, Marc and Rodolfo Monge Oviedo (1995), 'Costa Rica: Non-Market Roots of Market Success', in Fred Rosen and Deidre McFadyen (eds), *Free Trade and Economic Restructuring in Latin America,* New York: Monthly Review Press, pp. 62–77.

Edwards, Sebastian (1995), *Crisis and Reform in Latin America*, Oxford, NY: Published for the World Bank [by] Oxford University Press.

ESA Consultores (2001), *Honduras: Informe Marco Sobre la Infraestructura. Informe al Banco Mundial/PIAF*, Abril.

Esquivel, Gerardo and Felipe Larraín B. (2001), 'Fiscal Policy Reforms in Central America', in Felipe Larraín B. (ed.), *Economic Development in Central America, Vol. II: Structural Reform*, Cambridge, MA: John F.

Kennedy School of Government, Harvard University: Distributed by Harvard University Press, pp. 1–31.

Estache, Antonio, Vivien Foster and Quentin Wodon (2002), *Accounting for Poverty in Infrastructure: Learning from Latin America's Experience*, Washington, DC: World Bank.

Euraque, Dario A. (1992), 'Formación de Capital, Relaciones Familiares y Poder Político en San Pedro Sula: 1970–1958', *Polémica*, **18**, Septiembre–Diciembre, pp. 32–50.

Euraque, Dario A. (1996), *Reinterpreting the Banana Republic: Region and State in Honduras, 1870–1972*, Chapel Hill, NC: University of North Carolina Press.

Evans, Peter (1992), 'The state as problem and solution: predation, embedded autonomy, and structural change', in Stephan Haggard and Robert Kaufman (eds), *The Politics of Economic Adjustment. International Constraints, Distributive Conflicts, and the State*, Princeton, NJ: Princeton University Press, pp. 239–81.

Evans, Peter (1995), *Embedded Autonomy: States and Industrial Transformations*, Princeton, NJ: Princeton University Press.

Evans, Peter, Theda Scokpol and Dietrich Rueschemeyer (1985), *Bringing the State Back In*, Cambridge: Cambridge University Press.

Evans, Trevor (1995), 'Structural adjustment and the public sector in Costa Rica (1983–1992)', in Trevor Evans, Carlos Castro and Jennifer Jones (eds), *Structural Adjustment and the Public Sector in Central America and the Caribbean*, Managua: Cries, pp. 1–45.

Facio, Rodrigo (1978), *Obras de Rodrigo Facio*, Tomo I, San José: Editorial Costa Rica.

Ferraro Castro, Fernando (1998), *Estado y Desarrollo: El caso de Costa Rica*, San José, Costa Rica: Asamblea Legislativa, República de Costa Rica.

Fink, Carsten, Aaditya Mattoo and Randeep Rathindran (2002). 'An Assessment of Telecommunications Reform in Developing Countries', World Bank Policy Research Working Paper 2909, October.

Finnemore, Martha (1996), *National Interests in International Society*, Ithaca and London: Cornell University Press.

Flora, Jan L. and Edelberto Torres-Rivas (1989), *Sociology of 'Developing Societies': Central America*, New York: Monthly Review Press.

FOL (1996), *Exposición ante la Comisión Legislativa que analiza los proyectos de Ley de reforma del ICE y de transformación de la industria de energia y telecomunicaciones,* 10 de Diciembre.

Franklin, Cynthia Chalker (1998), 'Riding the wave: the domestic and international sources of Costa Rican democracy', Unpublished PhD dissertation, University of Pittsburgh.

Furlong, William (2000), 'Costa Rican Politics in Transition', Paper presented at the 22nd International Congress of the Latin American Studies Association, Miami, FL, 15–18 March.

Gasper, Des (1999), 'Ethics and the conduct of international development aid: charity and obligation', Working Paper Series No. 297, The Hague: Institute of Social Studies.

Gates, Leslie (2000), 'Privatization and union defection from centralized bargaining: lessons from the Mexican case', paper prepared for delivery at the 2000 meeting of the 22nd International Congress of the Latin American Studies Association, Miami, FL, 15–18 March.

Gayle, Dennis John (1986), *The Small Developing State: Comparing political economies in Costa Rica, Singapore and Jamaica*, Aldershot: Gower Publishing.

Geddes, Barbara (1994), *Politician's Dilemma: Building State Capacity in Latin America*, Berkeley, CA and Los Angeles, CA: University of California Press.

Gilbert, Christopher L., Andrew Powell and David Vines (2000), 'Positioning the World Bank', in Christopher L. Gilbert and David Vines (eds), *The World Bank: Structure and Policies*, Cambridge: Cambridge University Press, pp. 39-86.

Gilbert, Christopher and David Vines (2000), 'The World Bank: an overview of some major issues', in Gilbert, Christopher L and David Vines (eds), *The World Bank: Structure and Policies,* Cambridge: Cambridge University Press, pp. 10–36.

Gill, Stephen (2000), 'Knowledge, politics, and the neo-liberal political economy', in Richard Stubbs and Geoffrey R.D. Underhill (eds), *Political Economy and the Changing Global Order*, New York: Oxford University Press, pp. 48–59.

Gill, Stephen and David Law (1989), 'Global hegemony and the structural power of capital', *International Studies Quarterly*, **33**, pp. 475–99.

Gleijeses, Piero (1991), *Shattered Hope. The Guatemalan Revolution and the United States, 1944–1954,* Princeton, NJ: Princeton University Press.

Gobierno de Honduras (1999), *Plan Maestro de la Reconstrucción y Transformación Nacional: Estrategia para impulsar el desarrollo acelerado, equitativo, sostenible y participativo. Versión ampliada*, Reunión de Grupo Consultivo, Estocolmo Suecia, 25-29 Mayo.

Goldstein, Judith and Robert O. Keohane (1993), 'Ideas and foreign policy: an analytical framework', in Judith Goldstein and Robert O. Keohane (eds), *Ideas and Foreign Policy: Beliefs, Institutions and Political Change,* Ithaca and London: Cornell University press, pp. 3–30.

Gramsci, Antonio (1971), *Selections from the Prison Notebooks,* edited and translated by Quintin Hoare and Geoffrey Nowell Smith, New York: International Publishers.

Green, Duncan (1995), *Silent Revolution: The Rise of Market Economics in Latin America,* London: Cassel.

Grieb, Kenneth (1979), *Guatemalan Caudillo: The Regime of Jorge Ubico, Guatemala 1931–1944,* Athens, OH: Ohio University Press.

Guash, J. Luis and Pablo T. Spiller (1994), 'Regulation and private sector development in Latin America', World Bank. http://www.worldbank.org /html/lat/english/papers/trade/regpsd.txt, 27 May 1996.

Guatel (1993), Memoria de labores, Guatemala: Guatel.

Guatel (1994) *Llamado a presentar ofertas. Operación del servicio de telefonía móvil celular de Guatemala: Bases de licitación,* Octubre, Guatemala: Guatel.

Gudmundson, Lowell (1986), *Costa Rica Before Coffee: Society and Economy on the Eve of the Export Boom,* Baton Rouge, LA: Louisiana State University Press.

Haggard, Stephan (1986), 'The politics of adjustment: lessons from the IMF's Extended Fund Facility, in Miles Kahler (ed.), *The Politics of International Debt,* Itacha, NY: Cornell University Press, pp. 157–86).

Haggard, Stephan and Robert Kaufman (1992), 'Institutions and Economic Adjustment', in Stephan Haggard and Robert Kaufman (eds), *The Politics of Economic adjustment. International constraints, distributive conflicts, and the state,* Princeton, NJ: Princeton University Press, pp. 3-37.

Haggard, Stephan and Robert Kaufman (1995), 'Estado y Reforma Económica: La Iniciación y Consolidación de las Políticas de Mercado', *Desarrollo Económico – Revista de Ciencias Sociales,* **35** (139), pp. 335–72.

Haggard, Stephan, Jean-Dominique Lafay and Christian Morrison (1995), *The Political Feasibility of Adjustment in Developing Countries,* Paris: Development Centre OECD.

Handy, Jim (1984), *Gift of the Devil: A History of Guatemala,* Boston, MA, South End Press.

Harris, Richard L. (2000), 'The Effects of Globalization and Neoliberalism in Latin America at the Beginning of the Millennium', in Richard L. Harris and Melinda J. Seid, *Critical Perspectives on Globalization and Neoliberalism in Developing Countries,* Boston, MA: Brill, pp. 139–62.

Harris, Clive (2003) 'Private participation in infrastructure in developing countries: trends, impacts and policy lessons', World Bank Working Paper No. 5, Washington D.C: World Bank.

Hartlyn, Jonathan (1998), *The Struggle for Democratic Politics in the Dominican Republic*, Chapel Hill, NC: University of North Carolina Press.

Hayek, Friedrich A. (1960), *The Constitution of Liberty*, London: Routledge.

Hellman, Joel and Daniel Kaufmann (2001), 'Confronting the challenge of state capture in transition economies', *Finance and Development*, **38** (3), http://www.imf.org/external/pubs/ft/fandd/2001/09/hellman.htm

Hobson, John M. (1997), *The Wealth of States. A Comparative Sociology of International Economic and Political Change*, Cambridge: Cambridge University Press.

Holden, Robert H. (1999), 'Securing Central America against communism: the United States and the modernization of surveillance in the Cold War', *Journal of Interamerican Studies and World Affairs*, **41** (1), pp. 1–30.

Holden, Paul and Sarath Rajapatirana (1995), *Unshackling the Private Sector: A Latin American Story*, Washington, DC: World Bank.

Holiday, David (1997), 'Guatemala's Long Road to Peace', *Current History*, February , pp. 68–74.

Honey, Martha (1994), *Hostile Acts: US Policy in Costa Rica in the 1980s*, Gainesville, FL: University Press of Florida.

Hveem, Helge and Erik Reinert (1999), 'Utviklingsideenes utvikling', in Tor-Arve Benjaminsen and Hanne Svarstad (eds), *Samfunnsperspektiver på miljø og utvikling*, Oslo: Universitetsforlaget.

ICE (1988a), *Reestructuración del Instituto Costarricense de Electricidad*, 27 Mayo.

ICE (1988b), *Reformas legales propuestas para el I.C.E.*, Noviembre.

ICE (1994), *Memoria de los 30 años de las telecomunicaciones, 1963–1993*.

ICE (1995a), *ICE Towards the 21st Century: Framework Agreement for ICE's Renewal*.

ICE (1996a), *Anteproyecto Ley de Modernización y Fortalecimiento y del ICE*, Agosto.

ICE (1996b), *Anteproyecto Ley General de Telecomunicaciones*, Agosto.

ICE (1996c), *Anteproyecto Ley General de Electricidad*, Agosto.

IDB (1995), *Costa Rica: Loan 739/OC-CR for a public sector reform program. Release of the first tranche*, PR-1905-5, 31 October, Washington, DC: Inter-American Development Bank.

IDB (1997), *Costa Rica: Country Paper*, GN-1982, 8 July, Washington, DC: Inter-American Development Bank.

IDB (1998), *The Central American Economies on the Treshold of the 21st Century*, Regional Operations Department II, Washington, DC: Inter-American Development Bank.

IDB (2002), *Latin American economic policies*, Second Quarter, Vol. 18,

Research Department, Washington, DC: Inter-American Development Bank.

Ikenberry, John (1990), 'The international spread of privatization policies: inducements, learning, and "Policy Bandwagoning"', in Ezrat N. Suleiman and John Waterbury (eds), *The Political Economy of Public Sector Reforms and Privatization,* Boulder, CO: Westview Press, pp. 88–110.

IMF (1999), 'Honduras: initiative for heavily indebted poor countries', preliminary document, International Monetary Fund and International Development Association. November 23.

IMF (2000), 'IMF and World Bank Support Debt Relief for Honduras', press release, No. 00/41, 10 July 10.

Isacson, Adam (1997), *Altered States: Security and Demilitarization in Central America,* Washington, DC: Center for International Policy; and San José, Costa Rica: Arias Foundation for Peace and Progress.

ITU (2000), *Americas Telecommunication Indicators 2000,* Geneva: International Telecommunication Union.

Jiménez C, Wilburg (1992), 'Cambios ocurridos en las instituciones públicas costarricenses', in Juan Manuel Villasuso (ed.), *El Nuevo Rostro de Costa Rica,* Heredia, Costa Rica: CEDAL, pp. 385–396.

Johnson, Chalmers (1987), 'Political institutions and economic performance: the government–business relationship in Japan, South Korea and Taiwan', in Frederic C. Deyo (ed.), *The Political Economy of the new Asian Industrialism,* Ithaca, NY: Cornell University Press, pp. 136-164.

Johnson, Chalmers (1999), 'The developmental state: odyssey of a concept, in Meredith Woo-Cumings (ed.), *The Developmental State,* Ithaca, NY: Cornell University Press, pp. 32–60.

Jonas, Susanne (1991), *The Battle for Guatemala: Rebels, Death Squads, and US Power,* Boulder, CO: Westview Press.

Jordana, Jacint and David Levi-Faur (2004a), 'Towards a Latin American regulatory state? The diffusion of autonomous regulatory agencies across countries and sectors', in David Levi-Faur and Eran Vigoda-Gadot (eds), *International Public Policy and Management: Policy Learning Beyond Regional, Cultural and Political boundaries,* New York: Marcel Dekker, pp. 188–87.

Jordana, Jacint and David Levi-Faur (2004b), 'The politics of regulation in the age of governance', David Levi-Faur and Jacint Jordana (eds), *The Politics Of Regulation: Institutions and Regulatory Reforms for the Age of Governance,* Cheltenham, UK and Northampton, US: Edward Elgar, pp. 1–28.

Kahler, Miles (1992), 'External influence, conditionality and the politics of adjustment', in Stephen Haggard and Robert Kaufman (eds), *The Politics of Economic Adjustment. International Constraints, Distributive Conflicts, and the State*, Princeton, NJ: Princeton University Press.

Kahler, Miles (1995), 'Bargaining with the IMF: two-level strategies and developing countries', in Peter B. Evans, Harold K. Jacobson and Robert D. Putnam (eds), *Double-Edged Diplomacy: International Bargaining and Domestic Politics*, Berkeley, CA: University of California Press, pp. 363–95.

Keohane, Robert O. and Helen V. Milner (eds) (1996), *Internationalizaton and Domestic Politics*, Cambridge: Cambridge University Press.

Killick, Tony (1996), 'Principals, agents and the limitations of BWI conditionality', *World Economy*, **19** (2), pp. 211–229.

Killick, Tony (1998), *Aid and the Political Economy of Policy Change*, London: Routledge.

Klak, Thomas (1999), 'Globalization, neoliberalism and economic change in Central America and the Caribbean', in Robert N. Gwynne and Christobal Kay (eds), *Latin America Transformed. Globalization and Modernity*, London, Sydney and Auckland: Arnold Publishers, pp. 98–126.

Kohli, Atul (1999), 'Where do high-growth political economies come from? The Japanese lineage of Korea's "Developmental State"', in Meredith Woo-Cumings (ed.), *The Developmental State*, Ithaca, NY: Cornell University Press, pp. 93–136.

Krasner, Stephen D. (1999), *Sovereignty: Organized Hypocrisy*, Princeton, NJ: Princeton University Press.

Krueger, Anne O. (1993), *The Political Economy of Policy Reform in Developing Countries*, Cambridge, MA: MIT Press.

Lapper, Richard (1985), *Honduras: State for Sale*, London: Latin America Bureau.

Larraín B., Felipe and Luis F. López-Calva (2001), 'Privatization: fostering economic growth through private sector development', in Felipe Larraín B.(ed.), *Economic Development in Central America, Volume II: Structural Reforms*, Cambridge, MA: John F. Kennedy School of Government, Harvard University: Distributed by Harvard University Press, pp. 66–106.

Latinobarómetro (2004), *Informe: Resumen Latinobarómetro 2004: Una Década de Mediciones*, Santiago, Chile: Corporación Latinobarómetro.

Latour, Bruno (1986), 'The powers of association', in John Law (ed.), *Power, Action and Belief: A New Sociology of Knowledge*, London, UK, Boston and Henley, US: Routledge & Kegan Paul, pp. 264–80.

Leandro, José E., Hartwig Schafer and Gaspar Frontini (1999), 'Towards a more effective conditionality: an operational framework', *World Development*, **27** (2), pp. 285–99.

Lehoucq, Fabrice Eduard (1996), 'The institutional foundations of democratic cooperation in Costa Rica', *Journal of Latin America Studies*, **28**, pp. 329–55.

Lentner, Howard H. (1993), *State Formation in Central America: The Struggle for Autonomy, Development and Democracy*, Westport, CT: Greenwood Press.

Levi-Faur, David (2001), 'The politics of liberalization: privatization and regulation-for-competition in Europe's and Latin America's telecoms and electricity industries', unpublished paper, Centre for European Politics, Economics and Society and Nuffield College, University of Oxford.

Levy, Brian and Pablo T. Spiller (1996), *Regulations, Institutions, and Commitment: Comparative Studies of Telecommunications*, Cambridge: Cambridge University Press.

Lipset, Seymour Martin and Aldo Solari (1967), 'Preface', in Seymour Martin Lipset and Aldo Solari (eds), *Elites in Latin America*, London: Oxford University Press, pp. vii–x.

Longley, Kyle (1997), *The Sparrow and the Hawk: Costa Rica and the Untied States During the Rise of José Figueres*, Tuscaloosa, AL: University of Alabama Press.

López, Alvaro (1995), *Apertura Comercial, Libre Mercado y Proteccionismo en el Sector Agrícola Centroamericano*, Heredia, Costa Rica: Editorial Fundación Universidad Nacional.

Luján Muñoz, Jorge (1998), *Breve Historia Contemporánea de Guatemala*, Mexico, DF: Fondo de Cultura Económica.

Lukes, Steven (1974), *Power: a Radical View*, London: Macmillan Press.

Mann, Michael (1993), *The Sources of Social Power: Volume II, The Rise of Classes and Nation-States, 1760–1914*, Cambridge: Cambridge University Press.

Manzetti, Luigi and Charles H. Blake (1996), 'Market reforms and corruption in Latin America: new means for old ways', *Review of International Political Economy*, **3** (4), pp. 662–97.

Maravall, José María (1995), 'The myth of the authoritarian advantage', in Larry Diamond and Marc F. Plattner (eds), *Economic Reform and Democracy*, Baltimore, MD: Johns Hopkins University Press, pp. 13–27.

Marín-Guzmán, Roberto (2000), *A Century of Palestinian Immigration into Central America: A Study of Their Economic and Cultural Contributions*, San José, Costa Rica: Editorial de la Unviersidad de Costa Rica.

Martí, Werner J. (1994), 'The private sector, the state, and economic development: the Guatemalan experience', Unpublished PhD thesis, University of Texas at Austin.

Másis Iverson, Daniel (1999), 'Poder Político y Sociedad', in Juan Rafael Quesada Camacho, Daniel Masis Iverson, Manuel Barahona Montero,

Tobías Meza Ocampo, Rafael Cuevas Molina, and Jorge Rhenan Segura (eds), *Costa Rica Contemporánea: Raíces del Estado de la Nación*, San José, Costa Rica: Editorial de la Universidad de Costa Rica, pp. 45–84.

McCamant, John F. (1968), *Development Assistance in Central America*, New York: Praeger.

McCleary, Rachel M. (1999), *Dictating Democracy: Guatemala and the End of the Violent Revolution*, Gainesville, FL: University Press of Florida.

McKenzie, David and Dilip Mookherjee (2003), 'The distributive impact of privatization in Latin America: evidence from four countries', *Economía: Journal of Latin American Economy*, 3 (2), pp. 161–218.

Medard, Jean-François (1996), 'Patrimonialism, neo-patrimonialism and the study of the post-colonial state in Sub-Saharan Africa', in Henrik Secher-Marcussen (ed.), *Occasional Paper No. 17*, International Development Studies, Roskilde: Roskilde University Centre, pp. 76–97.

Meseguer, Covadonga (2003), 'The Diffusion of Privatization in OECD and Latin American Countries: What role for learning?' Paper presented at the Conference 'The Internationalization of Regulatory Reforms', Berkeley 25–26 April.

Mideplan (1992), *Costa Rica en Cifras 1950–1992*, San José, Costa Rica: Ministerio de Planificación Nacional y Política Economía.

Mideplan (1993), Documentos fundamentales de PAE III, San José, Costa Rica: Ministerio de Planificación Nacional y Política Economía.

Migdal, Joel S. (1988), *Strong Societies and Weak States. State-Society relations and State Capabilities in the Third World*, Princeton, NJ: Princeton University Press.

Molano, Walter (1997), *The Logic of Privatization: The Case of Telecommunications in the Southern Cone of Latin America*, Westport, CT: Greenwood Press.

Molina, Guillermo (1986), 'The Politics of Democracy in Honduras', in Mark Rosenberg and Phillip L. Sheperd (eds), *Honduras Confronts Its Future: Contending Perspectives on Critical Issues*, Boulder, CO: Lynne Rienner Publishers, pp. 23-36.

Monge, Ricardo (2000), 'La economía política de un intento fallido de reforma en telecomunicaciones', in Ronulfo Jiménez (ed.), *Los retos políticos de la reforma económica en Costa Rica*, San José, Costa Rica: Academía de Centroamérica, pp. 273–318.

Moore, Mick (1998), 'Death without taxes: democracy, state capacity, and aid dependence in the fourth world', in Mark Robinson and Gordon White, *The Democratic Developmental State: Politics and Institutional Design*, New York: Oxford University Press, pp. 84–121.

Morfín, Anabella and Mario Leonel Montenegro (2000), *Gestión del patrimonio del estado: Guatemala,* Colección de Educación Fiscal, No 2, Guatemala: FLACSO.

Morris, James A. (1984), *Honduras: Caudillo Politics and Military Rulers,* Boulder, US and London, UK: Westview Press.

Mosley, Paul, Jane Harrigan and John Toye (1991), *Aid and Power: The World Bank and Policy-Based Lending,* Volume 1, London: Routledge.

Murillo, M. Victoria (2003), 'Political bias in policy convergence: privatization choices in Latin America', *World Politics,* **54** (4), pp. 462–93.

Nellis, John (2003), 'Privatization in Latin America', Working Paper 21, Washington, DC: Center for Global Development.

Noé Pino, Hugo (1990), 'El Ajuste Estructural en Honduras', *Especial,* **45,** Mayo, Tegucigalpa: Centro de Documentación de Honduras (CEDOH).

Noé Pino, Hugo (1992), 'Consideraciones generales sobre el Ajuste Estructural en Honduras', *Especial,* **60,** Noviembre, Tegucigalpa: Centro de Documentación de Honduras (CEDOH).

North, Douglass C. (1990), *Institutions, Institutional Change and Economic Performance,* Cambridge: Cambridge University Press.

O'Donnell, Guillermo (1994), 'Delegative democracy', *Journal of Democracy,* **5** (1), pp. 55–69

Ordóñez Baca, Faustino (1999), *La Deuda Externa,* Parte I-VII, La Prensa de Honduras, 22–27 April 1999.

Oxhorn, Phillip and Graciela Ducatenzeiler (eds) (1998), *What Kind of Democracy? What Kind of Market? Latin America in the Age of Neoliberalism,* University Park, PA: Pennsylvania University Press.

Oxhorn, Phillip and Pamela K. Starr (eds) (1999), *Markets and Democracy in Latin America: Conflict or Convergence?,* Boulder, CO: Lynne Rienner Publishers.

Paige, Jeffrey M. (1997), *Coffee and Power: Revolution and the Rise of Democracy in Central America,* Cambridge, MA: Harvard University Press.

Palencia Prado, Mayra (1998), 'La Reforma Tributaria de 1992', in J. Fernando Valdez and Mayra Palencia Prado, *Los Dominios del Poder: la Encrucijada Tributaria,* Guatemala: FLACSO, pp. 177–249.

Peckenham, Nancy and Annie Street (1985), *Honduras: Portrait of a Captive Nation,* New York: Praeger Publishers.

Peet, Richard (2003), *Unholy Trinity: The IMF, World Bank and WTO,* Kuala Lumpur: SIRD, Johannesburg: Wits University Press; and London, UK and New York, US: Zed Books.

Petrazzini, Ben A. (1995), *The Political Economy of Telecommunication Reform in Developing Countries. Privatization and Liberalization in Comparative Perspective*, Westport, CT and London: Praeger.

Posas, Mario (1995), *La privatización en Honduras*, Tegucigalpa: Fundación Friedrich Ebert.

Posas, Mario and Rafael del Cid (1983), *La Construcción del Sector Público y del Estado Nacional en Honduras 1876–1979*, San José, Costa Rica: Editorial Universitaria Centroamericana.

Presidencia de la República de Costa Rica (1998), *Informe final de la comisión para la concertación nacional, San José*, Costa Rica: Presidencia de la República.

Presidencia de la República de Guatemala (1997), *De las palabras a las obras: Crónica de Gobierno 1996–2000, primer año*, Guatemala: Presidencia de la República.

Presidencia de la República de Honduras (1992), *Programa Global de Modernización del Estado*, Tegucigalpa: Presidencia de la República de Honduras.

Putnam, Robert D. (1988), 'Diplomacy and domestic politics: the logic of two level games', *International Organization*, **42** (3), pp. 427–60.

Ramamurti, Ravi (1992a), 'Why are developing countries privatizing?', *Journal of International Business Studies*, **23** (2), 225–49.

Ramamurti, Ravi (1992b), 'The impact of privatization on the Latin American debt Problem', *Journal of Interamerican Studies and World Affairs*, **34** (2), pp. 93–125.

Ramamurti, Ravi (ed.) (1996), *Privatizing Monopolies: Lessons From the Telecommunications and Transport Sectors in Latin America*, Baltimore, MD and London: Johns Hopkins University Press.

Ramírez, Miguel D. (2000), 'The evolution, rationale, and impact of Mexico's privatization program: a critical Assessment', in Melissa H. Birch and Jerry Haar (eds), *The Impact of Privatization in the Americas*. Miami, FL: North-South Center Press, pp. 51–76.

Ramírez-Arango, Julio Sergio (1985), 'The political role of the private sector associations in Central America: the cases of El Salvador, Nicaragua and Costa Rica', unpublished PhD thesis, Harvard University.

Raventós, Pedro (1997), 'Telecommunications in Central America', Discussion Paper No. 1, Central America Project, Harvard University, INCAE and the Central American Bank for Economic Integration.

Raventós, Pedro (2001), 'Deregulating telecommunications in Central America', in Felipe Larraín B. (ed.), *Economic Development in Central America, Vol. II: Structural Reform*, Cambridge, MA: John F. Kennedy School of Government, Harvard University: Distributed by Harvard University Press, pp. 107–56.

Remmer, Karen L. (1989), 'Neopatrimonialism: the politics of military rule in Chile, 1973–1987', *Comparative Politics*, January, pp. 149–70.

República de Honduras (1977), *Manual de organización y funciones de los organismos decentralizados*, Tegucigalpa: Secretaría Técnica del Consejo Superior de Planificación Económica.

Rivera, Eugenio (1982), *El Fondo Monetario Internacional y Costa Rica 1978–1982: Politica económica y crisis*, San José, Costa Rica: DEI.

Robinson, Walter I. (2003), *Transnational Conflicts: Central America, Social Change, and Globalization*, London, UK and New York, US: Verso.

Ropp, Steven (1974), 'The Honduran Army in the sociopolitical evolution of the Honduran state', *America*, **30**, pp. 504–28.

Rosenberg, Mark (1986), 'Honduras: an introduction', in Mark Rosenberg and Phillip L. Sheperd (eds), *Honduras Confronts Its Future: Contending Perspectives on Critical Issues*, Boulder, CO: Lynne Rienner Publishers, pp. 1–22.

Rosenberg, Mark (1995), 'Democracy in Honduras: the electoral and the political reality', in Mitchell A. Seligson and John A. Booth (eds), *Elections and Democracy in Central America Revisited*, Chapel Hill, NC: University of North Carolina Press, pp. 66–83.

Rottenberg, Steven (1993), *The Political Economy of Poverty, Equity and Growth: Costa Rica and Uruguay: A World Bank Comparative Study*, Oxford: Oxford University Press.

Rouquié, Alain (1973), 'Military revolutions and national independence in Latin America: 1968–71', in Philippe C. Schmitter (ed.), *Military Rule in Latin America: Function, Consequences and Perspectives*, Beverly Hills, CA: Sage Publications, pp. 2–56.

Rueschemeyer, Dietrich, Evelyn H. Stephens and John D. Stephens (1992), *Capitalist Development and Democracy*, Cambridge: Polity Press.

Rufín, Carlos and Evanán Romero (2001), 'Sustainability of regulatory reform in Latin America: a comparative analysis of Brazil, Bolivia and Panamá', paper presented to the 2001 meeting of Latin American Studies Association, Washington, DC, 6–8 September.

Ruhl, Mark J. (1984), 'Agrarian Structure and Political Stability in Honduras', *Journal of Inter-American Studies and World Affairs*, **26**, pp. 33–67.

Ruhl, Mark J. (1996), 'Redefining civil-military relations in Honduras', *Journal of Interamerican Studies and World Affairs*, **38** (1), pp. 33–66.

Salom Echeverría, Roberto (1992), *Costa Rica: deuda externa y soberanía*, San José, Costa Rica: Editorial Porvenir.

Salomón, Leticia (1992), *Política y Militares en Honduras*, Tegucigalpa, Honduras: Centro de Documentación de Honduras.

Salomón, Leticia, Julieta Castellanos and Dora Castillo (1996), *Corrupción y*

Democrácia en Honduras, Tegucigalpa: Centro de Documentación de Honduras.

Samper, Mario (1990), *Generations of Settlers: Rural Households and Markets on the Costa Rican Frontier, 1850–1935*, Boulder, CO: Westview Press.

SAPRIN (2004), *Structural Adjustment: The SAPRI report – the Policy Roots of Economic Crisis, Poverty and Inequality*, London and New York: Zed Books, Malaysia: TWN, India: Books for Change, Philippines: IBON.

Schirmer, Jennifer (1998), *The Guatemalan Military Project: a Violence Called Democracy*, Philadelphia, PA: University of Pennsylvania Press.

Schulz, Donald and Deborah Sundloff Schulz (1994), *The United States, Honduras and the Crisis in Central America*, Boulder, CO, San Francisco, CA, Oxford, UK: Westview Press.

Secretaria de Finanzas, *Memória de Labores* (annual reports), various issues, Tegucigalpa, Honduras.

Secretaria de Finanzas (2001a), *Análisis de la Deuda Pública Externa*, Dirección General de Crédito Publico Departamento de Gestión y Negociación de Deuda, Republica de Honduras, Mayo .

Secretaria de Finanzas (2001b), *Plan de Acción Estratégico de Reforma del Sector de Telecomunicaciones en Honduras*, República de Honduras, Mayo.

Segeplan (1996), *Programa de Gobierno 1996–2000*, Guatemala: Secretaria General de Planificación.

Segeplan (1999), *Guatemala hacia un nuevo milenio*, Guatemala: Secretaria General de Planificación.

Seligson, Mitchell A. (1980), *Peasants of Costa Rica and the Development of Agrarian Capitalism*, Madison, WI: University of Wisconsin Press.

Sieder, Rachel (1995), 'Honduras: the politics of exception and military reformism (1972–1978)', *Journal of Latin American Studies*, **27**, pp. 99–127.

Sikkink, Kathryn (1991), *Ideas and Institutions: Developmentalism in Brazil and Argentina*, Ithaca, US and London, UK: Cornell University Press.

Sikkink, Kathryn (1997), 'Development ideas in Latin America: paradigm shift and the economic commission for Latin America', in Frederick Cooper and Randall Packard (eds), *International Development and the Social Sciences: Essays on the History and Politics of Knowledge*, Berkeley, CA: University of California Press, pp. 228–57.

Skidmore, Thomas E (1977), 'The politics of economic stabilization in postwar Latin America', in James Malloy (ed.), *Authoritarianism and Corporatism in Latin America*, Pittsburgh, PA: University of Pittsburgh Press.

Sklair, Leslie (2001), *The Transnational Capitalist Class*, Malden: Blackwell Publishing.

Sojo, Carlos (1992), *La mano visible del mercado: La asistencia de Estados Unidos al sector privado costarricense en la década de los ochenta*, Managua: Ediciones CRIES/CEPAS.

Sojo, Carlos (1995), *Gobernabilidad en Centroamérica: la sociedad después del ajuste*, San José, Costa Rica: FLACSO.

Solís, Manuel A. (1993), 'El ascenso de la ideologia de la produccion en Costa Rica: El Partido Liberación Nacional', *Ciencias Sociales*, **60** (Junio), pp. 85–100.

Sosa, Lizardo A. (1991), 'La política económica del gobierno de Guatemala 1986–1990: una experiencia demócrata cristiana', *Panorama Centroamericana: Pensamiento y Acción*, **24** (nueva época), Octubre-Diciembre, pp. 60–70.

Stanley, William (1996), *The Protection Racket State: Elite Politics, Military Extortion, and Civil War in El Salvador*, Philadelphia, PA: Temple University Press.

Stokes, William S. (1950), *Honduras: An area study in Government*, Madison, WI: University of Wisconsin Press.

Stone, Samuel Z. (1990), *The Heritage of the Conquistadors: Ruling Classes in Central America from the Conquest to the Sandinistas*, Lincoln, US and London, UK: University of Nebraska Press.

Strange, Susan (1988), *States and Markets*, London: Frances Pinter.

Strange, Susan (1996), *The Retreat of the State: The Diffusion of Power in the World Economy*, Cambridge: Cambridge University Press.

Taussig, Michael (1997), *The Magic of the State*, New York and London: Routledge.

Tavares, José (2001), 'Crisis and Recovery: Central America from the Eighties to the Nineties', in Felipe Larraín B., *Economic Development in Central America, Vol. 1: Growth and Internationalization*, Cambridge, MA: John F. Kennedy School of Government, Harvard University: Distributed by Harvard University Press, pp. 53-87.

Teichman, Judith (2000), *Policy Networks and Policy Reform in Mexico: Technocrats, the World Bank and the Private Sector*, Paper presented at the 22nd International Congress of the Latin American Studies Association, Miami, FL, 15–18 March.

Toffler, Alvin (Undated), *Telecomuniaciones: Una llave para el Desarrollo*, San José, Costa Rica: SIECA/CINDE.

Toledo, José (2000), 'Las telecomunicaciones en Guatemala', Unpublished manuscript.

Toye, John (1993), *Dilemmas of Development*, 2nd ed., Oxford: Blackwell Publishers.

Trudeau, Robert H. (1993), *Guatemalan Politics: The Popular Struggle for Democracy*, Boulder, US and London, UK: Lynne Rienner Publishers.

Tsebelis, George (1995), 'Decision making in political systems: veto players in presidentialism, parliamentarism, multicameralism and multipartyism', *British Journal of Political Science,* **25**, pp. 289–35.

Ugarte, Justo (1999), *La Venta de Telgua S.A. Una Lesiva Privatización*, Guatemala: Bancada de Diputados, Frente Democratico Nueva Guatemala, Mayo.

UNAT (1998), *Una Evaluación del Proceso de Reforma Económica en Honduras 1990–1997,* Marzo, Tegucigalpa: Unidad de Apoyo Técnico (UNAT).

Valdez, J. Fernando (1998), 'La reforma tributaria de 1987', in J. Fernando Valdez and Mayra Palencia Prado, *Los Dominios del Poder: La Encrucijada Tributaria,* Guatemala: FLACSO, pp. 109–76.

Vega-Carballo, José Luis (1989), 'Parties, political development and social conflict in Honduras and Costa Rica: a comparative analysis', in Jan L. Flora and Edelberto Torres-Rivas (eds), *Sociology of 'Developing Societies': Central America*, New York: Monthly Review Press, pp. 92–111.

Veltmeyer, Henry, James Petras and Steve Vieux (1997), *Neoliberalism and Class Conflict in Latin America: A Comparative Perspective on the Political Economy of Structural Adjustment*, Houndmills and London: Macmillan Press.

Vickers, John and George Yarrow (1988), *Privatization: An Economic Analysis*, London: MIT Press.

Vilas, Carlos M. (1995), *Between Earthquakes and Volcanoes: market, state, and the revolutions in Central America*, New York: Monthly Review Press.

Villasuso, Juan Manuel (1992), 'La reforma democrática del estado costarricense', in Juan Manuel Villasuso (ed.), *El Nuevo Rostro de Costa Rica*, Heredia, Costa Rica: CEDAL, pp. 409–22.

Vinelli, Paul (1986), 'General characteristics of the Honduran economy', in Mark Rosenberg and Philip L. Sheperd (eds), *Honduras Confronts Its Future: Contending Perspectives on Critical Issues*, Boulder, CO: Lynne Rienner Publishers, pp. 97–110.

Vogelsang, Ingo and Bridger Mitchell (1997), *Telecommunications Competition: The Last Ten Miles*, Cambridge, MA: MIT Press.

Volio Guardia, Claudio A., Ricarcho Exhandi Zurcher and Germán Serrano Pinto (n.d.), *Estado Empresario: La participación del Estado costarricense en la economía y el proceso de privatización*, San José, Costa Rica: La Comisión Nacional para la Reestructuración de CODESA.

Wallsten, Scott (2002), *Does Sequencing Matter? Regulation and*

Privatization in Telecommunications Reforms, World Bank Development Research Group, Washington, DC: World Bank.

Weaver, Frederick Stirton (1999), 'Reform and (counter) revolution in post-independence Guatemala', *Latin American Perspectives*, **26** (2), pp. 129–58.

Weber, Max (1971 [1922]), *Makt og Byråkrati*, Oslo: Gyldendal.

Weiss, Linda (1998), *The Myth of the Powerless State. Governing the Economy in a Global Era*, Cambridge, MA: Polity Press.

Weiss, Linda and John Hobson, (1995), *States and Economic Development: A Comparative Historical Analysis*, Cambridge, MA: Polity Press.

Weyland, Kurt (2000), 'Neopopulism and Market Reform in Argentina, Brazil, Peru and Venezuela', Paper prepared for the 22nd International Congress of Latin American Studies Association, Miami, FL, 15–18 March.

Weyland, Kurt (2001), 'Clarifying a contested concept: populism in the study of Latin American politics', *Comparative Politics*, **34** (1), pp. 1–22.

Wilson, Bruce (1994), 'When social democrats choose neoliberal economic policies: the case of Costa Rica', *Comparative Politics*, **26** (2), pp. 149–68.

Wilson, Bruce M. (1998), *Costa Rica: Politics, Economics, and Democracy*, Boulder, CO: Lynne Rienner Publishers.

Woo-Cumings, Meredith (1999), 'Introduction: Chalmers Johnson and the politics of nationalism and development', in Meredith Woo-Cumings (ed.), *The Developmental State*, Ithaca, NY: Cornell University Press, pp. 1–31.

World Bank (1986a), *Project Completion Report: Guatemala. Second Telecommunications project* (Loan 1104-GU), Report No. 6493, November.

World Bank (1986b), Project Completion Report, Costa Rica, Fifth Telecommunications Project (Loan 1532-CR).

World Bank (1988), 'Report on Adjustment Lending', document R88–199, Country Economics Department, August.

World Bank (1992a) *Effective Implementation: Key to Development Impact* ('The Wapenhans Report'), report of the World Bank's Portfolio Management Task Force. Washington, DC: World Bank.

World Bank (1992b) *Consultative Group for Costa Rica,* 17–18 September, Chairman's Report of Proceedings.

World Bank (1992c), *Consultative Group for Costa Rica*, Washington, DC, 24 March, Chairman's Report of Proceedings.

World Bank (1992d), *Honduras: Prospects for Public Sector Reform,* Volume I: Summary of Main Findings and Recommendations, Washington, DC: World Bank, Latin America and the Caribbean Region.

World Bank (1992e), *Honduras: Prospects for Public Sector Reform,*

Volume II: The Main Report, Washington, DC: World Bank, Latin America and the Caribbean Region.

World Bank (1995a), *Bureaucrats in Business: The Economics and Politics of Government Ownership*, Oxford: Oxford University Press.

World Bank (1995b), *Country Assistance Strategy for the World Bank Group for Guatemala*, 5 May.

World Bank (1995c), *Honduras: Reforming Public Investment and the Infrastructure Sectors. A Joint World Bank and Inter-America Development Bank Study*, Washington, DC: World Bank, Latin America and the Caribbean Region.

World Bank (1996a), *El Salvador: Public Sector Modernization Technical Assistance Loan* (PSM-TAL).

World Bank (1996b), *Project Completion Note, Costa Rica, Third Structural Adjustment Loan*, Loan 3594-CR.

World Bank (1996c), *Report and Recommendation of the President of the International Development Associations to the Executive Directors on a proposed Public Sector Modernization Structural Adjustment Credit (PMSAC) to the Republic of Honduras. January 19, 1996*, Washington, DC: World Bank.

World Bank (1997), *World Development Report 1997: The State in a Changing World*, Washington DC: World Bank.

World Bank (2000) *Guatemala: Expenditure Reform in a Post-Conflict Country*, Central America Department/Latin America and the Caribbean Region, Report No. 19617-GU.

World Bank (2002), *Country – at a glance: Costa Rica and Honduras.* http://www.worldbank.org.

Yarrow, George (1999), 'A theory of privatization, or why bureaucrats are still in business', *World Development*, **27** (1), pp.157–68.

Yashar, Deborah (1997), *Demanding Democracy: Reform and Reaction in Costa Rica and Guatemala 1870s–1950s*, Stanford, CA: Stanford University Press.

Zack-Williams, Alfred B., Ed Brown and Giles Mohan (2000), 'The long road to structural adjustment', in Giles Mohan, Alfred B. Zack-Williams, Bob T. Milward, Ed Brown and Ray Bush (eds), *Structural Adjustment: Theory, Practice and Impacts*, London and New York: Routledge, pp. 3–23.

Index

agrarian reform 137–8, 139
agro-exporters 39–40, 42, 59–60, 61
agro-producer groups 13, 42
Agüero, Maria 153, 156–7, 164
Amador, José Luis 93
anti-privatization 121–4, 169
Arana Osorio, Colonel Carlos 46–7
Arbenz, Captain Jacobo 43–4, 134
Arévalo, Juan José 43
Arias Sánchez, Oscar 14, 97–8, 99, 101,
    108, 186
Armeringer, Charles 92
Arzú, Alvaro 56, 66–70, 72, 73, 76
Aurelio Soto, Marco 130
authoritarian regimes 5, 6, 39, 40
autonomous institutions (AIs)
    challenges to 175–6
    Costa Rica 85, 86–7, 88, 90, 91–5,
        103, 108, 125, 175
    Guatemala 67
    Honduras 135, 139, 141
    see also Guatel; Hondutel; ICE; SIT;
        state autonomy; Telgua
Ayau Cordón, Manuel 59–61, 64, 65, 66,
    70, 71, 72, 73, 117
Azcona Hoyo, José 143, 144, 145

banana companies, foreign-owned
    131–3, 136, 167
banana production 13, 40, 84, 131, 136,
    138
banks see Central Bank (Costa Rica);
    Central Bank (Guatemala); IDB;
    multilateral development banks
    (MDBs); World Bank
bargaining game 26–7, 37, 95–6, 124
Barrios, Justo Rufino 39–40
beliefs 29
BMCs (borrowing member countries)
    26–7, 28–9, 30

Bueso, Ricardo 77
bureaucracies 32
business elites 32–3

CACIF (Coordinating Committee of
    Agrarian, Commercial, Industrial
    and Financial Associations) 48–9,
    53, 54, 56, 57–9, 62, 63, 64, 79
CACM (Central American Common
    Market) 91–2
CAEM (Guatemalan Business Chamber)
    57, 59
Calderón Fournier, Rafael Angel 102–5,
    110, 186
Calderón Guardia, Dr Rafael Angel 85,
    86
Callejas, Rafael 145–8, 163
Cañas, Antonio 99–100
Carazo Odio, Rodrigo 95–6
Carías, Tiburcio 132–3
caudillismo 33, 130, 131, 133, 134, 138
CCIC (Chamber of Commerce and
    Industry of Cortés) 136, 144
CEES (Center for Social-Economy
    Studies) 59–60, 61, 71, 117, 171
cellular services 100–101, 105–6, 107,
    109, 147–8, 165, 174, 175, 177–8,
    179, 180, 186
    see also Celtel; Millicom
Celtel 147–8, 153, 154, 156, 157, 165,
    167, 185
Central America 11–15, 21–3, 39, 42,
    43, 140, 181–2
    see also Costa Rica; El Salvador;
        Guatemala; Honduras; Nicaragua
Central Bank (Costa Rica) 98, 108, 110
Central Bank (Guatemala) 55, 58, 70,
    176
Centro (Centre for the Study of National
    Problems) 85–6, 87–8

211